THE
RUSSIAN
IDEA

ESALEN INSTITUTE / LINDISFARNE PRESS
LIBRARY OF RUSSIAN PHILOSOPHY

The Meaning of Love, Vladimir Solovyov

War, Progress, and the End of History, Vladimir Solovyov

Sophia: The Wisdom of God, Sergei Bulgakov

Lectures on Divine Humanity, Vladimir Solovyov

THE
RUSSIAN
IDEA

Nikolai Berdyaev

Translated by R.M. French

LINDISFARNE PRESS

This book is a revised edition of the translation from the Russian by R.M. French
first published by Geoffrey Bles, Ltd., London, 1947.

This edition © Lindisfarne Press 1992.

Published by Lindisfarne Press
RR4, Box 94 A-1, Hudson, NY 12534

Library of Congress Cataloging-in-Publication Data

Berdiaev, Nikolai, 1874–1948.
    [Russkaia ideia. English]
    The Russian idea / Nikolai Berdyaev : translated by R.M. French.
    Translation of: Russkaia ideia.
    Includes bibliographical references and index.
    ISBN 0-940262-49-5 (paper)   ISBN 0-940262-54-1 (cloth)
    1. Soviet Union—Intellectual life—1801–1917.   I. Title.
DK189.2.B4613   1992   92–13324
947'.07—dc20   CIP

10 9 8 7 6 5 4 3 2

Printed in the United States of America

CONTENTS

INTRODUCTION

An angel flew through the midnight sky,
softly singing.
Moon, stars, clouds in a throng
listened to his holy song.

He sang of bliss of innocent spirits
sinless in paradise.
He sang of the great God,
his praise was unfeigned.

In his arms he bore a young soul,
destined for the world of sorrow and tears.
And the sound of his song stayed forever
wordless and alive in that young soul.

Long that soul languished in the world
filled with a wonderful longing.
The earth's dull songs could not replace
the sounds of heaven for it.

—Lermontov

Two images or metaphors come to mind to frame this reappearance of *The Russian Idea.*

In 1974, under the title *From Under the Rubble* (first published in Russian by the YMCA Press in Paris, of which Nikolai Berdyaev was editor-in-chief in the 30s and 40s) Alexander Solzhenitsyn edited a prophetic collection of essays calling for a renewal of spiritual values in the then Soviet Union. In his foreword, Solzhenitsyn spoke of the numbing, chaotic effect of the dark decades, in which free thought and discussion had been suppressed and study of the past been made impossible by the rewriting of history. The documents had seemingly perished, the voices had fallen silent, and an outsider could not penetrate into the dark depths beneath the piles of unsorted rubbish. And yet something was stirring.

It is from out of those dank, dark depths [Solzhenitsyn wrote], from under the rubble, that we are now putting forth our first feeble shoots. If we wait for history to present us with freedom and other precious gifts, we risk waiting in vain. History is us— and there is no alternative but to shoulder the burden of what we so passionately desire and bear it out of the depths.

These feeble shoots, if not yet tall trees, are now at least healthy saplings—and many things are possible that were impossible then. One of them is the fact that *The Russian Idea* is now available in Russia and that there is sufficient interest in the subject to reprint it here. And yet the rubble that Solzhenitsyn evoked was not entirely constituted by the objective conditions prevailing in the Soviet Union. Implicit in his title are also the resistances we find within ourselves when we attempt to approach the spiritual reality of human life and the destiny of individual peoples.

The title *From Under the Rubble* was not chosen solely for metaphorical reasons. There are other echoes, for Solzhenitsyn's volume had a forerunner in prerevolutionary Russia. In the spring of 1909, a group of seven prominent intellectuals, including Nikolai Berdyaev, who were in the process of moving away from Marxism toward a kind of Christian socialism or Christian communism, issued a collection of essays under the title of *Landmarks* (*Vekhi*). The experience of the defeat of the revolution of 1905-1906 had called into question many of its intellectual assumptions. The times indeed seemed to demand a rethinking of first principles. *Landmarks* was the result, a collection of essays that looked deeply and self-critically at Russian society and history and examined the failure of the intelligentsia to discover an authentically Russian solution to their problems. *Landmarks* was the third attempt to do this. More or less the same authors had previously collaborated on two other symposia—*Problems of Idealism* and *From Marxism to Idealism*. These marked an historic journey from materialistic positivism, populism, and Marxism toward a deeper, more religious-metaphysical understanding of cultural reality. But it was *Landmarks* that brought the realization that a "Russian" solution to the "Russian problem" had to be found: that a spiritual reform was necessary. The Foreword pointed out that, though the different authors differed with respect to fundamental problems of "faith," as well as in their practical suggestions, they were united in considering the traditional ideology of the intelligentsia mistaken in its assumption of the primacy of political and social forms. In its place, the contributors to *Landmarks* proposed "the theoretical and practical pre-eminence of the spiritual life over the external forms of society and social life." Believing that "the internal life of the human personality is the only creative force in human existence," they affirmed that spiritual life, not the self-sufficient principles of the political order, was the only solid basis for any social evolution.

Because the essays were arranged alphabetically, Berdyaev's came first. Called "Philosophic Truth and the Justice of the Intelligentsia," it distinguished between what he called the "circle" or "clique" intelligentsia—the ideologues—and the true intelligentsia "in the broad, national, historical sense." Berdyaev was critical of the wholesale adoption of European attitudes on the part of the former and called for a return to the Russian, and hence Christian, principles exemplified by the latter. Recent Russian thinkers, he claimed, had focussed too exclusively on European social, economic, and political concerns at the expense of their own creativity and indigenous spiritual resources. "Interest was placed above truth, the human above the divine." Taking full responsibility for the future of their country—rather than relying upon borrowed ideas—meant that a new soul could "be born in the intelligentsia." Looking to the deep stream of independent Russian thinking (exemplified by such seminal figures as Khomyakov, Kireevksy, Leontyev, Solovyov, Pushkin, Gogol, Dostoyevsky and Tolstoy), the contributors to *Landmarks* rejected both absolutism, autocracy, and political reaction on the one hand, and revolution on the other. Instead, they sought a means of evolutionary intellectual, cultural, and spiritual development, based on the principles of freedom, law, and order.

Landmarks created a considerable stir when it was published. It went into five editions in almost as many months and 217 articles on it appeared within the year of publication. Though Lenin had denounced it as "an encyclopedia of liberal apostasy," it continued to remain in people's minds throughout the Soviet years. Almost forgotten—but not by Solzhenitsyn—was the fact that in 1918 a similar symposium consisting of almost the same thinkers came together again to assess the Bolshevik revolution. Under the title of *From the Depths* or *De profundis* (*Iz Glubiny*), the authors saw the October revolution as the fulfillment of their premonitions in *Landmarks*.

Berdyaev spoke of Russia having been seized by evil spirits like those in Gogol's nightmarish tales. *From the Depths* was confiscated and banned almost immediately. But it made an impression. The Russian title of *From Under the Rubble* (*Iz Pod Glyb*) is, in fact, an intentional echo of *From the Depths* (*Iz Glubiny*). Max Hayward writes:

By modelling their collection of essays on *Landmarks*, Solzhenitsyn and his associates demonstrate their conviction that in order to talk meaningfully about present-day Russia it is essential to cross back over the intellectual void of the last sixty years and resume a tradition in Russian thought which is antithetical to the predominant one of the old revolutionary intelligentsia, particularly as it developed in the second half of the nineteenth century.

This is what Berdyaev does, and allows the reader to do, in *The Russian Idea*: he allows us to span seventy, and twice seventy, years and reach back into the living history of Russia's finest thinkers. In this book we can hear, as if rising from the depths, from under the rubble, the prophetic voice of the spirit of Russia as Berdyaev, in the mood of humility and pride characteristic of Christian mystical-philosophical existentialism, proclaims it. This spirit—which IS the Russian idea—speaks of a vision of the world very different from our own and very different from the ways in which recent history has allowed us to imagine Russia. It is intensely spiritual—apocalyptic, eschatological—and yet at the same time deeply personal, overflowing with character and experience, speaking in a unique voice from one heart to another. This voice of Russia, as Berdyaev utters it, speaks of first, last, and present things but in a way we are not used to—holistically, integrally, cosmically, and with a special emphasis on the *Sobornost* or all-togetherness of human beings viewed not as material entities but as spiritual images of the divine.

The Russian Idea is a mature work, written in the dark years of the Second World War and published in 1946 in Paris (1947, London and New York). It is one of his most systematically prepared works. As he himself says in his autobiography, *Dream and Reality*, it expresses his philosophical position more adequately than any of the

books written before his exile, with the possible exception of perhaps his own favorite work, *The Meaning of the Creative Act* (1916).

This image of the Russian idea rising from the depths suggests a
second metaphor: the story of the invisible city of Kitëzh. Almost
forgotten until conflated with other, related legends in W.J. Belski's
libretto for Rimski-Korsakov's opera *The Legend of the Invisible
City of Kitëzh and Lady Fevronia*, the story begins with Prince Yuri
Vsevolod who ascended the throne of Kievan Rus in 1163.

The tale in brief is this. Prince Yuri Vsevolod went to Prince
Michael Chernikovski to request permission to build churches in all
the cities of Russia. Having gained it, he travelled throughout the land
founding citadels and houses of God—Novgorod, Pskov, Moscow,
Rostov. Finally he came to Jaroslav, whence he sailed down the
Volga to the Forests of Murom and the town of Little Kitëzh, where
he also founded a church. From Little Kitezh, Prince Yuri Vsevolod
then journeyed overland, crossing four rivers, to Lake Svetlojar,
where, facing a forest of sacred oaks, he ordered a magnificent town
to be built, Great Kitëzh. This perfect city-community, where the virtues of hospitality and acceptance were paramount, was completed
September 30, 1168. But now came the savage invasion of the Tartars, under Khan Batu, the grandson of Genghis Khan. This was in
1239. The Russians were beaten back to Little Kitezh. Then the road
to Great Kitëzh was betrayed. Prince Yuri Vsevolod was murdered.
The Tartars advanced. According to one account they destroyed the
brilliant city of Kitëzh by the "bright lake." But according to another,
the city with all its inhabitants disappeared beneath the surface of
Lake Svetlojar—or rose to celestial heights. The city, the community,
of Great Kitëzh thus was hidden and protected by God's hand—some
say that it was the Mother of God who spread her mantle over it. It
became invisible, but will become visible again, like the New Jerusalem, when Christ returns.

In a sense, the Russian idea, the Russian soul, is a search for the
invisible city of Great Kitëzh. Its suffering and pain, its compassion
and love and wholeness, are driven by the heartfelt need to visit
that city and make it visible. Berdyaev's book, of course, is not that
city or even a glimpse of it, but in his story of the great Russian
thinkers of the nineteenth and twentieth centuries we can hear some
distant, suggestive echoes of how we all might make our way to a

true community of body, soul, and spirit. But who was Nikolai Berdyaev?

NIKOLAI ALEXANDROVICH BERDYAEV (sometimes spelt Berdyayev)—the best known Russian philosopher of the interwar period, many of whose works were then published in English translations—was born in 1874 of an aristocratic family. French on his mother's side (the revolution had forced his grandfather, Marie-Gabriel-Florent-Auguste, Comte de Choiseul-Gouffier, to emigrate to Russia) and Polish, Lithuanian, Russian, and Tartar on his father's side, Berdyaev grew up speaking French in the twilight of the gentry in comfortable, respected solitude in a household consisting of his father, his mother, and himself—his only brother was sixteen years his senior. Alexander Michailovich, his father, was a military man of considerably culture and learning. He was a Westernizer, a portrait of Lincoln stood on his desk, and his religion was Tolstoyan.

Berdyaev was uninterested in family life. He found family resemblances offensive. He was good-looking—which he got from his mother—but was marked by a nervous tic that would seize him in mid-sentence propelling his tongue forward. From earliest childhood, he felt himself "alone and rootless in this world." A year spent in bed with rheumatic fever confirmed this feeling of exile, giving him a lifelong, "almost mystic terror" of illness. Uninfluenced by the outside world, Nikolai Alexandrovich grew into a deep-rooted, almost congenital independence. He read a great deal. Tolstoy and, above all, Dostoyevsky became part of his being.

At ten, he was sent to military school. He disliked it and was a poor pupil. He resented having to absorb knowledge, preferring "communion with the world's thought." His aim was "a search for meaning and a search for eternity." On this basis he created his own curriculum for life:

One day, on the borderline between puberty and youth, I was shaken by the thought, "I may not know the meaning of life, but the search for meaning gives meaning to life, and I will consecrate my life to this search for meaning." This was a true inner transformation, which changed my whole life. I experienced it

with enthusiasm. This was my true conversion, the most powerful in my life, the turning to a search for Truth, which by this
very fact was a belief in the existence of Truth, spelled with a
capital letter. After this inner revolution, I began to read philosophical books with great enthusiasm, almost exaltation.

Berdyaev thus became a philosopher, reading Nietzsche,
Schopenhauer, Carlyle, Kant. His parents had intended him for a
military career, but now he left military school and began the arduous course of studies required for university. Despite his distaste for
external discipline, he set himself to it. He had found an inner
strength and will which would serve him well.

He entered the University of Kiev in 1894, a revolutionary time.
The air seethed with social ferment. Suddenly, Berdyaev found himself in the midst of life—socially, politically, philosophically. By
1897, he was a member of the Union for the Liberation of the Working Class and a trusted speaker at labor meetings. He even attended
the European meeting of trade unionists in Zurich, where he met
Plekhanov. He worked with leading Marxists. However, his insis-
tence on the independence of the intellect, each person's right to
personal judgment, and Truth, Beauty, and Goodness as absolute,
rather than relative, categories meant that this Marxist phase would
be just that.

In 1898, police authorities discovered the Union's secret printing
press. Names and addresses were found. Berdyaev was arrested—it
was the second time. He never returned to the university.

Prison intensified his "contempt for all false gods, all the false
greatness in history." He read Shestov's new book on Nietzsche and
Dostoyevsky, reread all of Schopenhauer, discovered Ibsen and
Maeterlinck. More than ever he was convinced "this civilized and
socialized life, with all its laws and comforts, is not the real, true
life." Berdyaev spent two years in prison, awaiting trial and sentenc-
ing. It was one of the happiest periods of his life. His sentence (on
May 23, 1900) was a three year exile to the northern city of
Vologda. Here he evolved rapidly away—in the words of Lunachar-
sky—from "an idealistically tinted Marxism into the dusk of mysticism, whence he plunged straight into the night of philosophical
Christianity." It was during this time, too, that he became a writer,

publishing *F. A. Lange and the Critical Philosophy* in 1900, and *Subjectivism and Individualism in Social Philosophy* in 1901.

Permitted to leave Vologda in late 1902, Berdyaev settled—after a spell of provincial life in Zhitomir (in the province of Volhynia) and a semester in Germany—in Kiev. Here he met his life's companions, Lydia and Eugenie Trushev, daughters of a prominent Kiev attorney, recently released from prison for "revolutionary activities." Berdyaev fell in love with Lydia "with a beautiful and ethical love," and married her. For most of their married lives, Eugenie lived with them. She once wrote, in response to a series of direct questions:

> Nikolai Alexandrovich based his attitude to marriage, as to all problems of human beings and their destiny, on revelation and on his own spiritual experience. Hence he understood marriage as the accomplishment, the realization, of the image and likeness of God in man, which image was divided in the fall into man and woman, which ought to unite for the attainment of one divine image in humanity. This sacrament is accomplished before God, in the human soul, and has no need of church sanction which in Nikolai Alexandrovich's view is a juridical act, and carried out for earthly, rather than heavenly, purposes. Nikolai Alexandrovich's marriage with my sister was a spiritual marriage. They lived as brother and sister, like the first apostles.

Donald Lowrie, who quotes this passage, comments: "All this is in line with Berdyaev's description of his attitude toward 'general, universally valid morality.' He felt all kinds of vows, marriage or monastic, even taking an oath in court, were actions against human freedom. All his life, he said, his attitude toward legalism had been one not merely of hostility but of moral indignation...."

In fall, 1904, Berdyaev moved to St. Petersburg to be the editor of a new periodical, *Questions of Life*. The plan had been worked out with Sergei Bulgakov, a good friend and former Marxist moving toward Christianity, who would soon become a priest and one of the leading Sophiologists.

This was the period of the "Russian cultural renaissance" and Berdyaev found himself participating in a maelstrom of literary, philosophical, and spiritual activity. There were the Merezhkovskys

(Dmitri Merezhkovsky himself and his wife, the poetess Zinaida Gippius) and their friend Dmitri Filosov, the "mystical anarchists" Geirgi Chulkov and Vyacheslav Ivanov, his old friend Lev Shestov, the extraordinary Rozanov, the poets of the "silver age" Alexander Blok and Andrei Biely—not to mention Sologub, Bryusov, Gershonsen, Frank, Struve, Prince Evgeni Trubetskoy and many others. The aim of *Questions of Life* was to bring cultural and social movements together. Berdyaev felt the limitations of aestheticism, of romanticism elevated into religion; similarly he saw the dangers of dialectical thinking and Nietzschean hubris. Thus he found himself increasingly inspired by Russian masters like Dostoyevsky and Tolstoy, and the great philosophers Vladimir Solovyov and Nikolai Fyodorov. Primary here was a deeply Russian understanding of the spiritual nature of humanity. Berdyaev was blessed with both a profound individualism and an equally profound sense of the unity of all human beings. This distanced him equally from any Wagnerian idea of "collective culture" and from Marxist collectivism. Finally, he would find the key to the social question in the unique reality of *Sobornost* (all-togetherness) as taught by the early slavophiles Khomyakov (on whom Berdyaev began to prepare a book) and Kireevksy. All of which is to say that *The Russian Idea* gestated almost half a century.

At this time, too, Berdyaev began reading deeply in Patristic and mystical literature. Indeed, we may recall, lest we assume anything provincial about him, his description of himself in the Introduction to *Freedom and the Spirit* (1935): "I regard myself as being a Christian theosophist, in the sense in which Clement of Alexandria, Origen, St. Gregory of Nyssa, Cardinal Nicholas of Cusa, Jacob Boehme, Staint-Martin, Franz von Baader, and Vladimir Solovyov were Christian theosophists."

In this mood he met Pavel Florensky, the author of *The Pillar and Foundation of the Truth*. Florensky, following Solovyov's philosophical lead, took Sophiology as the basis of theology. Berdyaev disagreed with Florensky in many things but recognized in him "a soul full of strife, pride, and boundless spiritual desire" whose descriptions of the agonizing torments of doubt qualify him as one of the first existentialists. But Berdyaev could not share the newly converted intelligentsia's sudden enthusiasm for the priesthood. He was too individualistic for that, but it would take him some time to work out his position. This he did in a number of small transitional works—*Sub Specie Aeternitatis* and *The New Religious Consciousness and Society* (1907), *The Spiritual Crisis of the Intelligentsia* (1910), *The Philosophy of Freedom* (1911), *A.S. Khomiakov* (1912), and *The Soul of Russia* (1915)—culminating in *The Meaning of the Creative Act* (1916). Here, above all under the influence of Jacob Boehme, the central ideas of creative freedom as definitive of human nature and human nature's essential religious vocation come together in a burst of visionary philosophy, a profound confession of faith: "For God's purposes in the world the genius of Pushkin is as necessary as the sainthood of Seraphim." "Revelation demands a creative act." Bulgakov called such ideas "demonic."

Berdyaev remained in Russia after the October Revolution. From the beginning, he hid nothing of his opinions. The revolution was barely two months old when he wrote: "The Russian revolution has turned out to be a consistent application to life of Russian nihilism, atheism, and materialism—a vast experiment based on denial of all absolute spiritual elements in personal and social life...." Experiencing the catastrophe as something happening within himself, Berdyaev responded to it with lectures and speeches. He disputed, stood up for what he believed. Because of this, and simply because it was his lot, his community service was arduous. Marched by guards at five in the morning, in twenty below zero weather, he was forced to clear the snow off the railroad tracks. It was the dead of winter. Throughout it all, he conducted seminars and wrote steadily—four books not to be published until his exile. "It would be better to be honest and die before a firing squad than to be careful and die in bed," he told Eugenie. He spent six weeks in the *Cheka* prison. After his release, he started the Author's Bookshop. Then, in 1922, he was banished. It was a deep blow. "I was born a Russian. My country is suffering. I ought to stay with my country." "Without love of country," he had written in 1915, "one cannot create." Berdyaev loved Russia and the Russian people. He was completely out of sympathy with the emigration. Yet, of course, he had to go.

He arrived in Berlin, to be met by rumors that he and the other exiles were Bolshevik agents. Berdyaev had no faith in or sympathy with the White Movement that hoped to overthrow Bolshevism. All that they dreamed of belonged to an irretrievable past. "I envisaged a wholly different way of saving Russia," Berdyaev wrote. "I believed in her regeneration from within, through a painful process of inner purification.... I was conscious that Russia in her revolutionary experience, and through her the whole world, was on the threshold of a new historical epoch, and that, as a result of that experience, she would come to learn her true vocation." For Berdyaev, Russian Marxism or communism marked the end of the historical period of the Renaissance—humanism had destroyed itself by its own dialectic. A new transitional "dark ages" had fallen upon the globe. Only a spiritual renewal would return the light.

In Berlin, Berdyaev continued to write, began to make contacts with European thinkers (Max Scheler and Count Keyserling among others), and helped establish the Russian Scientific Institute, becoming its dean and giving courses in ethics and the history of Russian thought. He also set up the Religious-Philosophical Academy, where he lectured on the philosophy of religion and the need for a spiritual renaissance. But in 1923 the German currency finally collapsed—his modest stipend from the YMCA became insufficient. In 1924, he moved to France where he would stay for the rest of his life.

No sooner was he in Paris than, with great courage, Berdyaev immediately began to make his powerful and individual vision known and felt. He became simultaneously Russia's most famous philosopher and a participant in the process and praxis of European philosophy. He edited the journal *Put* (*The Way*) for the YMCA and helped form and guide the YMCA Press, which published Russian works. He worked tirelessly—together with such as Jacques Maritain, Gabriel Marcel, Louis Massignon—to create an ecumenical, religious basis for the serious discussion of social, ethical, and philosophical questions.

He was an inspiration to younger figures like Henry Corbin. He met in dialog with peers such as Martin Buber. And in a continuing blaze of creative thinking he wrote those works whose titles clearly communicate his concerns—e.g., *Philosophy of the Free Spirit* (1926), *The Destiny of Man* (1931), *The Russian Revolution* (1931), *Christianity and Class War* (1931), *Man and the Machine* (1933), *Solitude and Society* (1934), *Spirit and Reality* (1937), *Slavery and Freedom* (1940).

The war came. Berdyaev's life was drawing to a close. He continued to write and participate actively in the spiritual renewal he so powerfully sought to bring down. It was a time of loss in an earthly way—the war, his beloved cat Muri, his wife, Lydia—but there was no loss inwardly. He wrote *The Russian Idea* and *The Beginning and the End*. In 1947, he was awarded an honorary degree by Cambridge University, a mark of esteem accorded only two other of his countrymen—Turgeniev and Tchaikovsky. He died on March 23, 1948, and was buried on Good Friday, March 26, in the little cemetery of Clamart, where he had lived for nearly a quarter of a century. An unfinished manuscript, *The Realm of the Spirit and the Realm of Caesar*, lay on his desk, its title attesting to a lifetime struggle to comprehend both human and divine realities.

The Russian Idea is a passionate, intensely personal book, at once cultural history, philosophy of history, and philosophy. As such, it has its faults and its critics. It has been accused of consisting of *a priori* ideas drawn from his own philosophy rather than from a thorough, systematic, and impartial study of Russian thought in its historical becoming. Berdyaev's Russian idea is eschatological and messianic; it is anarchist, as he is; and those who do not agree with him feel he takes his own beliefs on faith as those of his country. It is true that he omits Russia's long rationalist tradition, and is hostile to science as a form of knowledge, especially when allied to humanism. All the same, it is not quite true to say, as Alexander Vucinich said at the conclusion of his introduction to the 1962 Beacon Press edition, that "despite his own convictions of the value of prophecy, Berdyaev was more a representative of the past than a prophet of the future," precisely because, as Vucinich himself continued: "No person has outdone him in the forcefulness with which he studied and tied together the Russian mystical and antirationalist thought, based on messianism, unobstructed eschatology, ontological idealism, and supernatural ethics." For Russia now has a quite different future than it seemed to have in 1962—and it is destined to play a quite different role in the world. Indeed, the world itself is different, and those thinkers whom Berdyaev brings to life so vividly, so courageously, and so individualistically are also destined to play a new part. And, in this, Berdyaev's profound sense of human universality, freedom, and individuality will certainly prove admirably inspiring.

1

Definition of the Russian national type · East and West · Moscow the Third Rome · The Seventeenth Century Schism · Peter the Great's Reform · The Rise of the Russian Intelligentsia

1

THE ATTEMPT to define a national type and the individuality of a people is a matter of very great difficulty. It is a case in which it is impossible to give a definition in the strict and scientific sense. The mystery of individuality is in every instance revealed only in love, and there is always something in it which is incomprehensible in the last resort and in its final depth. What will interest me in the following pages is not so much the question: what has Russia been from the empirical point of view, as the question: what was the thought of the Creator about Russia, and my concern will be to arrive at a picture of the Russian people which can be grasped by the mind, to arrive at the "idea" of it. Tyutchev said "Russia is not to be understood by intellectual processes. You cannot take her measurements with a common yardstick, she has a form and stature of her own: you can only believe in Russia." It is necessary to bring to bear upon Russia the theological virtues of faith, hope and charity in order to comprehend her. From the empirical point of view there is so much that repels in Russian history. It is this which was so forcefully put into words by that devout believer and Slavophil Khomyakov in those poems of his which had Russia as their subject. The Russians are a people in the highest degree polarized: they are a conglomeration of contradictions.[1] One can be charmed by them, one can be disillusioned. The unexpected is always to be expected from them. They

---

1. I have written about this in an earlier study called "The Soul of Russia" which was printed in my book *The Destiny of Russia*.

are as a people capable in the highest degree of inspiring both intense love and violent hatred. As a people the Russians have a disturbing effect upon the peoples of the West. In every case the individuality of a people, like the individuality of any particular man or woman, is a microcosm, and, therefore, includes contradictions within it. But this happens in varying degrees. In respect of this polarization and inconsistency the Russian people can be paralleled only by the Jews: and it is not merely a matter of chance that precisely in these two peoples there exists a vigorous messianic consciousness. The inconsistency and complexity of the Russian soul may be due to the fact that in Russia two streams of world history—East and West—jostle and influence one another. The Russian people is not purely European and it is not purely Asiatic. Russia is a complete section of the world—a colossal East-West. It unites two worlds, and within the Russian soul two principles are always engaged in strife—the Eastern and the Western.

There is that in the Russian soul which corresponds to the immensity, the vagueness, the infinitude of the Russian land: spiritual geography corresponds with physical. In the Russian soul there is a sort of immensity, a vagueness, a predilection for the infinite, such as is suggested by the great plain of Russia. For this reason the Russian people have found difficulty in achieving mastery over these vast expanses and in reducing them to orderly shape. There has been a vast elemental strength in the Russian people combined with a comparatively weak sense of form. The Russians have not been in any special sense a people of culture, as the peoples of Western Europe have been; they have rather been a people of revelation and inspiration. The Russians have not been given to moderation and they have readily gone to extremes. Among the peoples of Western Europe everything has been much more prescribed and formulated, everything has been classified in categories, and that finally. The case has not been the same with the Russians. They have been less at the mercy of the prescribed life, more accustomed to facing infinitude, and unwilling to recognize classification by categories. The various lines of social demarcation did not exist in Russia; there were no pronounced classes. Russia was never an aristocratic country in the Western sense, and equally there was no bourgeoisie. Two contradictory principles lay at the foundation of the structure of the Russian soul, the one a natural, dionysian, elemental paganism an͏ ascetic monastic Orthodoxy. The mutually contradictory of the Russian people may be set out thus: despotism, the phy of the State, and on the other hand anarchism and li᷍___ elty, a disposition to violence, and again kindliness, humanity and gentleness: a belief in rites and ceremonies, but also a quest for truth: individualism, a heightened consciousness of personality, together with an impersonal collectivism: nationalism, laudation of self; and universalism, the ideal of the universal man: an eschatological messianic spirit of religion, and a devotion which finds its expression in externals: a search for God, and a militant godlessness: humility and arrogance: slavery and revolt. But never has Russia been bourgeois. In attempting a definition of the character of the Russian people and of its vocation some selection must needs be made from the material at one's disposal, and I shall call it an eschatological selection, in accordance with my final purpose. For this reason the choice of a particular period of its history as especially illustrative of the character of the Russian idea and the Russian vocation is also inevitable. I shall take the nineteenth century as such a period. It was a century of thought and speech and at the same time a century marked by that acute cleavage which is so characteristic of Russia. It was, too, the century which achieved interior freedom and it was a period of intense activity in spiritual and social enquiry.

Interruption is a characteristic of Russian history. Contrary to the opinion of the Slavophils the last thing it is is organic. There have been five periods in Russian history and each provides a different picture. They are: the Russia of Kiev; Russia in the days of the Tartar yoke; the Russia of Moscow; the Russia of Peter the Great; and Soviet Russia. And it is quite possible that there will be yet another new Russia. The development of Russia has been catastrophic. The Moscow period was the worst in Russian history, the most stifling, of a particularly Asiatic and Tartar type, and those lovers of freedom, the Slavophils, have idealized it in terms of their own misunderstanding of it. The Kiev period was better, so was the period of the Tartar yoke, especially for the Church. And of course the dualistic and separatist period of St. Petersburg, in which the creative genius of the Russian people flourished in a particular degree, was a better and more significant era.

The Russia of Kiev was not closed to influence from the West. It was more receptive and more free than the Moscow Tsardom, in the suffocating atmosphere of which even holiness was extinguished (during this period there were fewer saints than in any).[2]

A particularly significant fact which marks the nineteenth century is this, that then after a long period in which thought was at a discount the Russian people at length found itself in word and thought, and that it did this in the very oppressive atmosphere which accompanies the absence of freedom. I am speaking of outward freedom, for the inward freedom which existed among us was great. What is the explanation of this protracted lack of enlightenment in Russia, among a people, that is, who were highly gifted and capable of absorbing the highest culture? How are we to explain this backwardness in culture, and even illiteracy, this absence of organic links with the great cultures of the past? The idea has been put forward that the translation of the Sacred Scriptures into Slavonic was unfavorable to the development of Russian intellectual culture since it brought about a break with the Greek and Latin languages. Church Slavonic became the sole language of the clergy, that is to say, of the only Intelligentsia in those times. Greek and Latin were not needed. In my own view the backwardness of Russian enlightenment, the absence of thought and the inarticulateness of Russia before Peter the Great are not to be explained in this way. One must take into account the characteristic property of Russian history, that in the course of that history the strength of the Russian people remained for a long while in, as it were, a potential condition and not in a state of realization. The Russian people were crushed by a vast expenditure of strength, such as the scale of the Russian State required. The State grew strong, the people grew weak, as Kluchevsky says. The Russian expanses had to be subdued and defended. The Russian thinkers of the nineteenth century, pondering over the destiny of Russia and its vocation, continually draw attention to the fact that this potentiality, this lack of expression, this failure to actualize the strength of the Russian people, is a very pledge of the greatness of its future. They believed that the Russian people will, in the long run, say its word to the world and reveal itself. It is the generally accepted opinion that the Tartar

P. Fedotov, *The Saints of Ancient Russia.*

domination had a fatal influence upon Russian history and threw the
Russian people back. Byzantine influence at the same time subjugated Russian thought inwardly and made it traditional and conservative in character. The extraordinary, explosive dynamism of the
Russian people in its cultured class was revealed only upon its contact with the West after Peter's reform. Herzen said that the Russian
people answered the reform of Peter by the appearance of Pushkin.
We supplement this by saying: not of Pushkin only, but also of the
Slavophils themselves, and of Dostoyevsky and of L. Tolstoy and of
the searchers after truth, and also by the rise of original Russian
thought.

The history of the Russian people is one of the most poignantly
painful of histories. It embraces the struggle first against the Tartar
invasion and then under the Tartar yoke, the perpetual hypertrophy
of the State, the totalitarian regime of the Muscovite Tsardom, the
period of sedition, the Schism, the violent character of the Petrine
reform, the institution of serfdom—which was a most terrible ulcer
in Russian life—the persecution of the Intelligentsia, the execution
of the Decembrists, the brutal regime of the Prussian Junker Nicholas I, the illiteracy of the masses of the people, who were kept in
darkness and fear, the inevitability of revolution in order to resolve
the conflicts of contradictions, and the violent and bloody character
of the revolution, and finally, the most terrible war in the history of
the world. Folk tales and heroes are associated with the Russia of
Kiev and St. Vladimir. But chivalry did not develop on the spiritual
soil of Orthodoxy. In the martyrdom of St. Boris and St. Gleb there
was no heroism, the prevailing idea is that of sacrifice. The exploit
of non-resistance—that is the Russian exploit. Simplicity and humility—these are Russian traits.

Another characteristic of the spirit of Russian religion is what is
known as *yurodstvo*—being a fool for Christ's sake, accepting
humiliations at the hands of other people, acquiescing in the mockery of the world and thereby throwing out a challenge to it. Characteristic too is the fact that there ceased to be saintly monarchs after
the Grand Princes of Moscow became endued with sinful power.
Nor was it mere chance that a general impoverishment in the realm
of saintliness is to be observed during the Moscow Tsardom. The
burning of oneself alive, as an exploit in religion, is a Russian

national phenomenon, which is almost unknown among other peoples. What is known among us as the "double belief," that is to say, a combination of the Orthodox Faith with pagan mythology and folk poetry provides an explanation of many of the inconsistencies to be seen in the Russian people. Russian poetry always retained, and still retains down to the present time, an elemental, ecstatic dionysism. During the conflagration of the Russian Revolution a Pole said to me: "Dionysus is abroad in the Russian land." The enormous power of Russian choral singing and dancing is due to this. The Russians are by nature inclined to carousal and choral dancing. The same thing is to be seen among the popular mystical sects, among the adherents of *khlystovstvo*, for example. That the Russians have a leaning to debauchery and to anarchy with a loss of discipline, is well known. The Russian people have not only been subservient to an authority which enjoyed the sanction of religion, but it has also given birth to Stenka Razin and Pugachëv, whose praises it has sung in its folk songs. The Russians are fugitives and bandits: the Russians are also pilgrims in search of divine truth and justice. Pilgrims refuse obedience to the powers that be. The path of this earthly life presented itself to the Russian people as a way of truancy and a way of pilgrimage.

Russia has always been full of mystical and prophetic sects and among them there has always been a thirst for the transfiguration of life. Such was the case even with the repulsive and dionysiac sect of the *Khlysti*. In religious poetry a high value has been attached to indigence and poverty: a favorite theme in them is the suffering of the innocent. Social injustice is felt in a high degree in poems of devotion. A conflict is waged between truth and falsehood. But the pessimism of the people makes itself felt in them. In the popular conception of salvation, the bestowal of alms has the very highest importance. The religion of the soil is very strong in the Russian people; it lies deep down in the very foundations of the Russian soul. The land is the final intercessor. The fundamental category is motherhood. The Mother of God takes precedence of the Trinity and is almost identified with the Trinity. The people have felt the nearness of the interceding Mother of God more vividly than that of Christ. Christ is the Heavenly King and but scanty expression is given to His earthly image. Mother Earth alone is given a personal incarnation.

The Holy Spirit is frequently mentioned. G. Fedotov stresses the point that the religious poems reveal an inadequacy of belief in Christ as the Redeemer. Christ remains the Judge—that is to say, the people do not see, as it were, the *kenosis* of Christ. The people accept suffering themselves, but it seems as though they have little belief in the compassion of Christ. Fedotov explains this as due to the fatal influence of "Josephism" which has distorted the portrait of Christ among the Russian people, so that the Russian people wants to take shelter from the frightful God of Joseph Volotsky behind Mother Earth, behind the Mother of God. The image of Christ, the image of God, was overwhelmed by the image of earthly power and to the mind of the people took on a form analogous to it. At the same time there was always a powerful eschatological element in Russian religion.

If, on the other hand, the popular religion of the Russians created a link between the divine and the world of nature—yet, on the other hand, the apocryphal books, which had an enormous influence, spoke to them of the coming of Messiah in the future. The various basic elements in the spirit of Russian religion will be noted even in the thought of the twentieth century. Joseph Volotsky and Nil Sorsky are symbolic figures in the history of Russian Christianity. The clash between them arose out of the question of monastic property. Joseph Volotsky was in favor of the possession of property by the monasteries. Nil Sorsky was of the opinion that they ought not to be allowed to acquire it. But the difference of type between the two men went a great deal deeper than that. Joseph Volotsky was a representative of the Orthodoxy which had founded the Tsardom of Moscow and bestowed its blessing upon it, a state Orthodoxy which later became an imperial Orthodoxy. He was an adherent of a Christianity which was harsh almost to the point of sadism, and which loved power. He defended the use of torture and the execution of heretics. He was an enemy of every kind of freedom. Nil Sorsky took the side of a more spiritual and mystical interpretation of Christianity. He was a champion of freedom so far as it was understood in those days. He did not associate Christianity with power and he was opposed to the persecution and torture of heretics. Nil Sorsky was the precursor of the freedom-loving currents of thought among the Russian Intelligentsia. Joseph Volotsky was a fateful figure, a man of destiny, not only in the history of Orthodoxy, but also in the history of the Russian Tsardom. An attempt was made to canonize him, but he does not live on in the mind of the Russian people as the figure of a saint. Side by side with Ivan the Terrible he must be regarded as one of the principal founders of the Russian system of autocracy. Here we come into touch with the twofold nature of the Russian messianic consciousness and with the principal outbreak in which it found expression. Messianic consciousness is more characteristic of the Russians than of any other people except the Jews. It runs all though Russian history right down to its communist period. In the history of Russian messianic consciousness very great importance attaches to a conception which belongs to the philosophy of history, that of Moscow as the Third Rome, which was propounded by the monk Philotheus. After the fall of the Orthodox Byzantine Empire the Moscow Tsardom was left as the only existing Orthodox realm. The Russian Tsar—says the monk Philotheus—"is the only Christian Tsar in the whole earth." "In the God-bearing city of Moscow the Church of the Most Holy Mother of God stands as the representative of the Ecumenical and Apostolic Throne, it shines with light side by side with Rome and Constantinople, it is unique in the whole ecumenical world and shines brighter than the sun."

The people of the Moscow Tsardom regarded themselves as a chosen people. A number of writers, P. Milyukov, for instance, have drawn attention to the Slav influence emanating from Bulgaria upon the Muscovite ideology of the Third Rome.[3] But even if a Bulgarian source of origin be admitted for the monk Philotheus's idea, it still does not affect the importance of that idea for the destiny of the Russian people. In what respect was the conception of Moscow as the Third Rome twofold? The mission of Russia was to be the vehicle of the true Christianity, that is, of Orthodoxy, and the shrine in which it is treasured. This was a religious vocation. "Orthodoxy" is a definition of "the Russians." Russia is the only Orthodox realm, and as such a universal realm like the First Rome and the Second. On this soil there grew up a sharply defined nationalization of the Orthodox Church. Orthodoxy was in this view the religion of the Russians. In religious poetry Russ is the world; the Russian Tsar is a Tsar above

---

3. See P. Milyukov, *Sketches in the History of Russian Culture*, vol.III, "Nationalism and Europeanism."

all Tsars; Jerusalem is likewise Russ; Russ is where the true belief is. The Russian religious vocation, a particular and distinctive vocation, is linked with the power and transcendent majesty of the Russian State, with a distinctive significance and importance attached to the Russian Tsar. There enters into the messianic consciousness the alluring temptation of imperialism. It is the same duality as is to be seen in the messianic hope of the Jews in time past. The Muscovite Tsars regarded themselves as the successors of the Byzantine Emperors. They traced the succession back to Augustus Caesar. Rurik appeared in the light of a descendant of Prust, a brother of Caesar, who founded Prussia. Ivan the Terrible traced his descent from Prust, and was fond of calling himself a German. The Imperial Diadem passed to Russ. The line of descent went even further—it went back to Nebuchadnezzar. There is a legend about the sending of the imperial regalia to Vladimir Monomakh by the Greek Emperor Monomakh. These tokens of sovereignty from Babylon fell to the lot of the Orthodox Tsar of the whole world, since in Byzantium both Faith and Empire had met with shipwreck. Imagination set to work in the direction of fortifying the will to power. The messianic and eschatological element in Philotheus the Monk was weakened by solicitude for the realizations of an earthly Rome. The spiritual pit into which the idea of Moscow the Third Rome falls is due precisely to the fact that the Third Rome presented itself to their minds as a manifestation of sovereign power, as the might of the State. It was taken as expressed in the Tsardom of Moscow and then in the Empire and in the end as the Third International. The Tsar was regarded as the viceregent of God upon earth. To the Tsar belonged not only care for the interests of the State but also care for the salvation of souls. Ivan the Terrible was particularly insistent on this point. The synods of the Church were convoked by order of the Tsars. The pusillanimity and servility of the Synod of 1572 were astonishing. To the hierarchy, the will of the Tsar was law in ecclesiastical affairs. God's things were rendered to Caesar. The Church was subjugated to the State not only from the time of Peter the Great but even in the Russia of Moscow. Christianity was understood and interpreted in a servile spirit. It would be difficult to imagine a more perverted form of Christianity than the repulsive *Domostroi*. Ivan Aksakov even confessed himself at a loss to understand how the

Russian national character could give rise to a morale so debased as that of the *Domostroi*. The whole idea of Moscow as the Third Rome contributed indeed to the power and might of the Moscow State and to the autocracy of the Tsar, but not to the well-being of the Church and not to the growth of the spiritual life. The vocation of the Russian people was distorted and spoiled. As a matter of fact the same thing had happened in the case of the First Rome also and of the Second, for they did very little to realize Christianity in life. The Russia of Moscow moved on towards the Schism which became inevitable in view of the low level of education and enlightened thought. The Moscow Tsardom was in principle totalitarian in its outward expression. It was a theocracy in which the power of the Tsar was predominant over the priesthood, and at the same time there was no unified life in this totalitarian Tsardom. It was pregnant with a variety of clashes and cleavages.

The Schism of the seventeenth century was of much greater significance for the whole history of Russia than it is customary to suppose. The Russians are in fact schismatics. It is a deep-rooted trait in our national character. The conservatives should turn their attention to the past. The seventeenth century presents itself to them as the organic century in Russian history which they would like to imitate. Even the Slavophils were guilty of this same mistake. But it is an historical illusion. In actual fact it was a century of unrest and schism. It was a period of confusion which shook the whole of Russian life and brought about changes in the psychology of the people. It was a period which overtaxed the strength of Russia. In the course of it a deep-seated hostility within the life of society came into evidence—the hatred of the boyars on the part of the popular masses, and this found its expression in the struggles of the people to break a way through for their life and thought. The expression of this same struggle among the Cossacks was a very notable phenomenon in Russian history and they in particular bring to light the polarity and inconsistency of the character of the Russian people. On the one hand the Russian people meekly abetted the organization of a despotic and autocratic State, but on the other hand they also fled from it; they revolted against it and took refuge in the assertion of their liberty. Stenka Razin, who is a characteristically Russian type, was a representative of the "barbarian Cossacks," the ragamuffins. In the

Time of Troubles there already appeared a phenomenon analogous to that of the twentieth century and the period of revolution in Russia. Colonization was the work of the free Cossacks. It was Yermak who made a gift of Siberia to the Russian State. But at the same time the free Cossacks, among whom a number of different classes existed, represented the anarchic element in Russian history as counterweight to the absolutism and despotism of the State. They demonstrated that it is possible to find a way of escape from the State when it has become intolerable, into the free and open Steppes. In the nineteenth century the Russian Intelligentsia left the State, in a different sort of way and in other circumstances, but they also went out into the realm of free expression. Shchapov thinks that Stenka Razin was an offspring of the Schism. In the sphere of religion in the same way many sects and heresies represent a departure from the official ecclesiasticism of the Church within which there existed the same oppression as was to be found in the State, and wherein spiritual life had become torpid. It was among the sects and heresies that the element of truth and justice was to be found, over against the falsity and injustice which marked the State Church. In the same way there was right in the withdrawal of Leo Tolstoy. The greatest significance of all belongs to our Church Schism. From it dates that profound division of Russian life, and Russian history into two streams, the deep-seated spirit of division which was to last on until the Russian Revolution, and there is a great deal which finds its explanation in that fact. It was a crisis of the Russian messianic idea. It is a mistake to suppose, as has been frequently asserted in the past, that the religious Schism of the seventeenth century arose out of trivial questions of details of ceremonial or from the dispute between the advocates of unison and those of harmony in singing, or the use of two fingers or three in making the sign of the cross and so on. It is beyond dispute that no small part in our Schism was played by the low level of education, by Russian obscurantism. Rites and ceremonies did occupy too large a place in Russian Church life. From the historical point of view the Orthodox religion was of the type which is summed up as church-going devotion. Given a low level of thought and education this led to an idolatrous regard for forms of ceremonial which historically speaking were relative and temporary. Maxim the Greek was closely associated with

Nil Sorsky; he exposed this ignorant reverence for rites and ceremonies, and he fell a victim to it. His position in the midst of the ignorant society of Russia was a tragic one. In Muscovite Russia there existed a real fear of education. Science aroused suspicion as being "latinizing." Moscow was not the center of enlightenment. That center was Kiev. It was even the case that the schismatics were more literate than the Orthodox. The Patriarch Nikon was unaware of the fact that the Russian service books were versions of Greek originals into which the Greek themselves subsequently introduced modifications. The principal hero of the Schism, the Protopope Avvakum, in spite of having a certain amount of theological learning was, of course, an obscurantist, but at the same time he was the greatest Russian writer in the pre-Petrine period. The obscurantists' reverence for rites and ceremonies was one of the poles of Russian religious life, but at the other pole stood a quest for divine truth, the practice of pilgrimage and an ardent eschatological bent of mind, and in the Schism both the one and the other came into view. The theme of the Schism was the philosophical interpretation of history and it was linked with the Russian messianic vocation, the theme of the Kingdom. At the root of the Schism there lay the doubt whether the Russian Tsardom, the Third Rome, was in fact a true Orthodox Tsardom. The schismatics got wind of the change in Church and State and they ceased to believe in the sanctity of the hierarchical power of the Russian Tsardom. The feeling that God had forsaken the Tsardom was the chief directing motive of the Schism. The schismatics began to live in the past and in the future but not in the present. They found their inspiration in a social-apocalyptic utopia. Hence, even at the most extreme expression of the Schism—*Nyetovshchina*[4]—the phenomenon was purely Russian. The Schism was a way out of history because the prince of this world, antichrist, had reached the summit of power in Church and State and dominated history. The Orthodox Tsardom went underground. The true Kingdom is the City of Kitëzh which is to be found at the bottom of a lake. The left wing of the Schism, which is its particularly interesting aspect, assumes a pronounced apocalyptic color. From this

---

4. *Nyetovschina*. The name is derived from "nyet" the Russian word for "no" and expresses the negative attitude of this extreme section of the schismatics to the officials of both Church and State and their refusal of the demands such officials made upon them.

arises an intensified quest for the Kingdom of Righteousness as opposed to the present Tsardom of the day. That was the state of affairs among the masses of the people, and so it was to be among the Russian revolutionary Intelligentsia of the nineteenth century. They also were schismatics; they also were convinced that the powers of evil had got control of Church and State; they also were ardently bent upon the City of Kitëzh, but with a different feeling about it when *Nyetovshchina* had spread to the very foundations of religious life. The schismatics proclaimed the ruin of the Muscovite Orthodox Tsardom and the coming of the kingdom of antichrist. In the person of the Tsar Alexis Mikhailovitch, Avvakum saw the servant of antichrist. When Nikon said "I am a Russian but my Faith is Greek," he dealt a terrible blow to the idea of Moscow the Third Rome. The Greek Faith appeared in the light of a non-Orthodox Faith. Only the Russian Faith was the Orthodox, the true Faith. The true Faith was linked with the true Kingdom, and it was the Russian Tsardom which had to be the true Kingdom. Of this true Tsardom nothing any longer existed on the surface of the earth. In the year 1666 the reign of antichrist began in Russia. If the true Kingdom is to be sought, in space it must be looked for underground; in time, it had to be sought in the future, a future ringed with apocalyptic thought. The Schism imbued the Russian people with an expectation of antichrist, and from that time they will see antichrist both in Peter the Great and in Napoleon and in many other figures.

Communities of schismatics were organized in the forests. They fled from the kingdom of antichrist to the forests, the mountains, the desert. The *streltsi* were schismatics. At the same time the schismatics displayed an immense capacity for the organization of community life and for self-government. The people claimed freedom for their village affairs and their village affairs began to develop independently of State affairs. This opposition between the local community and the State, which was so characteristic of the nineteenth century among us, is little understood in the West. Very characteristic of the Russian people again is the appearance of pseudo-tsars from among the masses, and of prophets who were healers of body and spirit. Such imposture is a purely Russian phenomenon. Pugachëv could only meet with success by giving himself out to be Peter the Third. The Protopope Avvakum believed in himself as a chosen one and that he was possessed by a peculiar grace of the Holy Spirit. He regarded himself as a saint; he was called to be a healer. He said, "Heaven is mine and the earth is mine, the light is mine and mine is every created thing. God has bestowed them upon me." The tortures and the agonies of mind and body which Avvakum bore were beyond human strength to endure.

The Schism sapped the strength of the Russian Church. It lessened the authority of the hierarchy and made possible the Church reforms of Peter the Great as well as explaining them. But there were two elements in the Schism—the religious and the revolutionary. The importance of the left wing of the Schism, the group which dispensed with clergy, lay in the fact that it made Russian thought free and adventurous, it made it a separate thing and directed it towards an end; and an extraordinary property of the Russian people was brought to light, a capacity for the endurance of suffering and a mind directed ardently towards the other world, and the finality of things.

2

The reform of Peter the Great had been prepared for by the preceding trend of events, and it was both absolutely inevitable and at the same time imposed by force. It was a revolution which came from above. Russia had to emerge from the position of isolation and seclusion in which she found herself as the effect of the Tartar yoke and the whole character of the Muscovite Tsardom with its Asiatic aspect. Russia had to make her entry into the wide world. Without the violent reform of Peter which in many respects inflicted much suffering upon the people, Russia would not have been able to carry our her mission in world history, nor have been able to say her say. Historians who have had no interest in the spiritual side of the question have made it sufficiently clear that without the reform of Peter, the Russian State itself would have been incapable both of self-defense and of development. The point of view from which the Slavophils regarded Peter's reform cannot survive critical examination and is completely out of date; and the same is true of the purely Western point of view which denies the distinctive peculiarity of the Russian historical process.

For all the seclusion of the Tsardom of Moscow, intercourse with the West had already begun in the fifteenth century, and the West was all the while in fear of the growing strength of Moscow. A German quarter existed in Moscow. The German irruption into Russia began before the time of Peter. Russian commerce and industry was in the seventeenth century in the hands of foreigners, to begin with especially of the English and Dutch. There were already in Russia before Peter's time people who were the result of the totalitarian order of things in the Tsardom of Moscow. Such a one was the apostate Prince Khvorostinen, and another was the denationalized V. Kotoshikhin; still another was Ordyn-Nashchekin. The last was a forerunner of Peter, and in the same way the Croat Krizhanich was a predecessor of the Slavophils. Peter the Great, who hated the whole nature and style of the Muscovite Tsardom and had nothing but derision for its customs, was a typical "Russack." Only in Russia could such an extraordinary person make his appearance. The Russian traits to be seen in him were simplicity, coarseness, dislike of ceremony, of conventions and etiquette, an odd sort of democracy of his own, a love of truth and equity and a love of Russia, and at the same time the elemental nature of a wild beast was awake in him. There were traits in Peter which may be compared with the Bolsheviks. Indeed he was a Bolshevik on the throne. He staged burlesque travesties of ecclesiastical processions which remind us very much of the anti-religious propaganda of the Bolsheviks. Peter secularized the Russian Tsardom and brought it into touch with Western absolutism of the more enlightened kind. The Tsardom of Moscow had not given actual effect to the messianic idea of Moscow as the Third Rome, but the efforts of Peter created a gulf between a police absolutism and the sacred Tsardom. A breach took place between the upper governing classes of Russian society and the masses of the people among whom the old religious beliefs and hopes were still preserved. The Western influences which led on to the remarkable Russian culture of the nineteenth century found no welcome among the bulk of the people. The power of the nobility increased and it became entirely alien from the people. The very manner of life of the landowning nobility was a thing incomprehensible to the people. It was precisely in the Petrine epoch during the reign of Katherine II that the Russian people finally fell under the sway of the system of serfdom. The whole Petrine period of Russian history was a struggle between East and West within the Russian soul. The imperial Russia of Peter had no unity. It possessed no one style of its own, but during that period an extraordinary dynamism came within the bounds of possibility. Historians now recognize the fact that the seventeenth century was already a century of schism and the beginning of the process of introducing Western education and culture: it was the opening of a critical period. But with Peter we definitely enter upon the critical period itself. The empire was not organic and it imposed heavy burdens upon Russian life. From the reforms of Peter there arose the dualism which is so characteristic of the destiny of Russia and the Russian people and which is unknown in a like degree to the peoples of the West. If the Moscow Tsardom had already given rise to religious doubts in the minds of the Russian people, those doubts were very much strengthened in the face of the Petrine empire. At the same time the very widely accepted view that Peter, in establishing the Holy Synod on the German Lutheran pattern, enslaved and weakened the Church, is not true. It is more true to say that the ecclesiastical reform of Peter was in fact a result of the enfeeblement of the Church, of the ignorance of the hierarchy and of the loss of its moral authority. St. Dmitri of Rostov, who came to Rostov from the more cultured south (the level of education in Kiev was immeasurably higher), was appalled by the coarseness, the ignorance and the savagery which he found. It fell to the lot of Peter to work out and carry through his reforms in frightful darkness, in an atmosphere of obscurantism, and he was surrounded by thieves. It would be unjust to lay the blame for everything at Peter's door, but the aggressive character of Peter wounded the souls of the people. The legend was created that Peter was antichrist. We shall see that the Intelligentsia which took shape as the result of Peter's work was to adopt his universalism and his looking to the West, and to overthrow the empire.

The Western culture of Russia in the eighteenth century was a superficial aristocratic borrowing and imitation. Independent thought had not yet awakened. At first it was French influences which prevailed among us and a superficial philosophy of enlightenment was assimilated. The Russian aristocrats of the eighteenth century absorbed Western culture in the form of a miserable rehash of Voltaire. The effects of this Voltairian swoop upon the country lasted on among certain sections of the Russian nobility even in the nineteenth century, by which time more independent and deeper currents of thought had made their appearance among us. Generally speaking the level of scientific education in the eighteenth century was very low. The gulf between the upper classes and the people was all the time increasing. The intellectual tutelage of our enlightened absolutism achieved very little that was positive and only retarded the awakening of freedom of thought among the general public. Betsky said of the country squires that they said "I have no wish that those whose duty it is to serve me should be philosophers."[5] The education of the people was regarded as harmful and dangerous. Pobedonostzev thought the same thing at the end of the nineteenth century and the beginning of the twentieth, while Peter the Great said the Russian people had a capacity for science and intellectual activity like any other people. It was only in the nineteenth century that the Russians really learned to think. Our Voltairians were not free in their thinking. Lomonosov was a scholar and a genius, one who enthusiastically welcomed many of the discoveries of the nineteenth and twentieth centuries in physics and chemistry; he created the science of physical chemistry. But his loneliness in the midst of the darkness that surrounded him was tragic. For that aspect of the history of Russian self-consciousness which is of interest to us at the moment he did little that was significant. Russian literature began with satire but it achieved nothing worthy of note.

In the eighteenth century the one and only spiritual movement in our society was freemasonry, and its significance was enormous. The first masonic lodges had already arisen in the year 1731–2 and the best Russian people were masons. The first beginnings of Russian literature had their links with freemasonry. Masonry was the first free self-organized society in Russia; it alone was not imposed from above by authority. The freemason Novikov was the most active figure in the Russian enlightenment of the eighteenth century.[6] This broad-minded enlightening activity suggested danger to the Government. Katherine II was a Voltairian and reacted to the mysticism of freemasonry in a hostile way, and later on there were

5. See A. Shchapov, *The Social and Educational Conditions of the Intellectual Development of the Russian People.*
6. See Bogolyubov, *N.I. Novikov and his Times.*

added to this her political apprehensions as she inclined more and more towards reaction and even became a nationalist. The masonic lodges were suppressed in the year 1738. It was hardly for Katherine to question the Orthodoxy of Novikov, but in answer to the Empress's enquiry, the Metropolitan Platon said that he "says his prayers and prays that all over the world there may be Christians of the same sort as Novikov." Novikov was chiefly interested in the moral and social side of masonry. The ethical direction taken by Novikov's ideas was characteristic of the awakening of Russian thought. In Russia the moral element has always predominated over the intellectual. For Novikov freemasonry provided a way out "at the divergence of paths between Voltaire and religion." In the eighteenth century the spiritual view of life found shelter in the masonic lodges from the exclusive dominance of an enlightening rationalism and materialism. This mystical freemasonry was hostile to the philosophy of the Enlightenment of the Encyclopaedists. Novikov behaved to Diderot in a manner that suggested suspicion. He edited not only Western mystics and Christian theosophists but also the Fathers of the Church. Russian masons were searching for the true Christianity, and it is touching to note that Russian freemasons were all the time desirous of reassuring themselves upon the point whether there was anything in masonry which was hostile to Christianity and Orthodoxy. Novikov himself thought that freemasonry actually is Christianity. He stood nearer the English form of freemasonry, and the passion for alchemy and magic and the occult sciences was alien to his mind. Dissatisfaction with the official Church in which spirituality had become weakened was one of the causes of the rise of mystical freemasonry in Russia. In their discontent with the visible temple, they wanted to erect a temple which was invisible. Masonry among them was a striving after the inward Church. They looked upon the visible Church as a transitory condition. The molding of the cultured soul of Russia went on within freemasonry. It endowed that soul with an ascetic discipline. It worked out a moral ideal of personality. Orthodoxy, of course, had a more profound influence upon the souls of the Russian people, but it was within freemasonry that the cultured spirits of the Petrine period were born and in that environment they set up an opposition to the despotism of authority and obscurantism. The influence of masonry was later on replaced by that of German romanticism. Freemasonry was a preparation for the awakening of philosophic thought among us in the thirties, although there was no original philosophical thought in masonry itself. In the masonic atmosphere a spiritual awakening took place and we should remember the names of Novikov, Schwarz, I. Lopukhin and I. Gamalea. The outstanding man as a philosopher among the masons was Schwarz and it may be that he was the first person in Russia to practice philosophy. The Ukrainian theosophist philosopher Skovoroda stood apart in a position of his own in the eighteenth century. He was a remarkable man, a sage of the people, but he had no direct influence upon the intellectual tendencies among us in the nineteenth century. Schwarz had a philosophical training. He, in contrast to Novikov, was interested in the occult sciences and regarded himself as a Rosicrucian. Russian masons were always a long way from the radical illuminism of Weisshaupt. Katherine was always in a confused state of mind, it may be of deliberate purpose. She confused the Martinists with the illuminists. In actual fact the majority of the Russian masons were monarchists and opponents of the French Revolution. But social injustice troubled the masons and they wanted greater social equality. Novikov derived his ideas of equality from the Gospel and not from natural laws. I. Lopukhin, who was at first under the influence of the Encyclopaedists and translated Holbach, burned his translation. He was searching for a purified spiritual Christianity and he wrote a book about the inward Church. During the nineteenth century the struggle between Saint-Martin and Voltaire went on in the Russian soul, inoculated as it had been by Western thought. Saint-Martin had an enormous influence among us at the end of the eighteenth century and was translated in masonic editions at an early date. Jacob Boehme enjoyed an immense authority and he also was translated in masonic editions. The interesting point is that at the beginning of the nineteenth century when there was a mystical movement among us both in the cultured classes and in the masses, the influence of Jacob Boehme penetrated even to the masses of the people. In their quest for the spirit they took him to their hearts and he was so highly revered that they even called him "the holy Jacob Boehme among our fathers." There were people among us who also translated Pordage, the English follower of Boehme. Among Western mystics of the theosophist type who occupied more of a secondary place, Stilling and Eckhardt-Hausen were translated and they were very popular. The arrest of Novikov and the closing down of his press was a tragic moment in the history of freemasonry of the eighteenth century. Novikov was condemned to fifteen years in the Schlusselburg fortress; when he came out of it he was an absolutely broken man. The martyrology of the Russian Intelligentsia begins with the persecution of Novikov and of Radishchev. We must give separate treatment to the mystical period of Alexander I and the part played by masonry in his time.

The beginning of the nineteenth century, the time of Alexander, is one of the most interesting periods in the Petersburg epoch of Russian history. It was a period of mystical currents of thought, of masonic lodges, of interconfessional Christianity, of the Bible Society, of the Holy Alliance, of theocratic dreams, of the war for the fatherland, of the Decembrists, of Pushkin and the flowering of Russian poetry. It was a period of Russian universalism, which had so determining an influence upon Russian spiritual culture in the nineteenth century.[7] It was then that the Russian soul of the nineteenth century and its emotional life took shape. The figure of the Russian Tsar himself is of interest. One might call Alexander I a member of the Russian Intelligentsia on the throne. He was a complex figure, with two sides to his mind, able to combine opposites, in a spiritual turmoil and full of the spirit of enquiry. Alexander I had connections with freemasonry and in the same way as the masons he also stood for true and universal Christianity. He was under the influence of Baroness Krüdener. He worshipped with Quakers. He had sympathies with mysticism of the interconfessional type. There was no deeply laid foundation of Orthodoxy in him. He had in his youth passed through a stage of skeptical enlightenment; he hated slavery; he sympathized with republican ideas and with the French Revolution. He was educated by Laharpe who instilled in him a sympathetic feeling for liberty. The interior drama of Alexander I was due to the fact that he knew that the murder of his insane father was being plotted and he gave him no word of warning. A legend became current about the end of his life, to the effect that he became the pilgrim

7. See Pypin's book *Religious Movements in the Time of Alexander I,* also his book *Russian Masonry of the Eighteenth Century and the First Quarter of the Nineteenth Century.* See also a book by G. Florovsky called *The Ways of Russian Theology.*

Theodore Kuzmitz, a legend which was of just the kind that would arise in Russia. The first half of the reign of Alexander I was colored by the love of freedom and by efforts towards reform. But an autocratic monarch in that period of history could not remain true to the aspirations of his youth; it was a psychological impossibility. The instincts of despotism and the fear of the liberationist movement led to a situation in which Alexander handed over Russia to the power of Arakcheev, a grim and terrible figure. It was the romantic Russian Tsar who inspired the Holy Alliance which, according to his own idea, should have been an alliance of peoples on the basis of Christian universalism. It was a project which belonged to the realm of social Christianity. But this idea of it was not realized; as things worked out Metternich was victorious, and he was a politician of a more realist type of whom it was said that he turned an alliance of peoples into an alliance of princes against the peoples. The Holy Alliance became reactionary power. The reign of Alexander I led to the Decembrist rising. There was a sort of fatality in the fact that at that time the repellent obscurantists Runitch and Magnitsky were of a mystical and idealist bent; fatal too was the figure of the Archimandrite Photii, the representative of the "Black Hundred" of Orthodoxy, to whom even Prince Galitzin, the minister of religious affairs, was a revolutionary. A healthier phenomenon was Lovzin and his "Zionist Messenger." When the frightened reactionaries pointed out to Alexander I the danger of the masonic lodges and the liberationist movement among a section of the Guards, he was obliged to say that he himself sympathized with all this and was responsible for it. From the Alexandrine era with its interconfessional Christianity, the Bible Society and a mystical freedom of mind, there emerges also the figure of the Metropolitan Philaret who was a very gifted person, and there were two sides also to the part that he had to play.

The mystical movement which belonged to the reign of Alexander I was twofold. On the one hand the Decembrists were bred and trained in the masonic lodges which were tinged to a greater or less degree with mysticism. On the other hand the mystical movement was inclined to obscurantism. There was a dualism in the Bible Society itself and this duality was incarnate in the person of Prince Galitzin. The Bible Society was imposed from above by the Government. It was under orders to consist of mystics and interconfessional

Christians. It was even the case that books written in defense of the Orthodox Church were prohibited. But when the authorities issued orders in a reverse direction the society changed in a flash and began to say the sort of thing that was necessary to such people as Magnitsky. In actual fact the spiritual and liberationist movement existed only among a very small group of people. The Decembrists constituted an insignificant minority; they were without support either in the wider circles of the higher ranks of the nobility and bureaucrats or among the broad masses of the people who still believed in the religious consecration of the autocratic Tsar, and they were doomed to destruction. Chatsky was a typical Decembrist. He was surrounded by Famusovs with their cries of horror about "Farmasons" and Molchalins. It reflects extraordinary credit upon the Russian nobility that it created the Decembrist movement among the higher ranks of the aristocracy, the first liberationist movement in Russia, that is, and the one which opened the revolutionary century. The nineteenth century was to be the century of revolution. Members of the highest stratum in the Russian Guards, who at that time were particularly cultured men, displayed much disinterestedness. The wealthy landowners and the officers of the Guards could not reconcile themselves to the grievous position of the peasants and soldiers under serfdom. The arrival of the Russian armies from abroad after the year 1812 was of immense importance for the growth of the movement. They represented the most cultured stratum of the Russian nobility. There were names of people well known in Russia who took part in the Decembrist rising. A number of historians have pointed out that the people of the twenties, that is to say precisely those who took part in the Decembrist movement, were more hardened to life and less sensitive than the people of the thirties. There was more unity and clarity in the generation of the Decembrists. There was less unrest and agitation than in the following generation. A partial explanation of this is provided by the fact that the Decembrists were soldiers who had actual experience of war, and behind them stood the positive fact of the War for the Fatherland. The following generation was excluded from any possibility of practical social activity and behind them stood the horror of the atrocious way in which the Decembrist rising was suppressed by Nicholas I. There was an enormous difference of atmosphere between the epoch of

Alexander I and that of Nicholas. The minds of cultured Russians were being made ready during the Alexandrine period. But creative thought was awake in the time of Nicholas, and it was on its reverse side diametrically opposed to the politics of oppression and gloom. Russian thought was a light glimmering in the darkness. The first man of culture and lover of freedom in Russia was a mason and a Decembrist, but he was not as yet an independent thinker. A lofty and magnanimous mind was a natural property of the cultured stratum of the Russian nobility at the beginning of the nineteenth century. The Decembrists passed through the masonic lodges. Pestel was a mason; N. Turgeniev was a mason and even sympathized with the illuminism of Weisshaupt, that is to say of the extreme left wing of masonry. But masonry did not satisfy the Decembrists; it seemed too conservative; masons were obliged to be obedient to the Government. It was rather humaneness that the masons demanded than the abolition of serfdom. Beside the masonic lodges Russia was covered by secret societies which were actively making ready for political revolution. The first of these secret societies was "The Alliance of Safety." There were also "The Alliance of Virtue," "The Alliance of Prosperity."[8] Radishchev exercised some influence and so did the poems of Ryleev. They sympathized with the French Revolution and with the Greek Revolt. But there was no complete unity of thought among the Decembrists. There were various tendencies among them, some more moderate and others more radical. Pestel and the Southern Society represented the left radical wing of Decembrism. Pestel was in favor of a republic established by dictatorship, while the Northern Society was against a dictatorship. Pestel may be considered the first Russian socialist and his socialism was, of course, agrarian. He was a predecessor of the revolutionary movements in the Russian Intelligentsia. Attention was drawn to the influence upon Pestel of the "ideologist" Destutt de Tracey. The Decembrist Lukin knew Saint-Simon personally. It is a characteristic of Russia, and one which sharply distinguishes her from the West, that there has not been, nor will there be, among us any notable and influential bourgeois ideology. Russian thought of the nineteenth century was to be colored by social ideas. The failure of the

---

8. V. Semevsky, *The Political and Social Ideas of the Decembrists.*

Decembrists leads on to the corresponding and compensating idealism of the thirties and forties. The Russians suffered a great deal
from the impossibility of taking action. Russian romanticism was to
a notable degree a result of this impossibility of effective thought and
action, and an exalted emotionalism took its rise. The influence of
Schelling made itself felt, with the result that Dostoyevsky used the
name of Schelling as a symbol of "the noble and the beautiful." The
fatal failure of Pestel led to the appearance of the beautiful dreamy
youth of Stankevitch. The loneliness of the young people of the
1830s was to be more terrible than the loneliness of the generation of
the Decembrists; it was to lead to melancholia. The masons and the
Decembrists prepared the way for the appearance of the Russian
Intelligentsia of the nineteenth century, which is not well understood
in the West; confusion arose from the fact that in the West they are
called *intellectuelles*. But the masons and the Decembrists, themselves real members of the Russian nobility, were not yet typical
"intelligents," and they were possessed of only a few of the traits
which heralded the coming of the Intelligentsia. Pushkin, the greatest
phenomenon of the Russian language and Russian literature, was not
yet an "intelligent." A specially astonishing trait in Pushkin and one
which determined the spirit of the age was his universalism, his sympathetic responsiveness to the life of the whole world. Without Pushkin, Dostoyevsky and L. Tolstoy would have been impossible, but in
Pushkin there was something which belonged to the Renaissance,
and in this respect the whole of the great Russian literature of the
nineteenth century was different from him, for it was certainly not
Renaissance in spirit. The Renaissance element among us existed
only in the period of Alexander I and at the beginning of the twentieth century. The great Russian writers of the nineteenth century created not from the joy of creative abundance, but from a thirst for the
salvation of the people, of humanity and the whole world, from
unhappiness and suffering, from the injustice and slavery of man.
The coming themes of Russian literature are to be Christian even at
times when in their own thought Russian writers reject Christianity.
Pushkin is the one and only Russian writer of the Renaissance type
and he is evidence of the fact that every people of notable destiny is
a whole cosmos and potentially includes everything in itself. Goethe
is evidence of the same thing in the case of the German people.

Pushkin's poetry, in which the songs of Paradise are heard, is concerned with profound subject matter and above all with the subject of creation. Pushkin affirmed the creativeness of man, the freedom of creation, at the very time when at the opposite pole Gogol, Tolstoy and many others were calling human creativeness in question and expressing doubts about it. But the fundamental Russian theme will be not the creation of a perfect culture but the creation of a better life. Russian literature is to assume a moral character, and a somewhat concealed religious character, more than any other literature in the world. The moral problem is already felt strongly in Lermontov. His poetry is already not Renaissance in spirit. Pushkin was the singer of freedom and liberty, but his freedom is more profound and more independent of the political evil of the day than the freedom towards which the Russian Intelligentsia will turn their energies and aspirations. Lermontov also was bent upon freedom but with a great effort and with a many-sided mind. Lermontov perhaps was the most religious of Russian poets in spite of his wrestling with God. In connection with the problem of Russian Christianity it is a very interesting fact that during the Alexandrine period there lived both the greatest Russian poet, Pushkin, and the greatest Russian saint, St. Seraphim of Sarov—and they never heard a word about each other. And this too is the problem of the relation between genius and sanctity, between creativeness and salvation, which the old Christian consciousness was not able to solve.[9]

3

The Russian Intelligentsia is a quite special and peculiar thing; as a spiritual and social form of human life it existed only in Russia. The Intelligentsia is not a social class and its existence creates a difficulty for Marxist interpreters. The Intelligentsia was an idealistic class, a class of people wholly influenced by ideas and ready to face prison, hard labor and death for the sake of their ideas. Among us the Intelligentsia could not live in the present; it lived in the future and sometimes in the past. The impossibility of political activity led

---

9. This is the central problem of my book, *The Meaning of Creation, an Essa* *cation of Man*, in which I make use of Pushkin and St. Seraphim as examples.

to the profession of the most extreme social doctrines during a period of autocratic monarchy and serfdom. The Intelligentsia was a Russian phenomenon and had characteristically Russian traits, but its feeling about itself was that it had no ground beneath its feet. Such a feeling of having no basis is perhaps a national Russian trait. It is a mistake to regard as national only loyalty to conservative basic principles. Even a revolutionary spirit can also be national. The Intelligentsia had the feeling of freedom from the burden of history, against which they had revolted. It must be remembered that the awakening of Russian consciousness and Russian thought was a revolt against imperial Russia and this is true not only of the Westernizers but of the Slavophils also. The Russian Intelligentsia disclosed an exceptional capacity for appreciating the influence of ideas. Thus the Russians were influenced by Hegel, Schelling, Saint-Simon, Fourier, Feuerbach, Marx, as no one was ever influenced by them in their own countries. The Russians are not skeptics, they are dogmatists. Among them everything takes on a religious character; they have little understanding of what is relative. Darwinism, which in the West was a biological hypothesis, among the Russian Intelligentsia acquired a dogmatic character and so the question at issue was salvation for eternal life. Materialism was a matter of religious faith and its opponents were treated at a certain period as enemies of the emancipation of the people. In Russia everything was appraised and assessed according to the categories of orthodoxy and heresy. The attraction of Hegel had the character of a religious influence and it was expected that even the question of the faith of the Orthodox Church would be solved by Hegel's philosophy. They believed in the *phalanstery* of Fourier and in the coming of the Kingdom of God.

The young people made love in the language of Schelling's philosophy of nature. The same thing showed itself in the fascination exercised both by Hegel and by Büchner. Dostoyevsky was particularly interested in the fate of the "intelligent" Russian whom he called the "saunterer" of the Petersburg period of Russian history, and he was to reveal the spiritual reasons out of which this "sauntering" arose. Schism, apostasy, "sauntering," the impossibility of becoming reconciled to present realities, striving towards the future, towards a better and more righteous life—these are characteristic traits of the Intelligentsia. The loneliness of Chatsky, the lack of foundation in Onegin and Pechorin were phenomena which preceded the appearance of the Intelligentsia. The Intelligentsia was recruited from various social classes; to begin with it was derived in the main from the nobility; then from a variety of other classes: the "superfluous" person, the repentant noble and then the active revolutionary—these are the various stages in the existence of the Intelligentsia. During the thirties of the century there took place among us withdrawal from a present which was felt to be unendurable. There was at the same time an awakening of thought; what Father G. Florovsky wrongly calls an escape from history, that is to say enlightenment, utopianism, nihilism and the spirit of revolution, is also historical.[10] History is not only traditional and it is not only guardianship; a lack of basis has a basis of its own; revolution is a part of the flow of history. When in the second half of the nineteenth century the Intelligentsia of the left took final shape among us, it took on a character like that of a monastic order, and in this process the deep-seated Orthodox foundation of the Russian soul was brought to light: escape from the world which "lieth in wickedness," asceticism, a capacity for sacrifice and the endurance of suffering. It defended itself by intolerance and a sharp marking off of itself from the rest of the world. Psychologically it was an inheritance from the schism and on that account only was it able to survive in the face of persecution. It lived during the whole of the nineteenth century in acute conflict with the empire, with the power of the State. In this conflict the Intelligentsia were acting within their rights. It was a dialectic moment in the destiny of Russia. The idea of Russia to which the empire in its will to power and violence had been false was worn out. The first parent of the Russian Intelligentsia was Radishchev who heralded with enthusiasm its fundamental traits and gave them definite shape. When Radishchev in his *Journey from Paris to Moscow* wrote the words "I looked around me and my soul was lacerated by the sufferings of mankind," the Russian Intelligentsia was born. Radishchev was the most notable phenomenon in Russia in the eighteenth century. The influence of Rousseau is of course to be traced in him as well as the doctrine of natural law. He is notable not because of the originality of his thought but because of the originality of his

---

10. See G. Florovsky, *The Paths of Russian Theology.*

sensitiveness, his aspiration towards truth and righteousness and towards freedom. He was grievously wounded by the injustice of serfdom. He was the first to expose it and was one of the first Russian *narodniks*. He stood head and shoulders above those who surrounded him; he asserted the supremacy of conscience. "If the law," says he, "or the Tsar or any other authority on earth whatsoever, should compel you to do what is not right or constrain you to a violation of the dictates of conscience, then be immovable. Have no fear of humiliation, of suffering and torture or even of death itself." Radishchev sympathized with the French Revolution very deeply, but he protested against the lack of freedom of thought and of the press during the height of the French Revolution. He preached self-restraint in the matter of one's requirements and appealed for the relief of the poor. One may regard Radishchev as the first parent of the radical revolutionary tendencies of the Russian Intelligentsia. With him the principal matter was not the well-being of the State but the well-being of the people. His fate was a premonition of the fate of the revolutionary Intelligentsia; he was condemned to death but the sentence was commuted to ten years' exile in Siberia. The receptivity and the sensitiveness of the Russian Intelligentsia was in truth extraordinary. Russian thought will always be concerned with the transformation of the actual state of affairs. Recognition of the latter will go hand in hand with the changing of it. In their outburst of creativity, the Russians are in search of the ideal life and not only of the perfection of their own achievements. It is even true to say that the aspirations of Russian romanticism were bent upon the improvement of the actual and not simply upon its rejection. What the Russians were in search of in Western thought was above all the strength to change and to transform their own drab reality. They were looking first of all for an escape from the present. They found this strength in German philosophical thought and in French social thought. When Pushkin had finished reading *Dead Souls* he exclaimed: "Oh, Lord, how wretched our Russia is." This was the exclamation of the whole Russian Intelligentsia throughout the nineteenth century, and it endeavored to find a way out from the unbearable sadness of Russian reality into an ideal reality. This ideal reality was either the Russia before Peter's time, or the West, or the coming Revolution. The Russian emotional bent for revolution was the outcome of the unbearableness of the actual conditions in which they lived, of their wrongness and their ugliness. At the same time a revolution was taking place in the significance of political forms themselves. The Intelligentsia was placed in a tragic position between the empire and the people. It revolted against the empire in the name of the people. In the nineteenth century Russia became a vast realm of peasants in the shackles of serfdom, with an autocratic Tsar at the head, whose authority rested not only upon military power but also upon the religious belief of the people. It was an authority with a powerful bureaucracy which formed a separating wall between Tsar and people, with a gentry imposed upon the enslaved people, and taken as a whole themselves very uneducated, stubborn and stupid; and with a small class of cultured people which could easily be broken up and crushed. The Intelligentsia was in fact crushed between two forces— the power of the Tsar and the elemental strength of the people. This elemental strength of the people was a mysterious thing to the Intelligentsia. The Intelligentsia set itself over against the people; it was conscious of a feeling of guilt before the people and had a desire to serve the people. The theme "Intelligentsia and people" is a purely Russian theme and it is too little understood in the West. In the second half of the century the Intelligentsia, keyed up to a revolutionary frame of mind, was obliged to lead an existence which was almost heroic, and this terribly confused its consciousness and turned it away from many sides of the creative life of man. It led to its impoverishment. The people kept silence and awaited the hour when it should say its say. But when that hour struck the people came to the fore as persecutors of the Intelligentsia, in that very revolution which the Intelligentsia had been preparing for well-nigh a hundred years. It is a property of the Russian people to indulge in philosophy. The illiterate Russian loves to pose questions of a philosophic nature about the meaning of life, about God, about the future life, about evil and injustice, about how the Kingdom of God is to be realized in fact. Shchapov, under the influence of the natural sciences in accord with the tone of his period, particularly stresses the fact that it is a property of our people's *way of thinking* to take a realist and not a humanist direction.[11] If the natural sciences did not develop among

---

11. Shchapov's book—already quoted.

us it was due to the real opposition which came from the side of the Orthodox. But all the same in Shchapov's opinion, it was in accordance with the realistic makeup of the Russian people, that in the past applied and practical sciences had predominated among us. Russia in actual fact has a realistic makeup. The Russian has a great aptitude for technical inventions; but this is entirely capable of being combined with his spiritual quest and with his love of philosophizing about life. But Shchapov's opinion in any case is very one-sided. Partly it is connected with the fact that in Russia, as distinct from the West, a classical education was a reactionary force. Shchapov himself was a stranger to philosophy. The fate of the philosopher in Russia is painful and tragic. Philosophy was constantly exposed to persecution and was under suspicion. It found a refuge for itself in the main in the ecclesiastical academies. Golubinsky, Kudryavtsev, Yurkevitch represented philosophy with merit and dignity. But a breach occurred in Russian Orthodoxy, the one and only sort of breach that can occur in traditional philosophy. This even went to such a curious length that at one time the rationalistic and enlightened Wolf was considered particularly advantageous to Orthodox philosophy. The astonishing thing is that philosophy found itself under suspicion and became an object of persecution from the right, to begin with, from Russian obscurantism, but later on from the left, where it became an object of suspicion as spiritualism and idealism which were considered reactionary. Shado, a disciple of Schelling, was expelled from Russia. At one time during the period of Nicholas an ignorant and boorish general was appointed professor of philosophy. The obscurantists sharply attacked philosophical idealism. The climax was that in 1850 the minister of education, Prince Shirinsky-Shikhmatov, entirely prohibited lectures on philosophy in the universities. The odd thing is that he considered the natural sciences less dangerous. The nihilists of the sixties attacked philosophy from the other side because they thought its metaphysics would turn men aside from real action and from the duty of serving the people. In the Soviet period the communists started a persecution against every kind of philosophy except dialectic materialism, but all the same the idea of Russian nihilism and Russian communism itself is also a matter of philosophy. It is very important to note that Russian thinking has an inclination towards totalitarian doctrines and a totalitarian way of looking at life as a whole. That is the only kind of teaching which meets with any success among us. The religious makeup of the Russian people plays its part in this. The Russian Intelligentsia has always been bent upon working out a totalitarian and integral view of life in which truth shall be combined with justice. By means of totalitarian thinking they sought the perfect life and not only perfect works of philosophy, science or art. One might even say that this totalitarian character is a definite attribute of the Intelligentsia. Many notable and learned specialists like, for example, Lobachevsky and Mendeleev, could in no exact sense be reckoned as belonging to the Intelligentsia; while, on the other hand, many who in no way signalized themselves in intellectual work did belong to it. In the eighteenth century and at the beginning of the nineteenth, there was no real philosophy among us. It was in its infancy,[12] and for a long while yet no philosophical culture in the real sense was to arise among us. There were only lonely individual thinkers. We shall see that our philosophy is before all else a philosophy of history. It was precisely the historico-philosophical theme which was to give it a totalitarian character. A real awakening of philosophic thought went on among us under the influence of German philosophy. German idealism, Kant, Fichte, Schelling, Hegel had a determining significance for Russian thought. Russian creative thought began to show itself in an atmosphere of German idealism and romanticism. There was an astonishing duality in the German influence upon Russia. The penetration of Russian political life by Germans was injurious and fatal, but the influence of German philosophy and German spiritual culture was in the highest degree fruitful and creative. The first philosophers among us were disciples of Schelling and were under the influence of natural philosophy and aesthetics. To the school of Schelling belonged M. G. Pavlov, I. Davidov, Galos and Vellinsky. But especially interesting and particularly typical of Russian romanticism was Prince V. F. Odoevsky.[13] Russians travelled in order to hear Schelling. Schelling was very fond of the Russians and believed in Russian messianism. The brothers Kireevsky heard Schelling lecture. It is an interesting fact that Schelling learned about Saint-Mar-

---

12. See G. Shpet, *A Sketch of the Development of Russian Philosophy.*
13. See P. Sakulin, *History of Russian Idealism, Prince Odoevsky.*

tin and Pordage from Odoevsky. Schelling knew Chaadaev very well and valued him highly. Shevirev met Franz Baader who was very closely akin to Russian thought, and spread his opinions in Russia. In 1823 there arose in Russia the society of "The Love of Wisdom" which was the first attempt at an interchange of philosophical thought. After the Decembrist rising the society was suppressed. To the members of this society philosophy ranked above religion. Odoevsky popularized the idea of "The Love of Wisdom" in his contributions to *belles lettres*. To the members of this society it was not so much political as spiritual freedom which was precious. A. Koshelev and I. Kireevsky, who in the course of time became Slavophils, belonged to "The Love of Wisdom." The teaching of Schelling was not a creative movement of thought among us; independent philosophy was not yet born. His influence upon religious philosophy among us at the beginning of the twentieth century was more fruitful. The creative transformation of the teaching of Schelling and still more that of Hegel was not to be found among the disciples of Schelling in the proper sense, but among the Slavophils. In the thirties social mysticism made itself felt as an influence among us; that however was under the influence not of the Germans, but of the French and especially of Lamennais. The whole of the nineteenth century was to be permeated by striving after freedom and social justice. Religious, ethical and social subjects were predominant in Russian philosophical thought. There are two prevailing myths which are capable of becoming dynamic in the chorus of the peoples—the myth of the beginning and the myth of the end. Among the Russians it was the second myth, the eschatological myth, which prevailed. Thus we may define the theme of the Russian nineteenth century as tempestuous striving towards progress, towards revolution, towards the final results of world civilization, towards socialism and at the same time towards the profound and acute consciousness of the emptiness, the ugliness, the soullessness of bourgeois philistinism, of all the results of world progress, revolution, civilization and the rest. I will end this historical introduction with the words of St. Alexander Nevsky who may be regarded as characteristic of Russia and of the Russian people: "God is not in power but in truth." The tragedy of the Russian people lies in the fact that the Russian authorities were not true to those words.

2

The crucial importance of the problem of the philosophy of history • East and West • Russia and Europe • Chaadaev • The Slavophils and the Westernizers • The Two-sidedness of Russian Thought • Russian Universalism • State and People • The Russian Philosophy of History • Khomyakov • Ivan Kireevsky • K. Aksakov • Herzen • N. Danilevsky • Vladimir Solovyov • Narodnichestvo • Nationalism and Messianism

1

INDEPENDENT Russian thought was awakened by the problem of the philosophy of history. It had reflected deeply upon what the thoughts of the Creator were about Russia, about what Russia is, about what sort of destiny it has. It had long been a feeling which was native to Russians, (and I prefer to say "feeling" rather than "knowledge") that Russia has its own particular destiny, that the Russian people are a peculiar people. Messianism is almost as characteristic of the Russian people as it is of the Jews. Is Russia capable of going its own particular way, without repeating all the stages of European history? During the whole of the nineteenth century and even in the twentieth, there were to be controversies among us about which way Russia was to go and whether it would simply be a repetition of the paths of Western Europe. And our thought about the philosophy of history was to flow on in an atmosphere of profound pessimism in relation to Russia's past and especially to its present, and of optimistic faith and hope with regard to its future. Such was Chaadaev's philosophy of history. It was expounded in the celebrated philosophical letter to E. D. Pankova in the year 1829, which was printed in *The Telescope*. It was the awakening of independent original Russian thought. The results of this awakening are well-known. The government of Nicholas I replied to this awakening of thought with the pronouncement that Chaadaev was mad. A doctor had to go and see him every week. He was forbidden to write; he was compelled to keep silence. Later on he wrote *The Apology of a Madman,* which was a very notable production. It is characteristic of the history of Russian thought and of its irregularity that the first Russian philosopher of history, Chaadaev, was an officer of the Lifeguard Hussars, and the first original theologian, Khomyakov, was an officer of the Horseguards. Pushkin wrote of Chaadaev, "In Rome he would have been a Brutus, in Athens a Pericles, among us he is an officer of Hussars," and again he said of him, "He was always a wise man but sometimes a dreamer and an impartial observer of the giddy crowd." Herzen characterized Chaadaev later on as a shot going off in the darkness of the night. The whole of our philosophy of history was to be that challenging answer which Chaadaev expressed in his letter. Hershenson described Chaadaev as "a Decembrist who had turned mystic."[1] Chaadaev was particularly interested not in individual persons but in society. He insisted upon the historical nature of Christianity. He repeated the words of the Lord's Prayer—"Thy Kingdom come." His was a quest for the Kingdom of God upon earth. He handed on this theme to Vladimir Solovyov upon whom he had an undoubted influence. It is incorrect to think that Chaadaev became a Roman Catholic, just as it is incorrect also of Vladimir Solovyov; but he was shaken, and captivated, he says by the universalism of Roman Catholicism and by the active part it had played in history. Orthodoxy appeared to him to be too passive and not historical. There is no doubt that the theocratic ideas of Joseph de Maistre and de Bonald had a certain influence upon Chaadaev and so also had the philosophy of Schelling. To Western Europe these ideas were conservative. To Russia they seemed revolutionary. But Chaadaev was an independent thinker. He did not repeat Western ideas but elaborated them creatively. The disillusionment of Chaadaev in Russia and the disillusionment of Herzen in the West are basic facts in the theme of nineteenth-century Russia. The thirties were years of social utopias among us and a certain exaltation was characteristic of that decade. How did Chaadaev express his revolt against Russian history? "Love of one's native land is a beautiful thing but there is something still

---

1. See M. Hershenson, *P. Chaadaev.*

more beautiful, and that is the love of truth." "It is not through one's native land but through the truth that the way to heaven leads." "I have not learned to love my country with closed eyes, with bowed head and with sealed lips." "Now, the chief thing we owe to our country is truth." "I love my native land as Peter the Great taught me to love it." Chaadaev's thoughts about Russian history and about the past of Russia are expressed with the deepest pain; they are a cry of despair from a man who loved his country. Here is a particularly notable passage from his letter: "We do not belong to one of the great families of the human race; we do not belong either to the West or to the East, and we have no tradition either of the one or of the other. Standing, as it were, outside time, we have been untouched by the worldwide upbringing of the human." "We take our way within time in so strange a manner that with every step we make forward a preceding moment disappears for us irrevocably. This is the natural result of a culture entirely founded upon borrowing and imitation. We have absolutely no interior development, no natural progress. Every idea of ours shoulders out the old ones without leaving a trace." "We belong to the number of those nations which, so to speak, do not enter into the structure of mankind, but exist only in order to teach the world an important lesson of some sort." Chaadaev was disturbed by the "inarticulateness of the Russian." "At the present time we constitute a gap in the moral order of the world." "Looking at us it might be said that the general law of mankind had been abrogated so far as we are concerned. Leading a lonely life in the world we have given nothing to the world; we have taught it nothing; we have contributed no single idea to the aggregate of human ideas; we have not in any way taken a share in promoting the progress of human thought, and every element of that progress which has come our way we have marred and distorted." Russian self-consciousness had to pass through this bitter rejection of self. It was a dialectic moment in the development of the Russian Idea. What is more, Chaadaev himself in *The Apology of a Madman* arrives at an affirmation of the great mission of Russia. Chaadaev thought that the powers of the Russian people had not been given effect to in its history; they remained in a potential state, as it were. This was his line of thought even at a time when he was in revolt against Russian history. But there came into view a possibility of reversing this thesis and this he did in *The Apology of a Madman*. The ineffectiveness of the strength of the Russian people in the past, the absence of greatness in its history became for Chaadaev a pledge of the possibility of a great future, and in this he enunciates certain truths which are fundamental for the whole of Russian nineteenth-century thought. In Russia there is a preeminent example of virgin soil. Its very backwardness provides a possibility of choice. Hidden potential forces will be able to discover themselves in the future. "The past is no longer within our power," exclaims Chaadaev, "but the future depends upon us." "Let us avail ourselves of this immense advantage in the strength of which it is our duty to be obedient only to the voice of enlightened reason and of deliberate will." "Perhaps it would be an exaggeration to distress oneself, even if it be but for a moment, over the destiny of a people from the womb of which the mighty nature of Peter the Great has issued, the all-embracing mind of Lomonosov, and the grandiose genius of Pushkin." Chaadaev was penetrated by faith in the mystical mission of Russia. Russia may yet take a highest place in the spiritual life of Europe. In the second part of his life Chaadaev acknowledged also the greatness of Orthodoxy: "Concentrated upon itself, plunged deep in its own thoughts, locked up in its own life, thus the human mind was built up in the East. On the other hand it developed in the West by scattering itself about, twisting itself in all directions and striving against all hindrances." And finally Chaadaev enunciated the idea which was to be fundamental to all Russian currents of thought in the nineteenth century: "I have a profound conviction that we have a vocation to solve a great many of the problems of social order, to bring about the fulfillment of a great many of the ideas which have taken their rise in societies of the past, and to give an answer to questions of great importance with which mankind is concerned." In a word Chaadaev was permeated by the Russian messianic idea and in him this was combined with the expectation of the coming of the new era of the Holy Spirit. It is a characteristic Russian expectation and it gives expression to Russian pneumacentricism. Chaadaev was quite one of the most remarkable figures of the nineteenth century in Russia. His face was not blurred as the faces of so many Russians are. He had a sharply defined profile; he was a man of great mind and great gifts, but like the Russian people he gave inadequate effect to himself; he remained in a potential state; he wrote next to nothing. The

Westernizing of Chaadaev, his Roman Catholic sympathies remain characteristically Russian phenomena. He had a yearning for form; he revolted against Russian formlessness; he was a very Russian person of the upper classes of the Petersburg period of Russian history. He sought for the Kingdom of God on earth, and he waited for the new era of the Holy Spirit. He arrived at the belief that Russia will say its new word to the world. All this belongs to the problem which Russia has to face. It is true that he looked for historical greatness and that is not a typical Russian characteristic, but a form of compensation for other Russian traits.

Side by side with Chaadaev we must place the figure of Pechorin. He did finally go over to Roman Catholicism and became a Roman Catholic monk; he was one of the first of the Russian emigrants; he did not undergo the persecution of the period of Nicholas. It was a paradox that he went over to Roman Catholicism from liberalism and he loved all freedom of thought. In his revolt against the actual state of affairs by which he was surrounded, he wrote verses among which are these few lines: "How sweet it is to hate one's native land, and eagerly await its annihilation." Only a Russian could write this and what is more only a Russian who really loved his country passionately. His long journey through life as a Roman Catholic monk did not kill his nostalgia for Russia; it was only to grow more strongly within him; in spirit he could return to his native land, but he never saw Russia again. Herzen wrote to ask for an interview with Pechorin in his monastery and has given an account of it in *The Past and Reveries*. Pechorin's answer to Herzen's letter was very remarkable and it contains real foresight. He writes that the material civilization of the future will lead to a tyranny over the human spirit from which there will be no shelter anywhere. Chaadaev and Pechorin represent the religious aspect of the Westernizing movement among us, which preceded the actual rise of Westernizing and Slavophil currents of thought. But there were Slavonic elements also in these religious Westernizers. Pechorin believed that Russia together with the United States will inaugurate a new cycle of history.

The disputes of the Westernizers and Slavophils fill a great part of the century with us. Slavophil motifs existed already in Lermontov, but he thought that Russia lay wholly in the future. Doubts about Europe arose among us under the influence of the French Revolution.

The controversy between the Slavophils and the Westernizers was a dispute about the destiny of Russia and its vocation in the world. Both currents of thought in their historical form have become obsolete and may be considered as having been finally dealt with, but the actual theme remains. In its new forms it arouses passions even in the twentieth century. In the debating circles of the forties Slavophils and Westernizers could still carry on their disputes in the same salons. Khomyakov, a passionate disputant and a powerful dialectician, engaged in battle with Herzen. Herzen said of Khomyakov that he was like a mediaeval knight on guard before the Blessed Virgin; he slept weapon in hand. They carried on their dispute the whole night through. Turgeniev remembers that when a controversy was raging at its height and someone proposed they should have something to eat, Belinsky shouted out: "We have not yet decided the question of the existence of God and you want to eat!" The forties were a period of intense intellectual life. There were many gifted people among the Russians at that time. Speaking of the Westernizers and Slavophils of those times Herzen said: "We had one love, but it was not the same love." He called them a two-faced Janus, and both sides loved freedom, and both sides loved Russia. The Slavophils loved her as a mother, the Westernizers as a child. The children and grandchildren of the Slavophils and the Westernizers have now already grown so far apart that they would not be able to dispute in the same salons. Chernishevsky could still say of the Slavophils that they were among the most educated, the most well-born and the most gifted people in Russian society, but no one could imagine him taking part in a controversy with Khomyakov. The people of the forties belonged to one style of culture, to the same society of the cultured gentry. Belinsky alone was an exception; he belonged to the Intelligentsia but he was a commoner. Later on a sharp differentiation took place. The Russian philosophy of history was obliged before all else to solve the problem of the meaning and significance of Peter's reform which had, so to speak, sliced Russian history in two. It was above all about this that the clash took place. Is the historical path of Russia the same as that of Western Europe, that is to say, the path of common human progress, of common human civilization, and is the peculiarity of Russia to be found only in its backwardness? Or has Russia a special path of its own with its civilization belonging to another type? The Westernizers accepted Peter's reform entirely, and in their view the future of Russia lay in its taking the Western path. The Slavophils believed in a special type of culture springing out of the spiritual soil of Orthodoxy; Peter's reform and the Europeanizing of the Petrine period were a betrayal of Russia. The Slavophils absorbed the Hegelian idea of the vocation of peoples and what Hegel applied to the German people they applied to the Russian. They applied the principles of Hegelian philosophy to Russian history. K. Aksakov even said that the Russian people had a special vocation for understanding the philosophy of Hegel.[2] Hegel's influence was so great that in the opinion of Y. Samarin the fate of the Orthodox Church depended upon the fate of the Hegelian philosophy. Only Khomyakov persuaded him to the contrary of this by no means Orthodox thought, and he amended his dissertation under the influence of Khomyakov.[3] V. Odoevsky had already sharply criticized the West and accused its bourgeois life of being a desiccation of the spirit. Shevyrev, who represented, so to speak, all conservative and official Slavophilism, wrote of the decrepitude and decay of the West, but had close connections with the Western thinker F. Baader, whose mind faced towards the East. Among the classical Slavophils there was no complete rejection of the West; they did not use such language as "decay" in speaking of it; they were too good universalists for that. It was Khomyakov who used the words "The land of holy miracles" in speaking of Western Europe. But they enunciated the doctrine of the distinctive originality of Russia and its path, and it was their desire to explain the causes of its difference from the West. They endeavored to bring to light the primary foundations of Western history. The structure of Russian history as expounded by the Slavophils and in particular by K. Aksakov was entirely fantastic and cannot be maintained in the face of criticism. The Slavophils confused their ideal of Russia, their ideal utopia of the perfect order of society, with the historic past. It is interesting to note that it was principally the Westernizers and not the Slavophils, who worked out Russian historical science. But the Westernizers fell into an error of a different kind; they confused their ideal of the order

---

2. On the part played by Hegel's philosophy, see Chizhevsky, *Hegel in Russland.*
3. See the material of Kalyupanov's *Life of A. Koshelev.*

of life which was best for Russia with that of Western Europe in their own day, and that by no means corresponded with an ideal state of affairs. There was a visionary element in both the Slavophils and the Westernizers, they set up their dream in opposition to the intolerable reality of the regime under Nicholas. Both the Slavophil and the Westernizing points of view were mistaken in appraising the reform of Peter. The Slavophils did not understand the inevitability of that reform for the very mission of Russia in the world. They were unwilling to acknowledge that only with the Petrine era did thought and expression become possible in Russia. Only then did the very thought of the Slavophils itself and the great Russian literature become a possibility. The Westernizers did not understand the peculiar originality of Russia and would not acknowledge the unhealthiness of Peter's reform. They did not see wherein the singularity of Russia lay. The Slavophils were the first *narodniks* among us; they were *narodniks* on a religious basis. The Slavophils, like the Westernizers also, were lovers of freedom and like them did not see it in the actual environment in which they found themselves.

The Slavophils were bent upon the idea of the organic and upon integrality. The actual idea of the organic had been taken by them from their reading of the German romantics. The perfection of life, according to their ideal, consisted in its being organic, but they projected this ideal conception of the organic upon the historical past, upon the era before Peter; they could see no sign of it whatever in the Petrine period. It is impossible now not to feel astonished at the idealization of Muscovite Russia by the Slavophils; it led to nothing; it bore no resemblance to what the Slavophils loved; there was no freedom in it, no love, no enlightenment. Khomyakov had an extraordinary love of freedom and he connected the idea of the organic with it. But where indeed was freedom to be found in the Russia of Moscow? For Khomyakov the Church is the sphere of freedom. Was the Church of Muscovite Russia ecclesiastically free? The Slavophils put forward an integral and organic conception of Russia as a contrast to the dividedness and complexity of Western Europe; they fought against Western rationalism which they regarded as the source of all evils. This rationalism they traced back to Catholic scholasticism. In the West everything is mechanized and rationalized. The perfectly whole life of the spirit is contrasted with rationalistic segmentation. The conflict with Western rationalism was already a mark of the German romantics. F. Schlegel spoke about France and England, which were the West to Germany, in the same way that the Slavophils spoke about the West, including in it Germany too. But all the same Ivan Kireevsky in a remarkable essay *On the character of enlightenment in Europe and its relation to enlightenment in Russia* succeeded in formulating the typical marks of the difference between Russia and Europe, and this in spite of the wrongness of the Slavophil conception of Russian history. The same opposition exists also within Western Europe, for example, the antithesis between religious culture and godless civilization. But the type of Russian thinking and Russian culture was always very distinct from that of Western Europe. Russian thinking was much more totalitarian and integral than the thinking of the West, which is more differentiated and divided into categories. This is how Kireevsky formulates the distinction and states the antithesis: In the West everything has arisen from the triumph of formal reason; the tendency to rationalistic segmentation was, so to speak, the second fall of man. "Three elements belonging to the West—the Roman Catholic Church, the ancient Roman culture, and political government arising from the violence of conquest—were entirely alien from Russia." "Theology in the West took on a character of rational abstraction. In Orthodoxy it preserved the inward integrality of spirit. In the one case there was a development of the powers of the mind, in the other a striving after a living union. In the West there was a movement of the mind towards truth, by way of logical concatenation of concepts, while here in Orthodoxy is to be found a striving after truth by means of an inward raising of consciousness towards integrality of the heart and concentration of the mind. On the one hand it was the searching after an external and lifeless unity; on the other the striving towards something inward and living." "Sectionalism and integrality, rationality and wisdom, such are respectively the final expressions of Western Europe and the ancient Russian cultivation of the mind." The central philosophical idea from which Ivan Kireevsky starts is expressed by him in this way: "The inward consciousness which is to be found in the depths of the soul is a living general point of concentration of all the separate powers of the intellect and one which is capable of apprehending the loftiest truth. Such a consciousness is constantly raising the level of the very form of a man's thinking. While subduing his rational self-conceit it does not hamper the free operation of the natural laws of his thinking. On the contrary it fortifies his independent existence and at the same time subjugates him of his own accord to faith." The Slavophils sought in history, in society and in culture that same spiritual integrality which they found in the soul. It was their desire to bring to light the original type of culture and social order, and to do so upon the spiritual basis of Orthodoxy. "In the West," wrote K. Aksakov, "they kill souls and replace them by the perfecting of political forms and the establishment of good order and by police action. Conscience is replaced by law; regulations become a substitute for the inward impulse; even charity is turned into a mechanical business in the West; all the anxiety is for political forms." "At the foundation of the Russian State there lies spontaneity, freedom and peace." This last idea of Aksakov's is clamantly incompatible with historical reality and reveals the unhistorical character of the fundamental ideas of the Slavophils about Russia and the West. It is a typology; it is a description of spiritual types, not a description of actual history. How, from the point of view of the Slavophil philosophy of Russian history, are we to explain the rise of a colossal empire of the military type and the hypertrophy of the State at the expense of the free life of the people? Russian life was organized from above, as part of the life of the State, and it was organized by force. The independent action of social groups can be looked for only in the pre-Muscovite period. The Slavophils were bent upon the organic interpretation of history; and they valued the popular traditions. This conception of the organic existed only in their ideal of the future, not in the actual historical past. When the Slavophils said that *obshchina* and *zemshchina* were the foundations of Russian history, they must be understood as meaning that *obshchina* and *zemshchina* are their ideal of Russian life. When Ivan Kireevsky contrasted Russian theology with Western theology, this must be understood as a program, a plan of Russian theology, of a sort of Russian theology which had never yet existed anywhere; it only began with Khomyakov. But the Slavophils brought before the Russian consciousness the task of surmounting abstract thought, of passing over to concreteness; they made it aware of a demand for apprehension not only

by the mind but also by feeling and the will, and by faith. The force
of this remains even if the Slavophils' conception of history be
rejected. The Slavophils were not enemies and haters of Western
Europe as were the Russian nationalists of the obscurantist type;
they were enlightened Europeans; they believed in the great vocation of Russia and the Russian people; they believed in the truth
which was hidden in the Russian people, and they attempted to
describe a number of special marks of that vocation. It was in this
that their importance lay, and this was the service they rendered.

His friends said of Khomyakov that he would write some sort of
enormous work. It was his *Notes upon World History* which are
comprised in three volumes of his collected works.[4] The actual book
itself remained unwritten. These are only notes and materials for the
book. Aristocratic laziness, of which Khomyakov accuses himself,
prevented his writing the actual book, but from these notes we can
establish Khomyakov's philosophy of history. It rests as a whole
upon the contrast between two types and upon the conflict of two
principles in history, that is to say, it is consecrated to what is always
the same fundamental Russian theme, of Russia and Europe, of East
and West. Notwithstanding the fact that it is out of date and that frequently Khomyakov's views of history are untrue, the central idea of
the book is remarkable and holds one's interest. He sees the conflict
of two principles in history—freedom and necessity, spirituality and
materialism. Thus it is made clear that the principal thing, the thing
of highest value to him, was freedom. Necessity, the power of the
material over the spiritual was an enemy against which he fought all
his life. He saw this necessity, this power of materiality over the
spirit in pagan religion and in Roman Catholicism, in Western rationalism and in Hegel's philosophy. The principles which are seen in
conflict by him he expressed in terminology which is relative and
fruitful of misunderstanding. They are *iranstvo* and *kushitstvo*. *Iranstvo* is freedom and spirituality; *kushitstvo* is necessity and materiality, and of course it becomes clear that Russia is *iranstvo* and the
West is *kushitstvo*. To Khomyakov only the Hebrew religion is *iranstvo*; all pagan religions are *kushitstvo*. Characteristic of *iranstvo* are
theism and the Word; characteristic of *kushitstvo* is magic. Rome is

---

4. See my book, *A.S. Khomyakov.*

kushitstvo very particularly. Khomyakov paid due reverence to the freely creative spirit; but did free spirit exist, did freedom of the spirit exist or the spirit of freedom, in Muscovite Russia? Was not the stifled and fettered spirit of the Moscow Tsardom precisely more like *kushitstvo*, and was there not more freedom in the West where men were struggling for freedom and where that freedom of conscience and thought which were so dear and precious to Khomyakov were first asserted? Here the same thing happened with Khomyakov as with the Slavophil attitude towards history in general. Very valuable ideas are put forward, ideas which are characteristic of the strivings of the best of the nineteenth-century Russians. And these ideas are incorrectly applied to history. A real feeling for freedom existed in Khomyakov. But his doctrine of freedom, which lay at the very foundation of his philosophy and theology, was a possibility only after the doctrine of autonomy and spiritual freedom in Kant and German idealism had been made known. All the representatives of our reactionary and obscurantist thought had already pointed this out, but they lost sight of the fact that the sources of freedom of the spirit are embedded in Christianity, which guarantees them, and that without Christianity both Kant and all the defenders of freedom would have been impossible. It is very important for Khomyakov's philosophy of history that he regarded faith as the driving principle of history. Religious faith lies at the foundation of every civilization, of every path in history and of political thought, and by this also the difference between Russia and Western Europe is defined. The Orthodox Faith is the first principle of Russia. The Roman Catholic Faith is the first principle of Western Europe. Rationalism, that deadly sin of the West, has found a place in Roman Catholicism. And it is possible to find in Catholic scholasticism that same rationalism and that same power of necessity which exists in the European rationalism of the new age, in Hegel's philosophy, and in materialism. It was Russia, a Russia reduced to impotence as it was by the despotism of the regime of Nicholas, which was to pass on to the West the secret of freedom, being itself free from the sin of that rationalism which shackles men to necessity. In his verses, which are very mediocre as poetry but most interesting as revealing Khomyakov's thoughts, he exclaims, "Tell them the secret of freedom," and again, "Bestow upon them the gift of holy freedom"; by "them" he meant the West. At that same time many Russians were streaming away to the West in order to breathe the air of freedom; but after all there was a truth in Khomyakov which was not disproved by the empirical Russian reality. There is enshrined deep down in the Russian people greater freedom of spirit than there is among the more free and enlightened peoples of the West. There is enshrined a greater freedom in the heart of Orthodoxy than there is in Roman Catholicism. The vastness of this freedom is one of the polar principles in the Russian people and with it the Russian idea is connected. The inconsistency of Russia finds expression in Khomyakov's own writings too. He idealized ancient Russia less than any of them and spoke frankly about the wrongness of it. There are pages of his which remind one of Chaadaev: "Nothing good," he says, "nothing worthy of respect or imitation was to be found in Russia. Everywhere and at all times there was illiteracy, injustice, brigandage, sedition, oppression of the person, poverty, disorder, ignorance and moral corruption. The eye does not come to rest upon a single bright moment in the life of the people nor upon a single period of consolation." It would be difficult to find so vigorous an accusation even in the Westernizers. Of all the Slavophils, Khomyakov, who was quite the strongest character in that camp, idealized the historical past of Russia least and was least hostile to Western culture. He was even an Anglophile. The later Slavophil K. Aksakov, in contrast to N. Danilevsky, admitted the idea of a universal human culture. But one and all of them believe that Russia ought not to tread the way of the West and that the Slavonic Russian world was the world of the future. Repentance for the sins of Russia in the past was in the highest degree characteristic of Khomyakov. He calls upon God in prayer to forgive the "dark deeds of our fathers." Enumerating the sins of the past, he calls us to prayer and repentance and pronounces these words which still move us:

When drunk with fury, you summoned foreign mercenaries to the ruin of Russia.

Particularly well-known is his poem

Full of black injustice in thy tribunals and branded with the yoke of slavery.

While exposing the sins of the past and of the present he continues to believe that Russia, unworthy as it is of being chosen, has been chosen.

> Within thy bosom, Russia mine,
> There is a bright and gentle spring
> Which pours out living waters, thine;
> Hidden, unknown, a mighty thing.

In the national consciousness of Khomyakov there is a contradiction which belongs to all forms of national messianism. The vocation of Russia presents itself as connected with the fact that the Russian people are the most humble people in the world. But there exists among that people a pride in their humility. The Russian people are the least military-minded and a peace-loving people, but at the same time this people must rule in the world. Khomyakov accuses Russia of the sin of taking pride in external success and glory. Among the children and grandchildren of the Slavophils this contradiction becomes still stronger; they simply turned into nationalists, a thing which could not be said of the founders of Slavophilism. There was an inconsistency also in the attitude of the Slavophils to the West. I. Kireevsky was at first a Westernizer and the journal *The European* was suppressed because of his essay on the nineteenth century. But even after he became a Slavophil he wrote: "Even now I still love the West. I am bound to it by many unbroken ties of sympathy. I belong to it by my upbringing, by my way of life, by my tastes and by the argumentative make-up of my mind and even by the attachment of my heart." "Everything beautiful and noble and Christian we must make our own, even if it be European." He says that Russian culture is only the highest degree of Western culture and nothing more. In all this the universalism of the Slavophils, which later on disappeared, makes itself felt. I. Kireevsky was the most romantic of the Slavophils; to him belong the words: "the best thing to be found in the world is a vision." Every activity of his was paralyzed by the regime of Nicholas I. He was in particularly close touch with *Optina Pustyn*, the spiritual heart of Orthodoxy, and at the end of his life he finally steeped himself in Eastern mysticism and made a study of the writings of the Fathers. Khomyakov was of a more virile and realist

nature. I. Kireevsky had no desire for the return of the external peculiarities of ancient Russia but only for the spiritual wholeness of the
Orthodox Church. K. Aksakov, a grown-up infant, was alone in
believing in the perfection of pre-Petrine institutions.

What sort of ideal Russian principles had the Slavophils maintained? The Slavophils were originally Russian landowners, educated men, humanists, lovers of freedom, but they were deeply
rooted in the soil, very closely connected with a particular type of life
and they suffered from the limitations which that type of life,
imposed. This link between Slavophilism and a particular manner of
life could not fail to weaken the eschatological side of their Christianity. With all their animosity towards the empire they still felt the
solid earth under their feet and had no premonitions of the catastrophes which were to come. Spiritually they were still living before
Dostoyevsky, before the challenging appearance of Tolstoy, before
the crisis of man, before the spiritual revelation. In this respect they
differed greatly not only from Dostoyevsky, not only from Vladimir
Solovyov, who had closer connections with the elements of air than
with the element of earth, but even from K. Leontyev who was
already in the grip of a catastrophic feeling about life. In the era of
Nicholas I the volcanic nature of the ground had not yet been disclosed. Khomyakov and the Slavophils cannot be called in any exact
sense "messianic." The prophetic element in them was comparatively weak; they were aware of the profound opposition between
Holy Russia and the Empire, but the idea of Holy Russia was not
prophetic; it was directed to the past and to the cult of holiness
among the Russian people. The Slavophils likewise took very little
notice of Russian pilgrimage and Russian rebelliousness. So far as
they were concerned, Orthodox Christians, so to speak, have their
abiding City. The patriarchal organic theory of society was peculiarly theirs, i.e. that the basis of society is the family; and that society ought to be constructed upon the analogy of family relationships.
The Slavophils were very much family-minded; they were people
with a strong sense of family. But K. Leontyev was more in the right
when he denied the sense of family among the Russians, and recognized the great strength of the autocratic State. The peoples of the
West, the French in particular, have a greater sense of family than the
Russians and find much greater difficulty in breaking with family

traditions. K. Aksakov, the most naive of the Slavophils, says that "the ethical end ought to be achieved by ethical means, without help from without, and without the power of compulsion. The one way which is entirely worthy of man is the way of free persuasion, the way of peace, the way which the Divine Saviour revealed to us and which was followed by His Apostles." This does the highest honor to his moral consciousness and describes his ideal, but it is by no means compatible either with Russian history or with historic Orthodoxy; and it was always like that with the Slavophils. Khomyakov, for instance, always spoke about ideal Orthodoxy and set it up as a contrast to his ideal Catholicism. In the same way he was always speaking about an ideal of Russia, about the Russia of his ideal and for that reason he gave a wrong interpretation to the actual facts of history. Khomyakov, like the majority of Russians, like the best of Russians, did not hold the Roman conception of property. He thought that the whole people, who are the only owners of the land, handed over to him the wealth of the land, and entrusted him with the possession of it.[5] But all the same he lived the life of a very rich landowner and had the characteristics of that way of living. K. Aksakov taught that "the Russian people are not politically minded and what they want for themselves is not political freedom but freedom of the spirit." But they had neither political freedom nor freedom of the spirit, and least of all did they enjoy freedom of the spirit in the Russia of Moscow. The Slavophils looked upon the peasant commune as though it were one of the everlasting foundations of Russia and the guarantee of an originality of Russia's own; they contrasted it with Western individualism. But it can be taken as proved that the commune was not exclusively a peculiarity of Russia and that it belonged to all forms of economic life at a certain level of development. The Slavophils were under the influence of their *narodnik* illusions. To them the commune was not a fact of history but something imposing which stands outside the realm of history; it is the "other world" so to speak within this world. A sense of community does actually belong to the Russian people in a greater degree than to the peoples of the West; they have less of the Western individualism; but this is a spiritual aspect, a metaphysical property of the Russian people, and

---

5. On this point, see my book, *A.S. Khomyakov.*

it is not tied to any form of economic life whatever. When the Slavophils, and K. Aksakov in particular, stressed the importance of the choric principle among the Russian people, as distinct from the complacent self-sufficiency and isolation of the individual, they were right, but this belongs to the spiritual traits of the Russian people. "In the Russian commune personality was not crushed, it was simply deprived of its turbulence, its egoism, its exclusiveness; there was freedom in it, as there is in a chorus." This, of course, does not mean that the vocation of Russia in the world, the messianic consciousness of the Russian people, is linked to a backward form of economic life in the community. The Slavophils were monarchists and even supporters of the absolute monarchy. I shall write in a special chapter about Slavophil thought and its relation to the State and to authority and about the anarchic element in their thought. But at the moment it must be noted that in Khomyakov there was no religious conception of autocracy; he was a democrat in his idea of the source of authority, and he was opposed to the theocratic state and to Caesaro-papalism. But both Khomyakov and all the Slavophils regarded some form of monarchy which offered a contrast to Western absolutism, as an essential principle of Russian originality and the Russian vocation. They maintained that there are three basic principles of Russia: Orthodoxy, autocracy and the sentiment of nationhood. But they understood these things in a sense which was different from the official ideology of the government in which Orthodoxy and the sense of nationhood were in subjection to autocracy. In their classification Orthodoxy occupied the first place. Dostoyevsky adopted a critical attitude to the Slavophils and did not regard his own thought as a derivative from theirs. In actual fact the difference was indeed a great one. Dostoyevsky thought highly of the Westernizers for making a new experiment, for the dynamism of their will and for their complex ideas. In his opinion the Slavophils failed to understand the movement. He makes a stand for the tragic realism of life against the immobile idealism of the Slavophils.

The Slavophils had their own utopia and they regarded it as truly Russian. This utopia made it possible for them to live under the empire of Nicholas I, which they repudiated. Into this utopia there entered an ideal Orthodoxy, an ideal autocracy, an ideal sentiment of nationhood. Their view of the life of the people was organic and their view of the relation between the Tsar and the people was organic, and inasmuch as everything had to be organic, there must be nothing formal, or juridical, and no legal guarantees of any kind are necessary. This organic relationship was opposed to what is stipulated by contract; everything must be based upon reliance on good faith, upon love and upon freedom. The Slavophils, typical romantics in this respect, maintained that life should be based upon principles which stand on a higher level than that of legal contract. But the denial of legal principles depressed life below the level of legal principles. Guarantees of the rights of human personality are not necessary when the relationship is one of love, but the relationships which exist in human societies bear very small resemblance to the relationship of love. At the basis of Slavophil sociology lay Orthodoxy and German romanticism. The organic doctrine of society belongs to the same family of ideas as those of F. Baader, Schelling, Adam Müller and Görres, but on Russian soil this family of ideas took on a color which set it in sharp opposition to étatism. The Slavophils had no love for the State and for authority. We shall see that as distinct from the Catholic West, Slavophil theology denies the idea of authority in the Church, and in the mouth of Khomyakov proclaims a freedom which has never actually existed. Khomyakov's idea of *sobornost*, the meaning of which will be explained in another chapter, has an important bearing also upon his doctrine of society, but this is indeed the Russian sense and consciousness of community, the choric principle, the unity of love and freedom which has no external guarantees whatever; the idea is purely Russian. This community spirit the Slavophils set over against the chivalry of the West which they accused of an unchristian individualism and of pride. The whole Slavophil way of thinking was hostile to the spirit of aristocracy and was permeated by its own particular kind of democratic spirit. Legalism, formalism, aristocracy they ascribed to the spirit of Rome and it was with that that they were chiefly in conflict. They believed that Christianity had been absorbed by the Russian people with greater purity because the soil upon which the seed of Christian truth had fallen was more active. They very greatly minimized the element of paganism in Russian popular Orthodoxy, as they did also the influence of Byzantinism. K. Leontyev acknowledges that Khomyakov's is not authentic Orthodoxy, that it is too liberal and modernized, and

in opposition to it he contrasts ascetic monasticism and the severe
Byzantine Orthodoxy of Mount Athos. The Slavophil sociology and
Slavophil theology also underwent the influence of humanism.
Khomyakov was a decided opponent of the death penalty and of
harsh punishment, and it is doubtful whether he was able to reconcile
himself to the idea of the everlasting torments of hell. In this he was
very Russian. The rejection of capital punishment enters into the
Russian idea. It may be that Beccaria also had an influence upon
Russian penal legislation, but repugnance to the death penalty
entered into no single people to the extent that it entered into the
Russians, among whom there is no inclination to gaze upon an execution as upon a show. Turgeniev recorded the impression he got
from the execution of Tropman in Paris in these words: "Nobody
was looking on as a human being or as one who was conscious of
being present at the carrying out of a measure of public justice.
Everyone was trying to rid himself of responsibility for that murder." This is a Russian not a Western impression. In this respect the
Slavophils are in line with the Westernizers, with the revolutionary
socialists, with Tolstoy and with Dostoyevsky. Among the Russians
and it may be among the Russians only, there exists a doubt about
the righteousness of punishment. This is in all probability connected
with the fact that the Russians are people with a community spirit,
though they are not socialized in the Western sense, that is to say
they do not recognize the supremacy of society over man. The Russian legal pronouncements about property and theft are decisions
which rest not upon an attitude to property as a social institution but
upon an attitude to man. We shall see that there is a connection
between this and the Russian struggle against the bourgeois spirit
and the Russian refusal to accept the bourgeois world. "Repentant
gentlefolk" are a purely Russian phenomenon. There is not that hier-
archism among the Russians which exists in the Western peoples. It
is not to be found in any domain. The Russian opposition between
the Intelligentsia and the people and between the gentry and the people is also due to this fact. In the West the Intelligentsia is a function
of the life of the people and the gentry as a class are a function of the
national life viewed in terms of a hierarchy, whereas among the Russians one's consciousness of being a member of the Intelligentsia or
of the gentry was with the best people a consciousness of one's guilt

and of one's duty in regard to the people. This certainly means that as against the organic theory of the Slavophils, the ordering of life in the West was more organic than it was in Russia. But this form of the organic was bad. The Slavophils were, so to speak, insufficiently aware of the fact that the sense of the organic is already the sense of hierarchy. Tolstoy and even N. Mikhailovsky, in the conflict against the organic theory of society which they waged on behalf of the individuality of man, were more in the right than the Slavophils. But in any case the Slavophils desired "a Russia of Christ" and not "a Russia of Xerxes,"[6] which was what our nationalists and imperialists wanted. The "Idea" of Russia was always grounded in a prophetic view of the future and not upon what is at the moment, and indeed messianic consciousness cannot be otherwise.

An exceptional interest attaches to the letter which Franz Baader wrote to Count Uvarov, the minister of education. The letter is entitled *Mission de l'église Russe dans la décadence du Christianisme de l'Occident*. It was first published in a book by E. Susini called *Lettres Inédites de Franz von Baader.*[7] This was the first detailed systematic statement of Baader's general view of the world. Baader was a very remarkable and in his own day an inadequately appreciated thinker. He had particularly close connections with Russian thought. He was a free Catholic and at the same time a Christian theosophist. He revived interest in Jacob Boehme and had an influence upon Schelling in his latest period. He had a great deal of sympathy with the Orthodox Church and desired closer contact with it. In Russia he saw a mediator between East and West. Baader says a great deal which comes very near the Slavophils and Vladimir Solovyov. He decided to go to Russia after receiving an invitation from Prince Galitzin, but what happened to him provides a very Russian story. He was arrested at the frontier and turned out of Russia. Baader took great offense at this and wrote about it to Alexander I and to Prince Galitzin. But all the same he never got into Russia. In the letter to Uvarov he has put his remarkable thoughts about the mission of the Orthodox Church and of Russia. Great interest attaches to the letter from the fact that it reveals the existence in the West of thought

---

6. The reference is to some verses by Vladimir Solovyov, "What sort of East do you wish to be? The East of Xerxes or the East of Christ?"

7. Also in two volumes of a work of Susini's, *Franz Baader et le Romantisme Mystique.*

which was close to Russian thought. A great deal of it might stand over the signature of Khomyakov. The Russians have written much and have frequently written unjustly about the decomposition of the West, having particularly in view the anti-Christian West. But Baader speaks of the decomposition of even the Christian West and looks for the salvation of the West in Russia and the Orthodox Church. The letter, which is written in French, is of such interest that I reproduce a considerable part of it:

> If there is one fact that characterizes the present epoch, it is certainly the West's irresistible movement toward the East. In this great rapprochement, Russia, which possesses both western European and Eastern elements, must necessarily play the part of the intermediary who halts the deadly consequences of the collision. If I am not mistaken, the Russian Church for its part has a similar task to fulfil in the face of the the alarming and scandalous decadence of Christianity in the West. In the face of the stagnation of Christianity in the Roman Church and its dissolution in the Protestant Church, the Russian Church to my mind has an intermediary mission—one that is more connected than is usually thought with the country to which it belongs. Let me say something briefly about the decadence of Christianity in the West and the reasons why the Russian Church has managed to stand aside from this decadence and is thus able to exercise a liberating influence on the West. This influence will not be polemical but will result from its example and its doctrine, which is solidly founded on religious knowledge which the Roman Catholicism is far removed from by its destructive principle (by its science hostile to faith).... As a constitutive principle, the French have chosen and infected themselves with the destructive principle of revolution, just as the philosophers have adopted as their constitutive principle the destructive principle of Cartesianism, which at bottom is little better than scepticism.... I have been the first, and am still almost the only one, who has discoverecd this fundamental error in modern philosophy; I have shown that all philosophers since Descartes and his successor Spinoza

(including Leibniz) have started from this principle which is revolutionary and destructive as regards religious life and which, in the political sphere, has given birth to the constitutional principle. I have shown that a fundamental reform is possible only insofar as it works simultaneously in the two spheres of philosophy and politics. To my mind, the statesmen and leaders are dangerously wrong when they presume that the mode of thinking of a people (that is to say, their philosophy) is a matter of indifference and that science without prayer does not necessarily entail government without prayer—which is ruinous for governors and governed alike.... Until now, providence has kept the Russian Church outside this European movement whose effect has been to dechristianize philosophy as well as science. And precisely because it has defended ancient catholicism against the two enemies, Papism and Protestantism, and because it does not proscribe the use of reason like the Roman Church and yet does allow the abuses that can result from it, the Russian Church alone is capable of presenting itself as mediator, which should moreover occur by the sole help of science in Russia and "by Russians."

(S'il est un fait qui caractérise l'époque actuelle, c'est assurément ce mouvement irrésistible de l'occident vers l'orient. La Russie qui possède en elle l'élément Européen occidental aussi bien que l'élément oriental, doit, dans ce grand rapprochement nécessairement jouer le rôle de l'intermédiaire qui arrêtera les funestes conséquences du choc. L'église Russe de son côté a maintenant, si je ne me trompe, une tâche semblable à remplir à l'occasion de la décadence alarmante et scandaleuse du Christianisme dans l'occident: placeé en face de la stagnation du Christianisme dans l'église Romaine et de sa dissolution dans l'église protestante, elle reçoit à mon avis une mission intermédiaire qui est plus lieé qu'on ne le pense de l'ordinaire avec celle du pays auquel celle appartient. Qu'il me soit permis d'indiquer en peu de mots cette décadence du Christianisme dans l'occident et les causes pour lesquelles l'église Russe s'était maintenue à l'abri de cette

*décadence, est en état, par ci-même, d'exercer une influence
libératrice sur l'occident. Cette influence ne sera point
polémique, elle résultera de son exemple et de sa doctrine
solidement fondeé sur la science religieuse dont le catholicisme Romain est aussi loin par son principe destructif (par
sa science hostile à la foi)....Les Français ont choisi et inoculé
en eux comme principe constitutif le principe destructif de la
révolution, de même que les philosophes ont adopté pour
principe constituant le principe destructeur de deate
Carthésien, lequel dans le fond ne vaut pas mieux que le
scepticisme.... J'ai été le premier et je suit encore presque le
seul, qui ait découvert cette erreur fondamentale de la philosophie moderne; j'ai démontré que tous les philosophes (sans
en excepter Leibnitz) depuis Descartes et son successeur
Spinoza, sont partis de ce principe destructeur et revolution-
aire en ce qui tient à la vie religieuse, qui dans le sphère de la
politique a donné naissance au principe constitutionnel: j'ai
demontre qu'une reforme fondamentale n'est possible qu'en
tant qu'elle s'exercera simultanément dans les deux sphères
de la philosophie et de la politique. Ils se trompent à mon avis
d'une manière dangereuse ces hommes d'Etat et ces meneurs
qui présument que la mode de penser des peuples (c'est-à-dire
leur philosophie) est une chose indifférente, et qu'une science
sans prière n'entraîne pas après elle un gouvernement sans
prière—cette ruine pour gouverneur et gouvernés.... La
providence a tenur jusqu' à ce jour l'église Russe en dehors de
ce mouvement européen, dont l'effet a été de déchristianiser
aussi bien la science que la société civile; et précisement
parce qu'elle a défendu l'ancien catholicisme contre ces deux
ennemis, le papisme et le protestantisme, parce qu'elle ne
proscrit pas l'usage de la raison comme l'église Romaine sans
laisser passage, comme le protestantisme, aux abus qui en
peuvent résulter—elle seule est capable de se présenter
comme médiatrice, ce qui du reste devra se faire par le seul
secours de la science en Russie "par des Russes.")*

Baader supposes that a certain number of Russians will go to
Munich to study and to listen to his lectures in order to "Fill a gap

which still exists in Russia as in the West, at the same time as serving as a model for the West, and proving to it (which has not been done yet) that true science does not exist without faith and that true faith cannot subsist without science." Some mistaken judgments on Baader's part leap to the eyes: Roman Catholicism does not repudiate reason; Protestantism does not repudiate faith. The doubt of Descartes, and the French Revolution, were not merely destructive; they had a positive meaning as well. But the hopes which Baader placed on Russia are of immense interest. Of the Slavophils' philosophy I shall speak in another chapter, but for the moment it is to be noted that in Russia there was a double issue from philosophy—among the Slavophils it issued in religion and faith, among the Westernizers in revolution and socialism, and in both cases there was a striving towards integrality, towards a totalitarian view of the world, towards a union of philosophy and life, of theory and practice.

2

Occidentalism arose among us in the same connection—of Russia and its path and its relation to Europe. The Westernizers accepted the reforms of Peter and the Petrine era, but to the Empire of Nicholas I they reacted even more negatively than the Slavophils did. Occidentalism is more of an Eastern phenomenon than a Western. To the Western peoples the West was a reality and not infrequently a repugnant and hateful reality. To the Russians the West was an ideal, it was a vision. The Westernizers were just as much Russians as the Slavophils; they loved Russia and were passionately desirous of its highest good. Two tendencies rapidly formed themselves in Russian occidentalism—the more moderate and liberal tendency which was interested particularly in questions of philosophy and art, which submitted to the influence of German idealism and romanticism; and another tendency which was more revolutionary and concerned with social matters, and which absorbed the influence of French socialist currents of thought. And meanwhile Hegel's philosophy influenced both the one and the other. Stankevich, an outstandingly perfect example of the idealist of the forties, was one of the first of the followers of Hegel. Herzen, who had no connection with Stankevich's circle, and represents a sociallyminded occidentalism, also went through a period in which he was influenced by Hegel and regarded Hege's philosophy as the algebra of revolution. The revolutionary interpretation of Hegel preceded Marxism, it indicated a transition to Feuerbach. Ridiculing the influence of Schelling's philosophy, Herzen says: "The man who amused himself by going for a walk in Sokolniki went in order to give himself up to a pantheistic feeling of his unity with the cosmos." Herzen has left some remarkable reminiscences of the idealists of the forties who were friends of his: "What was it that had touched these people? Whose inspiration had re-created them? Not a thought did they have, not a care for their public position, for their personal advantage or for their security. All their life and all their strength were devoted to the common good, with no question of personal advantage. Some of them forget their wealth and others their poverty and they move forward without a halt towards the solution of theoretical questions. Interest in truth, in life, interest in the sciences and in the arts, interest in humanity, swallows up everything." "In what corner of the contemporary West will you find such groups of detached votaries of thought, of devotees of science, of fanatical adherents of their convictions, as these who hair is going grey but whose aspirations are eternally young?" That is indeed the Russian Intelligentsia. Herzen adds: "In contemporary Europe there is no youth; there are no young men." In Russia there was youth, and there were young men there. Dostoyevsky used to speak of Russian boys deciding cursedly difficult question. Turgeniev was studying Hegel's philosophy in Berlin, and he says this on the subject: "In philosophy we were searching for everything in the world except pure thought." The idealists of the forties were striving to achieve a harmony of individual feeling. In Russian thought the moral element predominated over the metaphysical; behind it was concealed an eagerness for the transformation of the world. The exceptional interest in the philosophy of Schelling and Hegel during the thirties and forties did not lead to the establishment of independent Russian philosophy. An exception must be made only in the case of a few philosophical ideas of the Slavophils, but these they did not develop. Philosophy was nothing but a way either of transforming the soul or of transforming society. There was a cleavage between all of them and the Empire. The problem of their relation to "reality" was a torment to them. We shall see later on the part that

Hegel's philosophy played in this. What is known as the idealism of the forties played an enormous part in the philosophy of personality which was held by cultured Russians. It was only in the sixties that the idealist type was replaced by the realist, but the traits of the idealist did not entirely disappear, not even when they began to be influenced by materialism and positivism instead of Schelling and Hegel. There is no need to attach too much significance to the considered formulae of thought. Granovsky was the most finished example of the humanist idealist type. He was a handsome man: he exerted charm and influence as a professor, but there was little originality about his thought. There was a very significant conflict between Granovsky and Herzen. The idealist Granovsky could not bear the transition from the philosophy of Hegel to that of Feuerbach, to whom Herzen attached so much importance. Granovsky desired to remain faithful to idealism. He set a high value upon belief in the immortality of the soul; he was an opponent of socialism because he considered it hostile to personality, at the very time when Herzen and Belinsky went over to socialism and atheism. Herzen and Belinsky have a central significance in the destiny of Russia. It was they who represented the left wing of the Westernizing movement which was pregnant with the future.

Belinsky is one of the most central figures in the history of Russian thought of the nineteenth century. He already differs from other Russian writers of the thirties and forties in the fact that he was not of gentle origin, and he had none of those aristocratic traits which were so strongly marked in the anarchist Bakunin. He was the first member of the Intelligentsia who came of the common folk, and he was a typical member of the Intelligentsia in the narrower sense of the second half of the nineteenth century, when our culture ceased to be exclusively the province of gentlefolk. Belinsky was a man of great gifts; his sensitiveness and receptivity amounted to genius; he had but little scholarship; he was almost without knowledge of foreign languages and was practically ignorant of German. He knew Hegel's philosophy not through reading Hegel's books himself but through what was said of Hegel by Bakunin, who read him in German. But his receptiveness was so extraordinary that he understood a good deal of Hegel by guesswork. He passed successively through Fichte, Schelling and Hegel and went over to Feuerbach and militant atheism. Belinsky, as a typical member of the Russian Intelligentsia, was at every stage of his life bent upon achieving a totalitarian world outlook. To him, with his passionate and sensitive nature, to understand and to suffer were one and the same thing. He lived exclusively by ideas and searched for truth "with stubbornness, agitation and haste." He was aflame, and quickly burned himself out. He believed that Russia is a synthesis of all the elements and he himself wanted to be a synthesis of all the elements, but did not achieve them all at one and the same time. He was always going to extremes, but successively, as time went on. Belinsky was the most significant of Russia's critics and the only one among Russian critics who was open to artistic impressions and aesthetic feelings. Literary criticism was to him only a form for the expression of an integrated world outlook; it was nothing but a conflict on behalf of truth. The vast importance which the literary criticism of the publicist acquired among us in the second half of the nineteenth century finds its explanation in the fact that under the conditions of censorship, it was only in the form of criticism of literary productions that it was possible to express philosophical and political ideas. Belinsky was the first really to appreciate Pushkin, and he sensed many of the geniuses who were being born. He was a Russian to the marrow. Only in Russia was he a possibility, but he was a passionate Westernizer and believed in the West. But at the time of his travels in Europe he became disillusioned about it. His disillusion is just as typically Russian as the fascination which he had previously felt. The first influence which was felt among us in the realm of ideas was that of Schelling. Later on we went over to Hegel. One can note three periods in the development of Belinsky's ideas: (1) moral idealism, heroism; (2) the Hegelian acceptance of the reasonableness of reality; (3) a revolt against reality in order to make radical changes for the sake of man. The path followed by Belinsky draws attention to the very great importance which Hegel's philosophy had among us. Of the two crises through which Belinsky passed it will be necessary to speak in the following chapter. At every stage Belinsky gave himself up completely to his idea of the moment. It was only by that idea that he could live; he was intolerant and exclusive, as were all members of the Russian Intelligentsia under the spell of an idea, and he divided the world into two camps. It was about ideas that he broke with his friend, K. Aksakov of whom he was very fond. He was the first to give up the possibility of relations with the Slavophils. He separated from Herzen, with whom he had had close associations, and from other friends, during the period in which he was under the spell of the Hegelian idea of the reasonableness of "reality," and he passed through a period of painful loneliness. The future anarchist Bakunin was under the influence of the Hegelian idea of the reasonableness of "reality," and it was he who lured Belinsky away with this idea. We shall see that Hegel was wrongly interpreted and that through this misunderstanding passions were brought into play. Only in his last period and towards the end of his life did Belinsky work out a perfectly defined world outlook, and he became a representative of the socialist tendencies of the second half of the nineteenth century. He was a direct predecessor of Chernishevsky and in the final outcome even of Russian Marxism. He was much less of a *narodnik* than Herzen; he was even in favor of industrial development. When Belinsky turns towards socialism we already see in him that narrowing of thought and displacement of many values, which are so painfully striking in the revolutionary Intelligentsia of the sixties and seventies. He was most conspicuously Russian in his revolt against the Hegelian world spirit, on behalf of the real concrete man. We see that same Russian theme in Herzen also. The execution of the Decembrists had a great effect upon the formulation of Herzen's views.

Herzen is of immense importance to the subject of the Russian philosophy of history. He was, if not the most profound, certainly the most brilliant of the men of the forties. He was the first of the revolutionary emigrants. This Russian Westernizer underwent profound disillusionment in Western Europe. After Herzen's experience the Westernizing movement was no longer possible in the same form as it had had in the forties. The Russian Marxists were Westernizers in another sense, and certain traits of Russian messianism were to be disclosed in the Marxism of the communists. In the person of Herzen the Westernizing group comes into touch with the Slavophils, and the same thing happens in the anarchism of Bakunin. Generally speaking the left socialistic wing of the Westernizing movement was to become more Russian and more original in its interpretation of the ways of Russia than the more moderate and liberal wing, which

becomes more and more colorless. The Russian theme of the peculiar path of Russia, and of its avoidance of the Western ways of
industrial capitalist development, will be revealed by *narodnik*
socialism which issues from the left wing of the Westernizing movement. Herzen is to be placed at the source of a socialism which was
narodnik and peculiarly Russian. The idea which had already been
put forward by Chaadaev that the Russian people, being more free
from the burden of world history, could create a new world of the
future, is developed by Herzen's and *narodnik* socialism. Herzen
was the first to give clear-cut expression to the Russian revolt
against the middle class view of life of the West. He saw in it a danger also to Western socialism itself. But this idea did not belong to
narodnik socialism only; there was a greater profundity in it and a
depth to which the superficial philosophy of Herzen himself did not
reach. It was a general Russian idea connected with Russian messianism. Herzen made his way through Hegel, as did everybody in the
forties and was one of the first to arrive at Feuerbach, with whom he
remained. This means that philosophically he had close associations
with materialism though not of a very profound type, and that he was
an atheist. But it would be truer to describe him as a humanist skep-
tic. He was not by nature a confessed enthusiast as Belinsky was. To
him materialism and atheism were not a religion. Given such a
philosophical world outlook it was difficult to justify a messianic
belief in the Russian people. It was difficult to find a basis for the
Herzen philosophy of history and for his ethics. French social mysticism like that of Pierre Leroux had a momentary influence upon
Herzen but it did not last long. Herzen justified his disbelief in the
higher meaning of life in the same way as it was done considerably
later by more subtle systems of thought. He says that science, being
an objective thing, is not concerned with human illusions and hopes.
He demands humility in the face of the sad truth. It was a peculiarity
of Herzen that truth presented itself to him as sad. There was a pessimistic element in his general outlook on life. He asks us to be
unafraid in the face of the meaninglessness of the world. His view is
anthropocentric. To him the highest thing in life and the dearest was
man, but such an anthropocentric position has no sort of metaphysical basis. N. Mikhailovsky was later on to make use of the expression "subjective anthropocentricity," contrasting it with "objective

anthropocentricity." This comes from Feuerbach too. Feuerbach was an optimist and professed the religion of humanity, but Herzen's ethics were decidedly personalist. To him the highest of all values, and one which must on no account be sacrificed, is human personality. Philosophically he could not establish personality as the highest value. His own particular philosophy of history was connected with his personalism. Herzen was an artist more than a philosopher, and one must not ask of him the grounding and development of a philosophy of history. He was a very well-read man; he read Hegel and even Jacob Boehme. He knew Cieszkowski, the philosopher of Polish messianism: but real philosophical culture he did not possess. In his case the subject of personality was linked with the subject of freedom. He is one of the most freedom-loving of Russians. He is unwilling to give up freedom even to his socialism, and it is left unexplained whence personality will acquire the strength to oppose its freedom to the power of nature and society, to the power of determinism. Herzen's revolt against the Western middle class view of life was connected with the idea of personality. He saw in Western Europe the enfeeblement and in the last resort the disappearance of personality. The shopkeeper has replaced the mediaeval knight, and for salvation from the triumphant bourgeois, he looked to the Russian peasant, to the grey sheepskin coat. The Russian peasant was more of a person than the Western bourgeois although he was a serf. He combines in himself the principle of personality with what belongs to the community. Personality stands opposed to the hidebound exclusiveness of egoism; it is possible only within the common life. Disillusioned by Western Europe, Herzen believes in the Russian peasant community; Herzen's socialism was of the *narodnik* type and at the same time individualist. He still makes no distinction between the individual and personality. "The chivalrous valor of the knight, the elegant aristocratic manners, the severe decorum of the protestant, the proud independence of the Englishman, the luxurious life of the Italian artist, the sparkling intelligence of the encyclopaedist, and the gloomy energy of the terrorist, all this was fused together and brought to life again in a whole conglomeration of other prevailing manners—those of the bourgeois." "As the knight was the prototype of the feudal world, so the merchant became the prototype of the new world. Lords were replaced by proprietors." "Under the influence of the bourgeois everything in Europe was changed. The knight's honor was replaced by the bookkeeper's honesty, humane manners by the manners of decorum; affectation took the place of urbanity; touchiness replaced pride; kitchen gardens became the substitute for parks; and instead of palaces there were hotels which were open to all (that is to say to all who had money)." It is the desire of everyone "to appear rather than to be." To the meanness of "the haves" is opposed the envy of the bourgeois "have-nots." Later on the reactionary K. Leontyev is to say the same thing as the revolutionary Herzen. Both alike rebelled against the bourgeois world and wanted to set the Russian world in opposition to it. Herzen put forward ideas of a philosophy of history which are exceedingly unlike the usual optimistic ideas of the progressive left of the camp. He opposes personality to history, to the fateful course of history. We shall see Belinsky's tempestuous experience of this theme and how acutely it was expressed by the genius of Dostoyevsky. Herzen proclaimed "a war of free men against the liberators of mankind." He was opposed to democracy and sympathized with anarchism. In his remarkable book *From the Other Side* he gave warning that the inward barbarian is coming, and he displayed much foresight in prophesying that life would become harder for the educated minority. "Explain to me, please," he says, "why it is ridiculous to believe in God, but not ridiculous to believe in man? Why is it not ridiculous to believe in humanity? Why is it stupid to believe in the Kingdom of Heaven but intelligent to believe in an earthly utopia?" Among the Western social thinkers Proudhon stood closest of all to him. He had nothing at all in common with Marx.

Herzen did not share the optimistic doctrine of progress which became the religion of the nineteenth century. He did not believe in a predetermined progress of mankind, in an inevitable movement of society upwards towards a perfect and happy state. He admitted the possibility of a retrograde movement and of a collapse. He thought the outstanding fact was that nature is completely indifferent to man and to his welfare and that truth is quite unable to speak any word of consolation to man. In contrast to his pessimistic philosophy of history he believed in the future of the Russian people. In a letter to Michelet, in which Herzen defended the Russian people, he writes that the past of the Russian people was dark, that its present is terrible;

there is left a belief in its future. This is a theme which was to be repeated throughout the course of the nineteenth century. At this same time Herzen, disillusioned by the revolution of the year '48, writes that the decay of Europe had begun. There is no guarantee of a better future for the Russian people, nor is there for any other people, because there exists no law of progress. But there remains the possibility of belief in the future. But what is most interesting in Herzen's criticism of the theory of progress is another theme, one which is very rarely met with in the group to which he belonged. This is the personalist motif. Herzen would not consent to sacrifice human personality to history, to the grandiose problems of history, as it were. He was unwilling to convert it into an instrument for the attainment of inhuman ends. He would not consent to sacrifice present generations for the sake of the generations that are to come. He grasped the fact that the religion of progress does not contemplate anybody or anything or any moment as a value in itself. Herzen's philosophical culture provided him with no possibility of giving basis and expression to his thoughts on the relation between the present and the future. He had no defined doctrine of time at all, but he sensed the truth that it is impossible to regard the present exclusively as a means for the future. He saw in the present an end in itself. His ideas were directed against Hegel's philosophy of history, against the crushing of human personality by the world spirit of history, by progress. It was a fight for personality, and this is a very Russian problem. It was posed very sharply in Belinsky's letter to Botkin, about which I shall speak in the next chapter. Herzen's socialism was individualistic; I should say now it was personalist. And he thought that this was Russian socialism. He belonged to the Westernizing camp, but he defended the special paths of Russia.

Slavophilism, concerned all the while with the same subject of Russia and Europe, in part changes its character and in part degenerates into nationalism of a very ugly kind. The liberal and humanitarian elements in Slavophilism begin to disappear. The idealists among the Westernizers are turned into "unwanted people" while the realists of the sixties had not yet made their appearance. The milder type is transformed into the harsher. The idealists among the Slavophils also take on a new life of a harsher type, and become the conservative nationals. This arose out of active contact with reality. Only a few, such as K. Aksakov, remain faithful to the ideals of strict Slavophilism. N. Danilevsky, who wrote a book called *Russia and Europe*, was already a man of an entirely different form of mind from the Slavophils. The old Slavophils were brought up intellectually on German idealism, on Hegel and Schelling, and they put their ideas for the most part in philosophical form. N. Danilevsky is a natural scientist. He is a realist and an empiricist. He put his ideas about Russia in a naturalistic form. In him the universalism of the Slavophils has disappeared. He divides mankind on a cultural basis into exclusive historical types. With him mankind has no one single destiny. The question is not so much the mission of Russia in the world as the formation of Russia into a peculiar cultural and historical type. Danilevsky is a predecessor of Spengler and puts forward ideas which are very like those of Spengler, though they were long before his time. But Spengler was not a Christian and it was easier for him to deny the unity of mankind than it was for Danilevsky who was a Christian. The Slavophils took their stand not only on philosophical universalism but also on Christian universalism. At the foundation of their world outlook there lay a certain interpretation of Orthodoxy and it was their desire to apply that organically to their own interpretation of Russia. The mission of Russia was to them a Christian mission. With Danilevsky on the other hand, there remains a complete dichotomy between his personal Orthodoxy and his naturalistic views on history. He sets up his cultural historical types as he sets up types in the animal world. There is no civilization which holds good for all mankind, no common history of man. All that there can be is a richer cultural historical type which associates more characteristics within itself, and on this ground Danilevsky recognizes the Slavic-Russian type. That type above all combined within it four elements: the religious, the cultural in the narrow sense, the political and the economic. This slavonic type of four elements is fundamental; but this classification of types is in itself highly artificial. The tenth type bears the name of Germano-Romance or European. The Russians were very much inclined to assign the German and the Romance to one type. But this is a mistake and rests upon an inadequate understanding of Europe. In actual fact there is a difference between France and Germany which is no less but even greater than that between Germany and Russia.

Classically Frenchmen consider the world beyond the Rhine, Germany, as the East, almost as Asia. An integral European culture does not exist. It is a fiction of the Slavophils. Danilevsky was absolutely right in saying that what is known as European culture is not the only possible culture and that other types of culture are a possibility, but he was not right in his understanding of the relation between genus and species. It is alike true to affirm that culture is always of a particular national sort and that there does exist a culture which is common to mankind. That which is universal and belongs to mankind in general is found in the individually national, and the latter becomes significant precisely by its original attainment of that which is universally common to all mankind. Dostoyevsky and L. Tolstoy were very Russian in their attitude to the West. It was by their own individual significance that they expressed the universal and common. German idealist philosophy is very German. It would have been impossible in France or in England, but its greatness lies in its attainment and expression of what is universal and common to mankind. Vladimir Solovyov in his brilliant book *The National Problem in Russia* subjected the ideas of Danilevsky and those who think with him to sharp criticism. He showed that Danilevsky's ideas about Russia were borrowed from the second rate German historian Rickert, but Vladimir Solovyov was criticizing not Danilevsky only but also the Slavophils in general. He said that it is impossible blindly to follow a national faith. One must believe not in the national faith but in the divine things themselves. But while this thought is indisputably true it is unjust to contrast it with Khomyakov, for instance, who believed above all in the divine things and was a universalist in his belief. But in any case the fact is that Danilevsky's notions constituted a breach in the conception of the Russian idea and cannot enter into that idea. Panslavism becomes inconsistent in the form in which he asserted it and his idea of a Russian Constantinople is erroneous, but it is characteristic that even Danilevsky believed that the Russian people and slavism in general would solve the social question better and sooner than the West of Europe.

Konstantine Leontyev modestly considered himself a follower of Danilevsky in the philosophy of history, but he stood at a very much higher level than Danilevsky, and his is one of the most brilliant of Russian minds. If Danilevsky can be considered as a precursor of Spengler then K. Leontyev was a precursor of Nietzsche. The ceaseless consideration of the development and fall of societies and cultures, a sharply defined predominance of aesthetics over ethics, a biological basis for the philosophy of history and sociology, belief in aristocracy, hatred of liberal equalitarian progress and democracy, *amor fati*, all these traits give Leontyev a family likeness to Nietzsche. It was entirely a mistake to reckon him as belonging to the Slavophil group. In actual fact he had little in common with the Slavophils and in many respects he was opposed to them. He had a different understanding of Christianity. His was a Byzantine, Monastic, ascetic interpretation which admitted no humanitarian element. His morality was other than that of the Slavophils, it was an aristocratic morality of power which did not stop short of violence, and it included a naturalistic understanding of the historical process. He certainly did not believe in the Russian people. He thought Russia exists and is great thanks simply to the fact that Byzantine Orthodoxy and Byzantine autocracy had been imposed upon the Russian people from above. His reaction to nationalism, and to the tribal principle was entirely negative; it leads in his opinion to revolution and to the democratic process of levelling. He was certainly not a *narodnik* whereas the Slavophils were *narodniks*. He loved Peter the Great and Katharine the Great, and in the era of Katharine he saw the flourishing complexity of Russian political and cultural life. He very much loved the old Europe, catholic, monarchical, aristocratic, complex and diversified. Most of all he loved not the Middle Ages, but the Renaissance. According to Leontyev's own broad theory human society inevitably passes through three stages: (1) a primitive simplicity, (2) a flourishing complexity and (3) a second period of simplification by a process of conglomeration. He regarded this process as fated; as distinct from the Slavophils he entirely disbelieved in the freedom of the spirit; to him human freedom does not operate in history. The highest point of development is in his view "the highest degree of complexity embraced by an interior despotic unity." Leontyev was in no sense a metaphysician; he was a naturalist and an aesthetic. He was the first Russian aesthetic. The results of liberal and democratic progress aroused aesthetic repulsion in him more than anything else. He sees in them the ruin of beauty. His sociology was completely amorąl; he does not admit moral values in relation to the life of society. He preached cruelty in politics. Here are some specially characteristic words of K. Leontyev: "Is it not horrible, would it not be insulting, to think that Moses went up Mount Sinai, that the Greeks built themselves an exquisite acropolis, that the Romans waged the Punic wars, that that genius Alexander, magnificent in a sort of plumed helmet, crossed the Granicus and fought at Arbela, that the Apostles preached and the martyrs suffered, that the poets sang, the painters limned and knights glittered in tourney, simply in order that the French or German or Russian bourgeois in his abominable and ridiculous clothes should complacently exist "individually" and "collectively" to the ruin of all this majesty that has gone before? Would it not be a shameful thing for mankind that this abject ideal of the common good, of petty labor and ignominious prose should be for ever triumphant?" [8] Leontyev taught that in the case of Europe the period of flourishing complexity lies in the past and that in its destiny it is moving towards the second period of simplification. Europe can no longer be counted upon; Europe is in decay and decomposition, but this decomposition is the fate of all societies. At one time Leontyev believed that in the East, in Russia, the culture of flourishing complexity was still possible, but in his case this was not connected with belief in a great mission of the Russian people. In the last period of his life he definitely lost belief in the future of Russia and the Russian people, and prophesied the coming of the Russian Revolution and the approach of the kingdom of antichrist. I shall speak of this again later on. In any case Leontyev occupies a quite peculiar place of his own in the history of Russian national consciousness. He stands apart. There is an element in his thinking which is not Russian. But the theme of Russia and Europe was fundamental to him. He was a reactionary romantic who did not believe in the possibility of stopping the process of decay and the destruction of beauty. He is a pessimist. There was much that he felt very keenly and much that he foresaw. After Leontyev it was impossible to return to the fair-souled Slavophilism of earlier days. Like Herzen whom he loved, he revolted against the

8. See my book, *Konstantine Leontyev: A Sketch of the History of Russian National Thought.*

middle class life and the bourgeois spirit of the West. This was his fundamental motif and with him it is a Russian motif. He hates the bourgeois world and desires its destruction. If he hates progress, liberalism, democracy, socialism, it is simply because all this leads to the sovereignty of the bourgeois and to a dull earthly paradise.

The national consciousness of Dostoyevsky is especially inconsistent and completely contradictory to his relation to the West. On the one hand he was a resolute universalist; to him the Russian is the all-man. The vocation of Russia is a world vocation. Russia is not shut up in itself and a self-sufficing world. Dostoyevsky gives particularly clear expression to the Russian messianic consciousness. The Russian people is a God-bearing people. A sensitiveness to the whole world belongs to the Russian people. On the other hand Dostoyevsky displays a real xenophobia; he cannot endure Jews, Poles, Frenchmen, and shows an inclination to nationalism. The duality of the Russian people reveals itself in him. There is a mingling of opposites. To Dostoyevsky there belong the most amazing words about Western Europe, words which were not equalled by a single Westernizer, words in which Russian universalism is revealed. Versilov, through whom Dostoyevsky expresses many of his own thoughts, says: "They [Europeans] are not free; we are free. In Europe, it was I and I alone with my yearning for Russia, who was free. A Frenchman thinks not only of his own France but even of mankind only on condition that he remains very much a Frenchman; the same is true of the Englishman and the German. The Russian alone, even in our own time, that is to say long before the whole account is made up, has the capacity of being especially Russian precisely and only at that time that he is especially European; and this is the most essential national difference between us and them. When in France, I am a Frenchman; among Germans, I am German; among the ancient Greeks, Greek; but at the same time very much a Russian, at the same time I am a real Russian and give my services especially to Russia, for I exhibit her chief thought." "To the Russian Europe is precious, just as Russia is precious; every stone in it is sweetly precious. Europe also has been our fatherland just as Russia has. Oh! more than that, it is impossible to love Russia more than I love it. But I have never reproached myself for the fact that Venice, Rome, Paris, those treasuries of their sciences and art and all their history are dearer to me than Russia. Those ancient foreign stones are dear to Russians; those wonders of the old divine world, those fragments of sacred marbles. They are even dearer to us than they are to them. Russia alone lives not for herself, but for thought; and it is a significant fact, that for more than a hundred years Russia has lived decidedly not for herself but simply for Europe alone." Ivan Karamazov says in the same spirit: "I want to go to Europe. Maybe I know that I shall go only to a cemetery, but it will be to the dearest of cemeteries. So there you are. Dear ones departed lie there. Every stone upon them speaks of such ardent life in the past and such a devoted belief in its own achievement, in its own truth, in its own struggle and its own science. But I know beforehand that I shall fall upon the earth and I shall kiss those stones and weep over them, at the same time convinced with all my heart that all this has already been a cemetery for a very long time and is nothing else whatever." In *The Diary of a Writer* we read: "Europe—is not this a terrible and a sacred thing—Europe? Do you know, gentlemen, how dear to us it is, to us dreamers, to us Slavophils, to us who in your opinion are haters of Europe? That same Europe, that country of 'holy wonders'—you know how dear to us are those wonders and how we love and revere them with more than brotherly love. We love and revere the great people who dwell in it and all the great and fine things that they have achieved, but do you know with what tears and throbbing of the heart the destinies of that land are dear and akin to us, moving us with sympathy and pain, how the gloomy clouds over them frighten us, clouds which ever more and more overcast its horizon? You, gentlemen, who are Europeans and Westernizers, have never loved Europe as much as we, the visionary Slavophils who in your opinion are its mortal foes." Dostoyevsky calls himself a Slavophil. He thought, as did also a large number of thinkers on the theme of Russia and Europe, that he knew decay was setting in, but that a great past exists in her, and that she has made contributions of great value to the history of mankind. Dostoyevsky himself was a writer of the Petersburg period of Russian history. As a writer he belongs more to Petersburg than to Moscow. He had a keen feeling for the special atmosphere of the city of Peter, that most fantastic of cities. Petersburg is another face of Russia than Moscow, but it is not less Russian. More than anything else Dostoyevsky witnesses to the fact that

Slavophilism and the Westernizing movement alike are liable to be surmounted, but both tendencies lead to the Russian Idea, as indeed always happens in creative forms of suppression (*Aufhebung* in Hegel's language).

Of the Russian thinkers of the nineteenth century V. Solovyov was the most universal; his thought had sources in Slavophilism but he gradually withdrew from the Slavophils, and when there was an orgy of nationalism among us in the year '80 he became a sharp critic of Slavophilism. He saw the mission of Russia in the union of the Churches, that is to say, in the assertion of Christian universalism. I shall speak about Solovyov in another connection. Russian reflections upon the subject of the philosophy of history led to the consciousness that the path of Russia was a special one. Russia is the great East-West; it is a whole immense world and in its people vast powers are confined. The Russian people are a people of the future; they will decide questions which the West has not yet the strength to decide, which it does not even pose in their full depth. But this consciousness is always accompanied by a pessimistic sense of Russian sin and of Russian darkness. Sometimes there is the feeling that Russia is falling into an abyss and the problem is always stated as a problem of the end and not an intervening one. Russian consciousness comes into contact with the eschatological consciousness. What kind of problems are they which the Russian consciousness poses?

3

The Problem of the clash between Personality and World Har-
mony · The significance of Hegel in the history of Russian
thought · Its relation to "reality" · Belinsky's revolt · The antici-
patory enthusiasm of Dostoyevsky · The individualistic socialism
of Herzen · The Problem of Theodicy in Dostoyevsky · The rise of
the great Russian Literature · The drama of Gogol · Metaphysical
themes in Tyutchev

1

HEGEL had an unprecedented career in Russia.[1] The immense
importance of Hegel's philosophy has lasted even into the period of
Russian communism. The Soviet publishes a complete edition of
Hegel's collected works and this in spite of the fact that to him philosophy was a doctrine about God. To the Russians Hegel was the
highest attainment of human thought and it was to him that they
looked for the solution of all world problems. His influence made
itself felt in Russian philosophical, religious and social thought. He
had the same sort of importance as Plato had for the Fathers and Aristotle for Scholasticism. Samarin at one time made the future of the
Orthodox Church to depend upon the fate of Hegel's philosophy, and
only Khomyakov induced him to see the inadmissibility of such a
conjunction of ideas. Among us Hegel was certainly not a subject of
philosophical investigation. The Russians put all their capacity for
giving a passionate welcome to influence in the sphere of ideas into
their acceptance of the ascendancy which his philosophy had over
them. Schelling's influence was that of the philosophy of nature and
the philosophy of art, but in Hegel it was a matter of solving problems

---

1. See Chizhevsky, *Hegel in Russland.*

which were concerned with the meaning of life. Stankevitch exclaimed: "I have no desire to live in the world unless I find happiness in Hegel." Bakunin takes Hegel as a religion. The problem of their relation to "reality," to their actual environment, tormented the Russian idealists of the Intelligentsia, deprived as they were of any possibility of taking effective action. This question of "reality" acquires an importance which is excessive and probably little understood by Western people. The Russian "reality" which formed the environment of the idealists of the thirties and forties was horrible. It meant the empire of Nicholas I, serfdom, the absence of freedom, illiteracy. The moderate conservative Nikitinko wrote in his *Diary*: "Our contemporary society presents a grievous spectacle; there are no magnanimous strivings in it; there is no justice, no simplicity, no loyalty to a code of manners; in a word, there is nothing to witness to a healthy, natural and energetic development of moral strength. Public depravity is so great that conceptions of honor and righteousness are regarded either as weak-spirited or as a sign of romantic exuberance. Our education is just an imposture. Why should we worry about the acquiring of knowledge when our life and society are antagonistic to all great ideas and truths, when every attempt to give effect to any sort of thought of righteousness or of goodness or of the common good is stigmatized and persecuted as if it were a crime?" "Everywhere there is violence added to violence. On all sides is constraint and limitation; nowhere is there scope for the poor Russian soul. And when will all this have an end?" "Will the people who are yet to come comprehend? Will they be able to appreciate all the horror and the tragic side of our existence?" In the last note in the *Diary* we read: "It is a terrible era for Russia in which we live and no way out of it is to be seen." This was written in the era of the "idealists" of the forties, a period which glittered with gifted men. But the remarkable people of the forties constituted a very small group who lived in an environment of darkness. This led in the end to the "unwanted people," to Rudin, the homeless wanderer, and to Oblomov. The stronger natures were obliged either to come to terms with "reality" in the realm of ideas by finding a meaning and a justification for it, or else to struggle against it. Belinsky, who was the central figure at the time, could not, on account of his quarrelsome disposition, simply withdraw from "reality" into philosophic and aesthetic contemplation. The problem presented itself to him with extraordinary painfulness. Bakunin introduced Belinsky to Hegel's philosophy, and from Hegel a reconciliation with reality was derived. Hegel said: "All reality is rational." In Hegel this thought had its reverse side. He regarded only the rational as real. The rationality of reality according to Hegel can only be understood in connection with his panlogism. Not every empirical reality was in his view reality. The Russians of that time had an inadequate understanding of Hegel and that gave rise to misapprehensions. But it was not all misunderstanding and misapprehension. Hegel did in any case decisively affirm the rule of the common over the partial, of the universal over the individual, of society over personality. His philosophy was anti-personalist. Hegel himself begot a Hegelianism of the right and a Hegelianism of the left. Conservatism and revolutionary Marxism alike found support in his philosophy. There was an extraordinary dynamism in this philosophy. Belinsky passed through a stormy crisis; he came to terms with "reality" in the Hegelian manner; he broke with his friends, with Herzen and the rest, and went away to Petersburg. A revolutionary by nature and disposed to protest and revolt, after no very long time he became a conservative; he wrote an essay on the anniversary of the Battle of Borodino, which perturbed and agitated everybody; and he insisted that terms must be made with "reality." He took the Hegelian philosophy to himself in totalitarian fashion. He exclaimed: "The world 'reality' has for me the same significance as the word 'God'." "Society," says Belinsky, "is always more in the right and stands higher than the individual person." He said this in a wrongheaded paper entitled "The Grief which comes of Intelligence." This might result in either a conservative or a revolutionary conclusion. Belinsky made the conservative exit and wrote an apology for power. He suddenly puts forward the idea that right is might and might is right; he produces justification for those who conquer; he preaches the submissiveness of reason in the face of the forces of history and he recognizes a special morality for conquerors, for great artists and the like. Reality is a very fine thing. Suffering is a form of blessedness. There was a time when poetry presented itself as the quintessence of life. Belinsky was decidedly an idealist; to him the idea stood higher than anything, the idea ranked higher than the living man. Personality must humble itself before truth, before reality, before the universal idea which operates in world history. The theme was stated trenchantly and experienced with passion. Belinsky could not hold this position for very long and he broke with "reality" in Petersburg and went back to his friends. After this break the revolt began, a decisive revolt against history, against the world process, against the universal spirit, on behalf of the living man, on behalf of personality. There were two crises of Hegelianism among us—the religious crisis in the person of Khomyakov, and the ethical, political and social crisis in the person of Belinsky.

2

The theme of the clash between personality and world harmony is very Russian. Russian thought experienced it with peculiar trenchancy and depth. In this connection the first place belongs to the revolt of Belinsky, and it found expression in the remarkable letter to Botkin.[2] Belinsky says of himself that he is a terrible person when some mystical absurdity gets into his head. There are a great many Russians who might say that of themselves. After he went through his crisis Belinsky expressed his new thoughts in the form of a reaction against Hegel, a revolt against him in the name of personality, on behalf of the living man. He moves on from pantheism to an anthropology which is analogous to the calmer philosophical process which occurred in Feuerbach. The power of the universal idea, of the universal spirit—that is the great foe. "To the devil with all your higher strivings and purposes," writes Belinsky. "I have particularly serious grounds for being angry with Hegel, because I feel that it was my belief in him which led me to come to terms with Russian reality. *The fate of the subject, of the individual, of the person, is more important than the fate of the whole world.* They say to me, develop all the treasures of your spirit with a view to untrammelled self-satisfaction through the spirit. Weep so that you may be consoled; grieve so that you may rejoice anew; strive after perfection; climb to the highest rung of the ladder of development, but flounder and fall, and the devil take you. . . . I humbly express my gratitude to Egor Fedorovitch [Hegel]; I reverence your philosopher's gown, but

---

2. See P. Sakulin, *The Socialism of Belinsky*, where the letter to Botkin is printed.

with all due respect to your philosophical philistinism I have the honor to inform you that if it were given to me to climb to the highest rung of the ladder of development, even there I would ask to be rendered an account for all the victims of chance, of superstition, of the Inquisition of Philip II, and so on and so on. Otherwise I would fling myself down headlong from that highest rung. I do not want happiness, even as a gift, unless I have peace of mind about every one of my brothers by blood.... This it seems to me is my final view of things and with it I shall die." "For me to think, to feel, to understand and to suffer are one and the same thing." "The fate of the subject, of the individual, of the person is more important than the fate of the whole world and the well-being of the Chinese Emperor, [that is to say, the Hegelian *Algemeinheit*]." This expression of Belinsky's thoughts strikes one by its likeness to the ideas of Ivan Karamazov, with his discussion on the tears of a child and world harmony. This is absolutely the same problem as that of the conflict between the individual person and the whole, the universal. It is the same gesture of returning the ticket to God. "To him [Hegel] the subject is not an end in itself, but a means to the momentary expression of the whole, and with him this whole in its relation to the subject, is Moloch." The fact that the rebellion of personality against world history and world harmony leads Belinsky to the cult of the social organization of life is of enormous and fundamental significance for the later history of Russian thought. Reality is not rational and ought to be radically altered for the sake of man. Russian socialism was primarily individualistic in its origin. "A sort of wild, frenzied, fanatical love for the freedom and the independence of personality has developed in me and that freedom and independence is possible only in a society which is founded upon right and chivalry. I have come to understand the French Revolution. I have come to understand even bloodthirsty hatred towards anyone who desires to separate himself from his brotherhood with mankind. I have now reached a new extreme—this idea of socialism, which has become a new idea to me, the way of all ways of living, the problem of problems, the alpha and omega of belief and knowledge. Everything arises from that, everything is for that and tends towards that. More and more I become a citizen of the whole world. More and more a mad longing for love devours me inwardly, a yearning which becomes more and more urgent and intractable. Human personality has become the point at which I am afraid of going out of my mind." "I am beginning to love mankind in the manner of Marat. To make the smallest part of it happy I think I would exterminate the rest of it with fire and sword." He exclaims: "The social organization of life, social organization, or death!" Belinsky is the predecessor of Russian communism to a much greater extent than Herzen and the *narodniks*. He was already asserting the bolshevik morality.

The subject of the clash between personality and world harmony is expressed in Dostoyevsky with the acumen of genius. He was tormented by the problem of theodicy. How is one to reconcile the fact of God with the creation of a world founded upon evil and suffering? Is it possible to acquiesce in the creation of a world, if in that world there is to be unmerited suffering, even if it be but the unmerited suffering of but one child? In his conversation with Alesha, Ivan Karamazov displays genius in his discussion of the tears of a child, and it reminds one very strongly of the theme as it is stated by Belinsky. It was expressed first with great acuteness in *Notes from Underground*. There the feeling of a person who will not acquiesce in being a mere pin in the world mechanism, a part of the whole, a means to the end of establishing world harmony, is brought to the point of madness. In this connection the genius of Dostoyevsky gives expression to the idea that man is certainly not a reasonable being who strives after happiness, but that he is an irrational creature who stands in need of suffering and that suffering is the one and only cause of the awakening of thought. The man underground will not agree with the world harmony, with the crystal palace towards the achievement of which he himself would be nothing but a means. "His own, his free and voluntary desire," says the man underground, "that which is his own, even if it be the slightest caprice, his own fancy, even though it be at times carried to the extent of madness, in that you have something which is the greatest of all gains, a thing which enters into no classification and for the sake of which all systems and theories will gradually be consigned to the devil." The man underground does not accept the results of progress, of compulsory world harmony, of the contented ant hill, when millions will be happy in refusing personality and freedom. This theme is developed most powerfully of all in the *Legend of the Grand*

Inquisitor.[3] The man underground exclaims: "Well now, I, for example, should not be in the least surprised if suddenly for no reason whatever, in the future state of general well-being, some gentleman emerges with an ignoble or rather a degenerate face, standing provocatively with arms akimbo, and says to us all: 'Well, gentlemen, wouldn't it be a good thing if we knocked all this rational well-being to bits with just one kick, reduced it to dust, with the one single aim that all these logarithms may take themselves off to the devil, and let us live once more according to our own stupid will?...'"

There was a duality in Dostoyevsky himself. On the one hand he was unable to come to terms with the world, founded as it was upon suffering, and unmerited suffering at that. On the other hand he does not accept a world without suffering but also without conflict. Freedom gives birth to suffering. Dostoyevsky does not want a world without freedom; he does not want even Paradise without freedom, he raises objections above all to a compulsory happiness. Ivan Karamazov's discussion of the tears of a child expresses Dostoyevsky's own thought, and at the same time this discussion is for him atheistic; it is a fighting against God, and this he overcomes by his faith in Christ. Ivan Karamazov says: "In the final result I do not accept God's world, and although I know that it exists I do not in the least degree permit it. The world may arrive at the highest degree of harmony, at a general reconciliation, but this will not atone for the innocent suffering of the past." "I have not suffered in order that through myself, through my evil deeds and through my suffering I may be the means of enriching some sort of future harmony." "I absolutely repudiate the highest harmony; it is not worth the tears of this one tortured child." Ivan Karamazov gives back to God his entrance ticket to world harmony. The problem of suffering stands at the center of Dostoyevsky's creativity and in this respect he is very Russian. The Russian has a greater capacity for enduring suffering than the man of the West, and at the same time he is especially sensitive to suffering; he is more sympathetic than the Western man. The rise of Russian atheism was due to moral causes; it was called into being by the impossibility of solving the problem of theodicy. A peculiar sort of Marcionism is to be found in the Russians. The Creator of this

---

3. See my book, *The World Outlook of Dostoyevsky*.

world cannot be good because the world is full of suffering, the suffering of the innocent. For Dostoyevsky the problem is solved by freedom, as the foundation of the world, and by Christ, that is to say, by the taking upon Himself the suffering of the world by God Himself. With Belinsky, who was very much of this world by nature, this theme led to individualistic socialism. This is how Belinsky expresses his social utopia, his new faith: "A time is coming, I ardently believe in this; a time is coming when no one will be burned, no one will have his head cut off, when the criminal will beg to be made an end of as an act of saving mercy, and there will be no punishment for him, but life will be left to him as a punishment, as death is now; when there will be no senseless forms and ceremonies, when no terms or conditions will be imposed upon feeling, when there will be no duty and obligation, and will yield not to will but to love alone; when there will be no husbands and wives, but lovers of both sexes; when the loved one will come to her lover and say: 'I love another' and he will answer 'I cannot be happy without you; I shall suffer for my whole life, but go to him whom you love'; and he will not accept her sacrifice, if through magnanimity she desires to remain with him, but like God, he will say to her, 'I will have mercy and not sacrifice.' There will be no rich; there will be no poor, neither tsars nor subjects; but there will be brothers, there will be people, and, in the tenor of the Apostle Paul's words, Christ will yield up His power to the Father, and the Father, the Divine Mind, will ascend to the throne anew but now over a new heaven and over a new earth."[4] Individualistic socialism was to be found also in Herzen who valued personality above everything, and during the seventies in N. Mikhailovsky and P. Lavrov as well. Russian thought cast doubts upon the justification of world history and civilization. The Russian progressive revolutionaries had their doubts about the justification of progress; they felt doubtful whether the coming results of progress would atone for the suffering and injustices of the past. But it was Dostoyevsky alone who understood that this question can be solved only within Christianity. Belinsky did not notice that after his revolt against the power of the common universal in Hegel he subjected human personality again to a common universal,

---

4. See N. Lerner, *Belinsky.*

that is to say to the social organization of life, no less harsh a master. Personalism and the spirit of community are alike native to the Russian; they are united in Dostoyevsky. The very revolt of Dostoyevsky against the revolutionaries, which was often very unjust, was made in the name of personality and freedom. He recalls that "Belinsky believed, with his whole being, that socialism not only does not destroy the freedom of personality but on the contrary raises it to unheard of majesty." This was not Dostoyevsky's own belief. The genius of what he writes on the subject, giving rise all the while, as it does, to contradictions, lies in the fact that man stands on his guard like one who has fallen away from the world order. And that was the revelation given by the experience of the underground, the submerged, in scientific language, in the sphere of the subconscious.

3

The great Russian writers who belong to the following period had already begun to write in the forties. Of Dostoyevsky and L. Tolstoy I shall speak later. But the creative work of Gogol belongs to the period of Belinsky and the men of the forties. Gogol belongs not only to the history of literature but also the history of the Russian religious and social quest. Religion was a subject which tormented the great literature of Russia. The theme of the meaning of life, of the salvation of man, of the whole Russian people and of all mankind from evil and suffering, prevailed over the theme of the creation of culture. The Russian writers could not restrain themselves within the limits of literature; they passed over these frontiers; they sought the transfiguration of life; and doubts arose among them about the justification of culture, about the justification of their own creativeness. Russian literature of the nineteenth century adopted a didactic tone; its writers wanted to be teachers of life; they summoned men to the betterment of life. Gogol is one of the most enigmatic of Russian writers.[5] He went through a very painful experience in the sphere of religion, and in the end he burned the second part of *Dead Souls* in circumstances which have remained a mystery. His drama of doubt about his own creative work reminds

---

5. See K. Mochulsky, *The Spiritual Path of Gogol.*

one, in the West, of the drama of Botticelli when he became a follower of Savonarola, and of the drama of the Jansenist Racine. Like
many other Russians he sought the Kingdom of God on earth; but in
him this search takes a repellent form. Gogol is one of the greatest
and most finished of Russian artists; he is not a realist, nor is he a
satirist, as used to be thought. He is a writer of fantasies that depicted
not real people but elemental evil spirits, and above all the spirit of
falsehood in whose power Russia lay. He even had but a feeble sense
of reality, and he was incapable of distinguishing truth from invention. The tragedy of Gogol lay in the fact that he never could see and
depict the human, the image of God in man, and this fact was a torment to him. He had a strong feeling for demonic and magical forces.
Gogol was the most romantic of Russian writers, and has close affinities with Hoffmann. He has no psychology at all, nor are living people to be found in his writings. It was said of Gogol that he sees the
world *sub specie mortis*. He recognized that he had no love for men
and women. He was a Christian and he experienced his Christianity
passionately and tragically, but the religion he professed was one of
fear and retribution. There was something which is not Russian in his
spiritual type. It is astonishing that the Christian writer Gogol was the
least humane of Russian writers, the least humane in the most
humane of all literatures.[6] Turgeniev and Chekhov who were not
Christian were more humane than Gogol who was. He was overwhelmed by the sense of sin; he was almost a man of the Middle
Ages; above all he was seeking salvation. As a romantic Gogol at
first believed that the transfiguration of life might be attained through
art. He lost this belief and gave expression to his disillusionment by
means of *Revizor*. Ascetic thought grew stronger in him and he is permeated by ascetic doubts about the justifiability of creative work.
There was a strong sense of evil in Gogol and this feeling of his was
certainly not exclusively due to the evil of public life, of the Russian
political regime; it was something deeper. He was inclined to public
repentance. At times there breaks out in him the acknowledgment
that he has no faith; he wants to give effective expression to religious
and moral service and to subordinate his artistic creative activity to

---

6. Rozanov could not bear Gogol on account of his inhumaneness and he wrote cuttingly
about it.

it. He printed *Select passages from correspondence with my Friends*, a book which called forth a storm of indignation among people of the left; they regarded him as a traitor to the liberation movement.

The fact that Gogol preached the pursuit of personal moral perfection and without that saw no possibility of the attainment of the highest level of public and social life may lead to a false interpretation of him. That idea of his, which is in itself true, could not arouse indignation against him. But in actual fact he, like many Russians, preached social Christianity, and this social Christianity of his was horrible. In his zealous sense of duty as a religious and moral teacher Gogol propounded his theocratic utopia, a patriarchal idyll. He desired to transform Russia by means of virtuous governor-generals, and their wives bearing the same title. From top to bottom the authoritarian regime is to be retained; even serfdom is to be preserved, but those who stand highest in the hierarchical scale are virtuous men; those who stand lowest are submissive and obedient. Gogo's utopia is abject and slavish; there is no spirit of freedom, no ardent call to rise; it is all permeated by an intolerable bourgeois moralizing. Belinsky did not understand Gogol's religious problem; that was a matter which lay beyond the limits of the things of which he was aware. But not without justification he took up a position of terrible indignation, such a one as only he was capable of. He wrote a celebrated letter to Gogol. He has had great respect for Gogol as a writer, but now suddenly this great Russian writer repudiates everything which was dear and sacred to Belinsky: "Preacher of the knout, apostle of ignorance, upholder of devilish darkness, eulogist of Tartar morals—What are you doing?" And in the course of the letter Belinsky's attitude to Christianity and to Christ is set forth. "That you should rely upon the Orthodox Church as a support for such teaching, that I can understand; it has always been a support for the knout, and a fawner upon despotism. But Christ—why do you bring Him into all this? He was the first to bring to men the doctrine of freedom, of equality, of brotherhood, and by His suffering He sealed it and affirmed the truth of His teaching." "If you had in actual fact been filled with the truth of Christ and not with a doctrine which is devilish, you would certainly not have written what is in your new book. You would have said to the landowner that since his peasants are his brothers in Christ and as a brother cannot be a slave to his brother, he ought either to give them their freedom or at the very least to make use of their labors in a way which is as advantageous as possible for them, recognizing deep down in his conscience the fact that he stands in a false position in regard to them." Gogol was overwhelmed by this reception which his book *Select passages from correspondence with my Friends* met with. Gogol is one of the most tragic figures in the history of Russian literature and thought. Leo Tolstoy was also to preach the pursuit of personal moral perfection, but he did not construct a servile doctrine of society. On the contrary he exposes the falsity of that society. Yet all the same, in spite of the repellent character of Gogol's book he shared in the idea that Russia is called to express the brotherhood of man. The quest for the Kingdom of God upon earth was in itself a Russian quest. From Gogol the religious and moral character of Russian literature, its messianism, takes its beginning; and the great importance of Gogol lies in that fact apart from his importance as an artist. From his time onwards there will be found among Russian artists a longing to go beyond the production of artistic work to the creation of the perfect life. The subject of religion and metaphysics and of religion and social life is a torment to all Russian writers of importance.

Tyutchev, one of the most profound of Russian poets, gives expression to the metaphysical cosmic theme in his poetry, and he even foresaw world revolution. Behind the outward shell of the cosmos he saw the quivering movement of chaos. He is the poet of the night of the soul of nature.

> The abyss now yawns across the path we tread
>   With all its terrors and its gloomy mist.
> Between the gulf and us no barriers exist
>   And hence to us the night is filled with dread.

This world is

> A carpet flung over the abyss
> And we float, by the flaming abyss
> Surrounded on all sides.

A very remarkable poem entitled "Of what are you blowing, O wind of the night?" finishes with the lines:

> O! rouse not sleeping storms,
> Beneath us quivering chaos moves.

Tyutchev feels this same chaos also behind the outward shell of history and forsees catastrophe. He is no lover of revolution and does not desire it, but he considers it inevitable. The spirit of prophecy enters into Russian literature with a force which is not to be found in other literatures. Tyutchev sensed the imminent approach of "the fateful moments" of history. In a poem written in an entirely different connection there are these amazing lines:

> O happy he whom fate has called to live
>   At the world's fateful moments. Him they meet
>   And him most graciously they call and greet
> A glad companion at the feast they give.

We at the present time are such "happy companions," but Tyutchev foresaw this a hundred years ago; he foresaw the catastrophes which were coming upon Russia.

> Wilt thou for long behind a cloud
>   Conceal thyself, O Russian star?
> Wilt thou thyself for ever shroud
>   In forms that mere illusion are?
> And to the eager eyes that seek
>   With longing search throughout the night
> Thy rays be merely scattered, weak,
>   Like some vain meteor to the sight?
> The gloom grows ever deeper, grief
> Profounder: still the all-afflicting woe.

Tyutchev had a complete theocratic doctrine which in its grandiose scale reminds us of the theocratic doctrine of Vladimir Solovyov. Many Russian poets experienced the feeling that Russia is moving towards catastrophe. It was already to be seen in Lermontov who

expressed what was almost a Slavophil belief in the future of Russia.
He wrote the terrible verses:

> The day will come, for Russia that dark day
> When the Tsar's diadem will fall, and they,
> Rabble who loved him once, will love no more,
> And many will subsist on death and gore.
> Downtrodden law no shelter will provide
> For child or guiltless woman. Plague will ride
> From stinking corpses through the grief-stricken land
> Where fluttering rags from cottages demand
> Help none can give. And famine's gnawing pangs
> Will grip the countryside with ruthless fangs.
> Dawn on the streams will shed a crimson light.
> And then will be revealed the Man of might
> Whom thou wilt know; and thou wilt understand
> Wherefore a shining blade is in his hand.

In the self-same Lermontov there is to be found the Russian drama of
creativity, that is, doubt of its justification on religious grounds.

> But grant me, O Creator, Thy release
> And free me from the direful thirst for song
> Then on the narrow path of saving peace
> I turn anew to Thee for Whom I long.

These words already give an indication of the religious drama which
Gogol went through. Lermontov was not a man of the Renaissance
as Pushkin, and it may be Pushkin alone, was, and even he not completely. Russian literature underwent the influence of romanticism,
which is a Western-European phenomenon. But in reality neither
romanticism nor classicism existed among us. Among us there took
place an ever-increasing return to religious realism.

4

1

WHEN in the course of the nineteenth century philosophical thought came to birth in Russia, it was preeminently religious, ethical and social in character. This means that its central theme was man, the fate of man in society and in history. Humanism in the European sense of the word formed no part of the experience of Russia. There was no Renaissance among us, but we did experience, and it may be with some particular sharpness, the crisis of humanism, and its inner dialectic was disclosed. The very word humanism was used inaccurately among us and may give ground for some surprise among the French, who consider themselves the humanists par excellence. The Russians always confused humanism with humanitarianism and connected it not so much with antiquity, with a certain attitude towards Greco-Roman culture, as with the religion of humanity which belonged to the nineteenth century; not so much with Erasmus as with Feuerbach. But, nevertheless, the word humanism is connected with man and indicates the assignment of a special role to man. Primarily European humanism by no means meant an acknowledgment of the self-sufficiency of man and the deification of humanity; it had its sources not only in Greco-Roman culture but also in Christianity. I have already said that Russia had almost no knowledge of the joy of creative abundance which belonged to the Renaissance. It was a Christian humanism which the

Russians understood. It was precisely Russian thought which had its own feeling of doubt, religious, ethical and social doubt, about the justification of creative culture. It was a doubt which was both ascetic and eschatological. Spengler described Russia very acutely and very well when he said that it is "an apocalyptic revolt against antiquity."[1] This defines the profound difference between Russia and Western Europe. But if humanism in the sense of the Western European Renaissance was not native to Russian thought, humaneness was very much so, that is, what is sometimes spoken of conventionally as humanitarianism, and there is to be seen in Russian thought the dialectic of the self-affirmation of man. Since the Russian people is polarized, elements of cruelty also may be mingled with the humaneness. But humaneness, all the same, remains one of the characteristic Russian traits. It bears upon the Russian idea at the highest points of its manifestation. The best Russians, both among the higher cultured classes and among the masses of the people, cannot bear the thought of the death penalty and of harsh punishments; they feel pity for the criminal. The Western cult of cold-blooded justice is not to be found among them. To them man is a higher principle than property, and this is the defining factor in Russian social morality. Pity for the fallen, for the humiliated, for the insulted, and compassion are very Russian characteristics. Radishchev, the father of the Russian Intelligentsia, was extraordinarily compassionate. Russian moral valuations were to a notable degree defined by the protest against serfdom, and this is reflected in Russian literature. Belinsky has no desire for happiness for himself, for one out of thousands, if his brethren are suffering. N. Mikhailovsky does not want rights for himself if the peasants are not to have them also. Russian *Narodnichestvo* as a whole arose out of pity and compassion. The repentant gentry of the seventies were repudiating their own privileges and went to the people in order to serve them and mingle in their lives. That Russian genius and wealthy aristocrat L. Tolstoy suffered from his privileged position all through his life. He felt repentant about it and desired to renounce everything and become one of the common folk, to become a *muzhik*. Another Russian genius, Dostoyevsky, was driven mad by suffering and compassion.

---

1. See Spangler, *Der Untergang des Abendlandes*, vol. II.

It is the basic theme of his creative work. Russian atheism was born of compassion, of the impossibility of enduring the evil of the world, the evil of history and civilization. It was a peculiar form of Marcionism which was experienced by the thought of the nineteenth century. God, the Creator of this world, is rejected in the name of righteousness and love. Power in this world is evil, the government of the world is vile. A different sort of government of the world and of man must be organized, one in which there will be no unmerited suffering, in which man will not be a wolf to his fellow men, but a brother. Such is the primary emotional basis of the Russian religious spirit; it is that which underlies the Russian social theme. In this way Russian life becomes dominated by an acute dualism. Inhumanity, cruelty, injustice and the slavery of man were objectivized in the Russian State, in the Empire; they were alienated from the Russian people and turned into an external power. In a land of autocratic monarchy, an anarchic ideal was asserted; in the land of serfdom the socialist ideal was affirmed. Feeling the wounds caused by human suffering, resting their case on pity, and permeated by the pathos of humanity they refused to accept the Empire; they would have no authority, no might, no force. The Third Rome was not to be a mighty state. But we shall see what the dialectic process was which led Russian humaneness to inhumaneness.

Humaneness lay at the basis of all the tendencies of our social thought in the nineteenth century, but they led to the communist Revolution which in its emotional content refused to recognize humaneness. The metaphysical dialectic of humanism (for the sake of convention I retain this word of two meanings) was revealed by Dostoyevsky. He drew attention not only to the Russian but also to the world crisis of humanism, as Nietzsche also did. Dostoyevsky rejected the idealistic humanism of the forties; he rejected Schiller, the cult of "the lofty and the beautiful" and the optimistic view of human nature. He went over to "the realism of actual life," to a realism, however, which was not superficial but profound and which revealed the secret depths of human nature in all its contradictions. In Dostoyevsky there was a twofold aspect of humanism (humanitarianism). On the one hand he penetrated into the very depths of humaneness; his compassion was unbounded and he understood the revolt against God which arises from the impossibility of bearing the suffering of the world. In the fallen creature, man, he revealed the image of man, that is to say the image of God. The very least considered of people possesses a significance which is absolute; but on the other hand he exposes the ways of humanistic self-assertion and reveals its final results, which he calls man-as-God. The dialectic of humanism is revealed as the destiny of man in freedom, when he had dropped out of the world order which was represented as eternal. In Dostoyevsky there is to be found a very lofty idea of man. He interceded for man, for human personality; he is ready to defend man before God; his anthropology is a new thing in Christianity; he is the most passionate and extreme defender of the freedom of man which the history of human thought has ever known. But he also discloses the fatal results of human self-affirmation, of godlessness and empty freedom. Compassion and humaneness in Dostoyevsky are turned into inhumanity and cruelty when man arrives at the stage of man-as-God, when he reaches self-deification. It was not without reason that they called him "a cruel genius." Dostoyevsky, nevertheless, may be called a Christian humanist in comparison with the Christian or rather the pseudo-Christian anti-humanism of Leontyev, but all the same he announces the end of the realm of humanism. European humanism was an intermediate realm; that which belongs to the limit, to the end, did not appear in it. It had no knowledge of the problem of eschatology and was not troubled by it. This intermediate realm wanted to strengthen itself forever. It was also preeminently the realm of culture. In the West, the end of this reign of humanism was the phenomenon of Nietzsche, who read a certain amount of Dostoyevsky and upon whom he exerted some influence. Nietzsche is a phenomenon of enormous importance for the fate of man. He wanted to experience the divine when there was no God, when God was killed, to experience ecstasy when the world was so base, to experience exaltation to the height when the world was flat and there were no heights. In the final analysis he expressed his religious theme in the idea of the super-man in whom man finishes his existence. Man was but a transition; all he had to do was to manure the soil for the appearance of the super-man. There a breach takes place with Christian and humanist morality, humanism passes over into anti-humanism. There is greater religious depth in Dostoyevsky's statement of this problem. Kirillov, a man of the loftiest spirit, of

great purity and detachment, expressed the final results of the path
of the godless self-affirmation of man: "There will be a new man,
happy and proud," says Kirillov, as though in a frenzy, "who will
conquer pain and fear and that same one will be God; God is the pain
of fear and death. Whoever conquers pain and fear, he becomes God.
Then there will be a new life; then there will be a new man; everything will be anew." "Man will be God and will be changed physically and the world will be changed and actions and thoughts and all
feelings will be changed." "He will bring the world to an end who
bears the name of man-God. God-man? asks Stavrogin again. Man-
God, answers Kirillov. There is the difference." The way of the man-
God leads, according to Dostoyevsky, to the system of Shigalev and
the Grand Inquisitor, that is to say, it is a denial of man who is an
image and likeness of God, it is the denial of freedom. Only the way
of God-manhood and the God-man leads to the affirmation of man,
to human personality and freedom. Such is the existential dialectic
of Dostoyevsky. Humaneness disrupted from God and God-man, is
reborn in inhumaneness. Dostoyevsky sees this transition in the case
of the atheist revolutionary Nechaev who completely breaks away
from humanist morality, from humanitarianism and makes a demand
for cruelty. It must be said in this connection that Nechaev, whom
the author of *The Possessed* inaccurately describes, was a real
ascetic and a hero of the revolutionary idea, and in his *Revolutionary
Catechism* writes, so to speak, an instruction for the spiritual life of
the revolutionary and requires from him a denial of the world. But
the problem, as stated by Dostoyevsky, is a very profound one. The
term "man-deity" which was misused among us in the twentieth century, may give rise to misunderstanding and it is difficult to translate
into foreign languages. It is indeed a Christian idea that man ought
to attain deification, though not through self-assertion and self-satisfaction. Humanism is to be superseded (*aufhebung*) and not
destroyed. There was truth in it and sometimes great truth in comparison with the falsity of historical Christianity. There was in it a great
truth as against bestiality.[2] But the eschatology of humanism is
revealed as an intermediate realm, and that is disclosed especially by

2. Max Scheler is mistaken in opposing Christianity and humanism (humanitarianism) which
he connects with *ressentiment*. See his *L'Homme du Ressentiment*.

Russian thought. It is impossible to remain in this intermediate cultural realm as the humanists of the West would wish; it disintegrates and lays bare in their finality the ultimate conditions.

Vladimir Solovyov may be called a Christian humanist, but his humanism is altogether a peculiar one. In controversy with the right wing of the Christian camp Vladimir Solovyov was fond of saying that the humanistic process of Russian history is not only a Christian process, even although it was not recognized as such, but that the unbelieving humanist actually gave more effective expression to Christianity than the believing Christians who did nothing for the betterment of human society. The unbelieving humanists of the new history tried to establish a society which was more human and free, while the believing Christians acted in opposition to it and defended and preserved a society which is based on violence and robbery. Vladimir Solovyov gave particular expression to this in his essay "On the Collapse of the Mediaeval World Outlook" and aroused violent indignation in K. Leontyev who was at that time disillusioned in his theocratic utopia. He considered the idea of God-manhood as the basic idea of Christianity. I shall say something about this when I come to speak about Russian religious philosophy. It is a fundamental idea of that philosophy. Humanism (or humanitarianism) enters into the religion of God-manhood as a constituent part. In the Person of Jesus Christ there took place the union of divine and human nature and the God-man appeared. The same thing ought to take place in humanity, in human society and in history. The realization of God-manhood, of divine-human life, presupposes the activity of men. In the Christianity of the past there was not sufficient activity on the part of man, especially in Orthodoxy, and man was often crushed. The liberation of human activity in the new history was necessary for the realization of God-manhood. Hence the humanism which can in thought be non-Christian and anti-Christian takes on a religious meaning. Without it the purpose of Christianity would not be effectively realized. Vladimir Solovyov tried to give a religious meaning to the experience of humanism; it is one of the principal services that he rendered. But his thought moved in the direction of reconciliation and synthesis. In him there were no tragic conflicts and yawning gulfs, such as are disclosed in Dostoyevsky. Only towards the end of his life did a pessimistic and apocalyptic frame of mind and the expectation of the speedy coming of antichrist take control of him. Solovyov's thought enters into the Russian dialectic of man and humaneness and is inseparable from it. His religious philosophy is permeated with the spirit of humaneness, but it was too cold in its outward expression. In it the personal mysticism which was inherent in him was rationalized.

Bukharev was one of the most interesting of the theologians who were the product of our spiritual environment; he was an archimandrite and left his monastery. He also integrated humaneness and Christianity as a whole; he demands the acceptance of Christ in human life in all its fullness; to him all true humaneness is of Christ; he is opposed to the tendency which lays less stress upon the human nature of Christ; he is against every monophysite tendency. One cannot call L. Tolstoy a humanist in the Western sense; his religious philosophy was in certain of its aspects more akin to Buddhism than to Christianity, but Russian humaneness was very much a part of him; it finds expression in his revolt against history and against all violence, in his love for simple laboring folk. Tolstoy's doctrine of non-resistance and his repudiation of the violence of history could only grow out of Russian spiritual soil. Tolstoy is the exact opposite of Nietzsche; he is the Russian antithesis of Nietzsche and of Gogol also. Considerably later V. Rozanov, when he belonged to the Slavophil conservative camp, says with indignation that man has been turned into a means for the historical process, and asks when indeed man would be seen to be an end.[3] In his view the significance of human personality is only revealed in religion. Rozanov thinks that a feeling for the majesticgreatness of history does not belong to the Russian people and this fact he deems an advantage in the face of the people of the West who are possessed by the idea of historical greatness. K. Leontyev alone thought otherwise than the majority of Russians, and in the name of beauty rebelled against humaneness. But for the sake of intellectual richness and variety the people should have a counterweight to the fundamental direction of its thought.

K. Leontyev was a man of the Renaissance; he loved flourishing culture; beauty was to him a more precious thing than man, and for the sake of beauty he was ready to acquiesce in any sort of suffering

3. V. Rozanov, *The Legend of the Grand Inquisitor.*

and torment for men. He preached an ethic of values, the values of beauty, of the flourishing culture of the mind, and of the might of the State, in opposition to an ethic based upon the supremacy of human personality, upon compassion for man. Without being a cruel man himself he preached cruelty in the name of the highest values, just as Nietzsche did. K. Leontyev was the first Russian aesthete. "Humanity," in his thought, "is not a sufferer but a poet." As distinct from the majority of Russians he liked the power of the State. In his view there are no humane States, and that view may be correct but it does not alter our judgments of value. A humanistic State is a State in a condition of disintegration. Everything hurts on the tree of life; to accept life is to accept pain. Leontyev preaches naturalism in sociology; he sees God not in the freedom of the spirit but in the laws of nature and history. Leontyev not only does not believe in the possibility of a kingdom of truth and righteousness upon earth, but does not even desire the realization of truth and righteousness, supposing—as he does—that in such a kingdom there will be no beauty, which, in his view, is everywhere connected with the greatest inequalities and injustice, with violence and cruelty. The audacity and radicalness of Leontyev's thought lies in the fact that he dared to admit things which others do not dare to admit. Pure good is not beautiful. In order that there may be beauty in life, evil also is necessary; the contrast of darkness and light is necessary. Above all Leontyev hated eudemonism. He rebels against the idea of the happiness of people; he professes an ascetic pessimism; he considers a liberal equalitarian process ugly, but at the same time fated; he does not believe in the future of his own ideal. This distinguishes him from the usual type of reactionary and conservative. The world is moving towards an ugly and confused simplicity. We shall see how in his opinion naturalistic sociology passes into apocalyptic; and aesthetic values coincide in his view with religious values. Brotherhood and humanism he acknowledges only as a means to the salvation of the individual soul. He preaches a transcendent egoism. During the first half of his life he was seeking for happiness in beauty; in the second half of his life he was seeking for salvation from ruin.[4] But he is not seeking the Kingdom of God, and

---

4. See my book, *Konstantine Leontyev*.

in particular he is not seeking the Kingdom of God on earth. The Russian idea of the brotherhood of man, and the Russian search for universal salvation are alien to him and Russian humaneness is alien to him also. He attacks the "rosy Christianity" of Dostoyevsky and L. Tolstoy. It is a strange accusation to bring against Dostoyevsky whose Christianity was tragic. Leontyev is a lonely dreamer; he stands apart and expresses the opposite pole to that at which the Russian idea took shape. But even he desires a special path for Russia. He is distinguished by a great perspicacity and he foresaw and foretold much. The destiny of culture was a theme which he stated in great acuteness. He foresaw the possibility of a decadence of culture and said much which anticipated Nietzsche, Gobineau and Spengler. There was an eschatological current of thought in him. But it is impossible to follow Leontyev; his followers became repulsive.

As I have already said, there is an inner existential dialectic by the force of which humanism passes into anti-humanism. The self-assertion of man leads to the denial of man. In Russia the last word in this dialectic of humanism was communism. That also had humanitarian sources, it desired to fight for the liberation of man from slavery; but in the result, the social collective, within which man ought to be liberated from exploitation and violence, becomes an agency for the enslavement of human personality. The primacy of society over personality is affirmed, the primacy of the proletariat, or rather of the idea of the proletariat, over the worker, over the concrete man. Man in liberating himself from the idolatry of the past falls into a new idolatry. We see this already in Belinsky. Having made its escape from the power of the "common," personality is again subjected to the power of a new "common," that is of the social organizing of life. For the sake of the triumph of social organization violence may be done upon human personalities, any sort of means becomes permissible in order to realize the highest end. In our socialistic movement Herzen was the most free from idolatry. How was it with Marx himself? In this connection the works which Marx produced as a young man, but which were published comparatively late, are most astonishing.[5] His sources were humanistic; he fought for the liberation of man. His revolt against capitalism was based upon the fact that in

---

5. Especially interesting are the essays, *Philosophia und Nazionaleconomie.*

capitalist society there takes place an alienation of the human nature of the worker, a dehumanizing process, the turning of him into a thing. The whole ethical pathos of Marxism was founded upon a struggle against that alienation and dehumanization. Marxism demanded the return of the fullness of his human nature to the worker as a man. In these early works Marx kept in view the possibility of an existential social philosophy. Marx melted down the frozen categories of classical bourgeois political economy; he denies that there are eternal economic laws; he denies that there is any objective reality of things which lies behind economics. Economics are nothing but the activity of people and the relations among people. Capitalism means nothing more than the relations of living people to one another in the sphere of production. The activity of man can change the relations among men, can change economics which are no more than a form which has taken shape in the course of history and is in its very nature transient. The primary and original ground upon which Marxism rested was certainly not that socialistic determinism which later on began to be affirmed both by its friends and by its enemies. Marx still stood near to the German idealism from which he issued. But he originally accepted the absolute supremacy of man, and in his view man was the supreme value which was not subordinated to anything higher, and therefore his humanitarianism was exposed to the existential dialectic process of disintegration. His notable doctrine of the fetishism of goods is an existential sociology which sees the primary reality in laboring human activity, and not in the objectivized realities or quasi realities of things. Man accepts as the exterior reality, and it ends by enslaving him, that which is his own product, an objectivization and alienation which is produced by himself. But the philosophic and religious foundations of his world outlook do not allow Marx to go further along the true path. In the last result he saw man as exclusively a product of society, of class, and subordinated the whole man to the new society, the ideal social body, instead of subordinating the society to man and so liberating man finally from the categories of social class. Russian communism drew extreme conclusions from this and the rejection of Russian humaneness took place. And so it will always be if they affirm man outside God-manhood. Dostoyevsky understood this more profoundly than anyone, although his way of putting it is open to criticism. There remains the eternal truth that man will preserve his highest value, his freedom and independence from the power of nature and society only if God exists and if God-manhood exists. This is the theme of Russian thought

2

Within historical Orthodoxy in which the monastic ascetic spirit prevailed, the subject of man has not been, and could not be adequately revealed. The tendency to deviate towards monophysitism predominated. The anthropology of the Fathers was deficient. There was no correspondence with christological truth in it; it did not contain what in my book *The Meaning of Creation* I have called the christology of man. Christianity teaches almost exclusively that man is a sinner and needs to be taught about salvation. Only in St. Gregory of Nyssa can one find a loftier doctrine of man, but even in him the creative experience of man is still not comprehended.[6] The truth about man and about the central part he plays in the created world, even when it has been disclosed outside Christianity, has had Christian sources, and apart from Christianity cannot be comprehended. In Russian Christian thought of the nineteenth century, in Khomyakov's doctrine of freedom, in Solovyov's doctrine of God-manhood, in all the creative work of Dostoyevsky, in the genius of his discussion on freedom, in Nesmyelov's remarkable anthropology, in N. Fedorov's belief in the resuscitating activity of man, something new about man was revealed. But official Orthodoxy, official ecclesiasticism was unwilling to listen to it. In historical Orthodoxy the Christian truth about man has remained, as it were, in a potential state. It is the same potentiality, the same lack of disclosure which belonged to the Russian people in general in the past. The Christian West used up its strength in human activity of various kinds. In Russia the revelation of the creative forces of man lies in the future. Chaadaev had already brought forward this subject and later on it was constantly repeated in our intellectual and spiritual history. Within Russian Orthodoxy but not in its official form, the promulgation of a new doctrine of

---

6. See an interesting book by the Jesuit Hans von Balthasar, *Présence et Pensée. Essai sur la Philosophia Religieuse de Grégoire de Nysse.*

man may be a possibility; but that means also a new doctrine of the history of society. It is a mistake to put Christianity and humanism in opposition to each other. Humanism has a Christian origin. The ancient Greco-Roman humanism, which was long ago integrated with Christianity by Catholicism, was unaware of man's highest dignity and loftiest freedom. In Greek thought man was dependent upon cosmic forces; the Greek view of the world was cosmocentric. In Roman thought man was in entire dependence upon the State. Christianity alone is anthropocentric, and in accordance with its principles liberates man from the power of the cosmos and of society. The antithesis between God-humanity and man-deity, as stated by Dostoyevsky, has a profound meaning. But the actual terminology may give rise to doubt and requires critical reexamination. Man ought to become God and to deify himself, but he can do this only through the God-man and God-humanity. God-humanity presupposes a creative activity of man. The movement goes from man to God also and not only from God to man, and this movement from man to God must certainly not be understood in the sense of choice, a choice made by man through his freedom, as, for example, traditional Roman Catholic thought understands it. It is a creative movement which continues world creation. But the loftiest idea of man among us arises out of duality, out of what Hegel calls an unhappy consciousness. Gogol is a clear example of the "unhappy consciousness," but it has made itself felt also in Tolstoy and Dostoyevsky. Russian philosophy, having developed outside an academic framework, has always been existential in its themes and in its approach, whereas the social theme among us was but the giving of concrete form to the theme of man.

5

1

THE SOCIAL THEME occupied a predominant place in Russian nineteenth-century thought. It might even be said that Russian thought in that century was to a remarkable extent colored by socialistic ideas. If the word socialism is not taken in its doctrinaire sense, one might say that socialism is deeply rooted in the Russian nature. There is already an expression of this truth in the fact that the Russian people did not recognize the Roman conception of property. It has been said of Muscovite Russia that it was innocent of the sin of ownership in land, the one and only landed proprietor being the Tsar: there was no freedom, but there was a greater sense of what was right. This is of interest in the light that it throws upon the rise of communism. The Slavophils also repudiated the Western bourgeois interpretation of private property equally with the socialists of a revolutionary way of thinking. Almost all of them thought that the Russian people was called upon to give actual effect to social truth and righteousness and to the brotherhood of man. One and all they hoped that Russia would escape the wrongness and evil of capitalism, that it would be able to pass over to a better social order while avoiding the capitalist stage of economic development. And they all considered the backwardness of Russia as conferring upon her a great advantage. It was the wisdom of the Russians to be socialists during the period of serfdom and autocracy. Of all peoples in the world the Russians have the community spirit; in the highest degree the Russian way of life and Russian manners are of that kind. Russian hospitality is an indication of this sense of community.

The forerunners of Russian socialism were Radishchev and Pestel. The latter's socialism, of course, was of an agrarian character. Social mysticism was of original growth among us, as for instance in Pechorin under the influence of Lamennais. The fundamental influence was that of Saint-Simon and Fourier. The Russians were passionately enthusiastic disciples of these two men. This form of socialism was at first free from politics. M.V. Petrashevsky, a Russian landowner, was a convinced follower of Fourier and installed a *phalanstery* at his home in the country. The peasants burnt it as an innovation and contrary to their way of life. His socialism was of a peaceful sort, non-political and idyllic. It was a belief in the possibility of a happy equitable and right-minded life. A circle of Petrashevsky's friends used to meet together for quiet and dreamy discussions about the ordering of mankind "under new management" (the phrase is Dostoyevsky's). Petrashevsky believed in the possibility of actually putting Fourier's type of socialism into effect in Russia while the autocratic monarchy was still in being. These remarkable words are his: "Finding nothing worthy of my attachment either among women or among men, I have vowed myself to the service of mankind." All this ended very sadly and in a manner very characteristic of power in history. In 1840 the Petrashevites, as they were called, were arrested; twenty-one of them (Dostoyevsky was among the number) were condemned to death, a sentence which was afterwards commuted to one of hard labor. Of the members of the circle Speshnev was the most revolutionary in tendency and may be regarded as a precursor of communism. He came nearest to Marxist ideas and he was a militant atheist. A wealthy landowner, an aristocrat and goodlooking, he served Dostoyevsky as a model for Stavrogin. The first Marxists were Russians. Almost the very first of the followers of Marx was a Russian country squire from the Steppes named Sazonov, who lived in Paris. Marx was not very fond of the Russians, and was astonished at the fact that he found followers among the Russians earlier than among the Western peoples. He did not foresee the role that he was to play in Russia. Among the Russians, socialism had a religious character even when it was atheistic. Three periods of Russian socialist thought are to be distinguished: utopian socialism, which was due to the influence of the ideas of Saint-Simon and Fourier; *narodnik* socialism—the most Russian of all, and nearer to the thought of Proudhon; and scientific or Marxist socialism:[1] To this I would add another—a fourth period—communist socialism, which may be defined as the free exaltation of the revolutionary will. A primary fact about Russian socialism was the decisive predominance in it of the social over the political. This was the case not only in utopian socialism, but also in the *narodnik* socialism of the seventies. It was only at the end of the seventies when the party known as the People's Will was organized that the socialist movement became political and entered upon a terrorist struggle. It has sometimes been said that the social question in Russia has a conservative and not a revolutionary character. This was due in the main to those traditional features of Russian life, the peasant commune and the workers' association. It was the ideology of the small producer. The socialist *narodniks* were afraid of political liberalism on the ground that it brings in its train the triumph of the bourgeoisie. Herzen was an opponent of political democracy. At one time he even believed that a useful part was played by the Tsar and was prepared to give his support to the monarchy if it would protect the masses of the people. What the socialists desired more than anything was that Russia should avoid the Western path of development, that whatever happened it might escape the capitalist stage.

---

1. K. A. Pazhitov, *The Development of Socialist Ideas in Russia*, and P. Sakulin, *Russian Literature and Socialism*.

2

Narodnichestvo is a phenomenon which is peculiar to Russia just as Russian nihilism and Russian anarchism are peculiarly Russian phenomena. It had many different manifestations. There was a conservative *Narodnichestvo* and a revolutionary; there was a materialist form of it and a religious. The Slavophils and Herzen were *narodniks*; so were Dostoyevsky and the revolutionaries of the seventies. But all the while at the root of it was a belief in the people as the guardian of truth and right. A distinction was drawn between the people and the nation, and the two ideas were even set in opposition to each other. *Narodnichestvo* is not the same thing as nationalism, although it might take on a nationalist color. In religious *Narodnichestvo* the people is a sort of mystical organism which goes deeper into the soil and deeper into the spirit, than the nation, which is a rationalized, historical organization in connection with the body politic. The people are a concrete community of living persons, whereas the nation is a more abstract idea. But even in religious *Narodnichestvo*, among the Slavophils, with Dostoyevsky and L. Tolstoy, the people meant especially the peasants and the working classes of society. While to the *Narodnichestvo* which was non-religious and revolutionary the people were identified with the social category of the working class, and their interests were identified with the interests of labor. The spirit of the *narodniks* and the spirit of democracy (in the social sense) were mingled together. The Slavophils thought that among the simple people, among the peasantry, the spirit of the Russian *narodniks* and the Orthodox faith were preserved to a greater extent than among the educated and ruling classes. A negatory attitude to the State was characteristic of Russian *Narodnichestvo* as distinct from nationalism. It had an anarchic tendency and this was to be found in Slavophilism also, just as it was in the left wing of the *narodniks*. The State was regarded as a vampire which sucked the blood of the people, as a parasite on the body of the people. *Narodnik* thought was connected with the idea of breaking away, with opposition and with the absence of unity. The people is not the only complete constituent part of the historical nation. For over against the people stands on the one hand the Intelligentsia and the educated classes, and on the other hand the nobility and ruling classes. As a rule the *narodnik* who was a member of the Intelligentsia did not feel himself an organic part of the whole mass of the people or that he fulfilled a function in the life of the people. He was conscious of the fact that his position was not normal, not what it ought to be, and even sinful. Not only truth was hidden in the people but there was also hidden a mystery, which it was necessary to unravel. *Narodnichestvo* was the offspring not of the organic character of Russian history of the Petrine period, but of the parasitic character of the mass of the Russian nobility; and it does great honor to the best part, a comparatively small part, of the Russian nobility that *narodnik* thought was brought to birth in it. This *narodnik* thought was the "work of conscience"; it was a consciousness of sin and repentance. This sense of sin and repentance reaches its highest point in the person of L. Tolstoy. Among the Slavophils it took another form and was connected with a false idyllic view of the period of Russian history before Peter, as being organic. On the other hand the social question was not expressed among them with sufficient clearness. It might be said that Slavophil social philoso-phy replaced the Church by the commune and the commune by the Church; but the social ideology of the Slavophils bore a *narodnik* and anti-capitalist impress. In accordance with their manner of life the Slavophils remained typically Russian gentry, but since they saw truth and right among the simple people, among the peasantry, they endeavored to imitate the way of life of the people. This was naively expressed in a sort of popular Russian dress which they tried to wear. In this connection Chaadaev produced the witticism that K. Aksakov dressed in the Russian style to such an extent that people in the street took him for a Persian. Among the repentant gentry of the seventies who "went to the people" the consciousness of guilt before the people, and their repentance, went very deep. But in any case the Slavophils believed that her own special path belonged to Russia, that there would be no development of capitalism among us, no formation of a powerful bourgeoisie, that the community spirit of the Russian people's way of life in distinction from Western individ-ualism would be preserved. The triumphant bourgeoisie in the West repelled them, albeit less acutely perhaps than it repelled Herzen.

During his last period Belinsky arrived at a world outlook which may be regarded as the basis of Russian socialism. After him, in the

history of our socialistic thought the leading part was played by articles and criticism in the press. Behind them our social thought was
concealed from the censorship. This had grievous consequences for
literary criticism itself, which did not reach the highest level of Russian literature. It has already been said that Belinsky's new device
was social organization—"social organization or death!" Belinsky
loved literature and in him as a critic there was much delicacy and
sensitiveness. But on the ground of compassion for the unfortunate
he rejected the right to think about art and learning. The social utopia dominated him, the passionate belief that there will be no more
rich and poor, no more Tsar and subjects, that people will be brothers and finally that man will arise in the whole fullness of his stature.
I use the word "utopia" by no means to indicate something which
was not actually realized, but only to indicate a maximum ideal. It
would be an error to suppose that Belinsky's socialism was sentimental; he was passionate but not sentimental and in him there
sounded that ill-omened sinister note: "People are so stupid that it is
necessary to bring them to happiness by force." And for the realization of his ideal Belinsky did not stop short of violence and blood-
shed. Belinsky was by no means an economist; he had little learning,
and this makes him a contrast with the very well-equipped Chernishevsky; but, as I have already said, one can regard him as one of
the predecessors of the Russian Marxist socialists and even of the
communists. He is less of a typical *narodnik* than Herzen. It is to
Belinsky that the words belong: "A liberated Russian people would
not go to Parliament, but they would hurry to the pub to have a drink,
to smash windows and hang the gentry." He acknowledged the positive importance behind the development of the bourgeoisie in Russia, but he also thought that Russia would solve the social problem
better than Europe. Belinsky is interesting for this reason that in him
the primary ethical basis of Russian socialism in general is revealed.
Herzen is much more characteristic of *narodnik* socialism. He had a
passion for freedom and he defended the value and dignity of personality, but he believed that the Russian peasant would save the
world from the triumph of the bourgeois spirit which he saw even in
Western socialism and among the workers of Europe. He sharply
criticized parliamentary democracy, and this is typical of the *narodniks*. He saw two aspects in the European bourgeois world: "On the

one hand the bourgeois proprietors who stubbornly refuse to surrender their monopoly; on the other hand the bourgeois have-nots who want to wrest their property from their hands but have no power to do so; that is to say, on the one hand avarice and on the other envy. Since in actual fact no moral principle is involved in all this, the position of any person on one side or the other is fixed by the outward circumstances of his status and the position he occupies in society. One of the opposing wolves fighting the other gains the victory, that is to say property or place, and only passes over from the side of envy to the side of avarice. Nothing could be more advantageous for this transition than the fruitless exchanges of parliamentary debate; it gives movement and sets limits; it provides an appearance of getting things done, and provides a setting for the common interests, which is favorable to the attainment of its own personal ends."[2] Here Herzen shows great perspicacity. There were anarchic tendencies in Herzen, but this anarchism stood nearer to Proudhon, a social thinker who was more akin to him than to Bakunin. The astonishing thing is that the skeptical and critical Herzen looked for salvation in the village commune, in the economic backwardness of Russia. He saw its great advantage in solving the social question. This is a traditional motif. Russia cannot tolerate the development of capitalism, of a bourgeoisie and proletariat. There are in the Russian people germs which are an earnest of community, of common life, of a possible brotherhood of man, things which are not yet to be found among peoples of the West. In the West a falling into sin has taken place, and its results are being lived down. In many respects Herzen is like the Slavophils, but he did not share their religious foundations. Herzen found a special difficulty in combining the principle of community with the principle of personality and freedom. Herzen remained true to his social ideal but he had no faith, and historical pessimism was one of his traits. He had experience which Belinsky had not, and the enthusiastic belief of the latter had no place in him. He had acute powers of observation, and the world presented a picture which was but little favorable to optimistic illusions. A typical *narodnik* in his social outlook in general, he remained an individual and original thinker in the history

---

2. The quotation is from *The Past and Reveries*.

of Russian social thought. In a letter to Michelet in which he defends the Russian people, Herzen wrote: "Russia will never make a revolution with the purpose of getting rid of the Tsar Nicholas and replacing him by representative-tsars, judge-tsars, policeman-tsars." He meant by this that in Russia there will be no bourgeois, no liberal revolution, but there will be a social revolution and in this his foresight was remarkable. During the sixties the character and type of the Russian Intelligentsia changed; it has another social makeup. In the forties the Intelligentsia was still for the most part recruited from the gentry; in the sixties it comes from other classes as well. The appearance on the scene of these other classes was a very important phenomenon in the history of Russian social currents of thought. The proletariat member of the Intelligentsia comes into being in Russia and is to become a revolutionary fermenting agent. Members of the Intelligentsia who came from the ranks of the clergy will still play a great part; men who have been seminarists become nihilists. Chernishevsky and Dobrolyubov were the sons of priests and were trained in the seminary. There is something mysterious in the growth of movements in public life in Russia during the sixties. "Society" made its appearance; public opinion began to form. This was still not the case in the forties when there were figures who stood alone and small circles. The central figure of Russian social thought of the sixties was M. G. Chernishevsky. He was a leader in the realm of ideas. It is essential to know the moral character of Chernishevsky. Such people as he constitute moral capital of which less worthy people who come after will avail themselves. In personal moral qualities he was not only one of the best of Russians but also he came very near to being a saint.[3] Yes—this materialist and utilitarian, this ideologist of Russian "nihilism" was almost a saint. When the police officers took him into penal servitude in Siberia they said, "Our orders were to bring a criminal and we are bringing a saint." The case of Chernishevsky provided one of the most revolting falsifications perpetrated by the Russian Government. He was condemned to nineteen years' penal servitude; it was necessary to get Chernishevsky out of the way as a man who might have a

---

3. See the extraordinarily interesting book *Love among the people of the sixties*, where Chernishevsky's letters are quoted and especially those which he wrote to his wife from penal servitude.

harmful influence upon the young. He bore his penal servitude hero-
ically; it might even be said that he endured his martyrdom with
Christian humility. He said "I fight for freedom, but I do not want
freedom for myself lest it should be said that I am fighting for interested ends." It was thus that the "utilitarian" spoke and wrote. He
wanted nothing for himself; he was one whole sacrifice. At that time
far too many Orthodox Christians successfully arranged their
earthly affairs with their heavenly. Chernishevsky's love for his
wife, from whom he was separated, is one of the most amazing manifestations of love between man and woman; it is even a loftier love
than that of Millet for his wife or of the love of Lewes for George
Eliot. One must read the letters which Chernishevsky wrote to his
wife from penal servitude in order to arrive at a complete appraise-
ment of his moral character and of the almost mystical character of
his love for his wife. The case of Chernishevsky is striking in virtue
of the lack of correspondence between his rather pitiable materialist
and utilitarian philosophy and the ascetic attainment of his life and
his lofty character. Here we must remember the words of Vladimir
Solovyov: "the Russian nihilists have a sort of syllogism of their
own—man is descended from a monkey, consequently we shall love
one another." The Russian revolutionaries who were to be inspired
by the ideas of Chernishevsky present an interesting psychological
problem. The best of Russian revolutionaries acquiesced during this
earthly life in persecution, want, imprisonment, exile, penal servitude, execution, and they had no hope whatever of another life
beyond this. The comparison with Christians of that time is most
disadvantageous to the latter; they highly cherished the blessings of
this earthly life and counted upon the blessings of heavenly life.
Chernishevsky was a very learned man; he knew everything; he
knew theology, Hegel's philosophy, natural science, history, and he
was a specialist in political economy. His type of culture was not
particularly high; it was lower than that of the idealists of the forties.
Such was the result of democratization. Marx started to learn Russian in order to be able to read Chernishevsky's works on economics, so highly did he value them. Chernishevsky was forgiven his
lack of literary talent. There was nothing at all outwardly attractive
about his writings; he cannot be compared with the more brilliant
Pisarev. Chernishevsky's socialism had close affinities with the *nar-*

odnik socialism of Herzen; he also desired to rely upon the peasant commune and the workers' guild; he also wanted to escape capitalist development in Russia. In his *Criticism of the Philosophical Prejudices against Communal Land Ownership* he availed himself of the terminology of Hegel's dialectic and endeavored to show that it is possible to avoid the intermediate capitalist period of development or to reduce it to the extreme minimum or even to almost nothing at all. His fundamental social idea was the antithesis between the wealth of the nation and the well-being of the people. At the same time Chernishevsky was in favor of industrial development, and in this respect he was not a *narodnik*, if by *Narodnichestvo* we understand the demand to remain exclusively an agricultural country and not enter upon the path of commercial development. But he believed that commercial development can be achieved by other ways than Western capitalism. The primacy of distribution over production remained a belief which he held in common with the *narodniks*. Chernishevsky was ready even to see something in common between the Slavophils and himself. But how great the psychological difference is between Chernishevsky and Herzen, in spite of their similarity in regard to social ideals! It was the difference between the spiritual makeup of the gentry in contrast with other classes, between the democrat and the man of aristocratic culture. Chernishevsky wrote of Herzen: "What a clever man! What a clever man and how behind the times! He actually thinks at this time of day that he is going on sharpening his wits in the salons of Moscow, and sparring with Khomyakov. But time is passing with terrible rapidity; a month is equal to a decade in times gone by. Look at him—everything that belongs to the Moscow gentleman is still to be seen in him." This hits the center of the target as an expression of the difference between the generations, which always played so enormous a part in Russia. In his spiritual makeup Herzen remained an "idealist" of the forties in spite of Feuerbach and his own skepticism. The milder type of "idealist" of the forties was replaced by the harsher type of the "realist" of the sixties. In the same way in the course of time the milder type of *narodnik* was replaced among us by the harsher type of Marxist, the milder type of menshevik by the harsher type of bolshevik. At the same time Chernishevsky was in no respect a harsh type of person; he was extraordinarily human, full of

126 ❖ THE RUSSIAN IDEA

love and self-denial; but his thought took on a different color and his will a different direction. Those who belonged to the Intelligentsia of the sixties, to the thinking "realists," did not recognize the play of abundant creative forces; they did not recognize all that was being born of abundance of leisure; their realism was poor; their thought was narrow and dull and focused upon what was to them the one chief thing. They were "Jews" and not "Hellenes." They fought against all subtleties; they even fought against the subtle skepticism which Herzen allowed himself; they fought against the play of wit; they were dogmatists. Among the "nihilists" of the sixties an ascetic mentality made its appearance, which was characteristic of the subsequent revolutionary Intelligentsia. Without that ascetic spirit a heroic revolutionary struggle would have been impossible. Intolerance and isolation of self from the rest of the world grew much stronger. This led to Nechaev's *Revolutionary Catechism*. This ascetic element found expression in Chernishevsky's *What is to be done? What is to be done?* belongs to the type of utopian novels. This novel has no artistic worth. It was not written with talent. The social utopia which is depicted in Vera Pavlovna's dream is elementary enough. Cooperative needlework businesses can cause no alarm to anybody in these days, nor can they arouse enthusiasm, but Chernishevsky's novel is, nevertheless, remarkable and it had an immense influence. This influence was in the main moral; it was the preaching of the new morality. The novel, recognized as a catechism of nihilism, was calumniated by the representatives of the right wing, and those in whom such an attitude was least of all becoming cried out against its immorality. In actual fact the morality of *What is to be done?* is very high, and in any case it was infinitely higher that the abominable morality of the "Domostroi," which was a disgrace to the Russian people. Bukharev, one of the most notable of Russian theologians, acknowledged *What is to be done?* as Christian in the spirit of the book. This book is above all ascetic; there is in it that same ascetic element with which the Russian revolutionary Intelligentsia was permeated. The hero of the novel, Rakhmetov, sleeps on nails in order to prepare himself to endure suffering, and is ready to deny himself everything. It was the preaching of free love which gave rise to the principal attacks upon the book, and the repudiation of jealousy, as being based upon the vile sense of property.

These attacks came from the right, the conservative, side, which was in practice particularly addicted to hedonistic morality. Sexual license flourished chiefly among the Guards' officers, the idle land-owners and important functionaries, not among the revolutionary Intelligentsia with their ascetic frame of mind. It ought to be acknowledged that the morality of *What is to be done?* was very pure and detached. The preaching of free love was the preaching of sincerity of feeling and of the value of love as the one justification of relations between a man and a woman. Discontinuation of love on one of the two sides is the discontinuation of the meaning of the relation. Chernishevsky rebelled against any kind of social violence upon human feelings and was moved by love for freedom, reverence for freedom and all sincerity of feeling. The unique love for a woman which Chernishevsky experienced in his own life was a pattern of ideal love. The theme of free love in Chernishevsky had nothing in common with the theme of "justification of the flesh" which played its part among us, not among the nihilists and revolutionaries, but among the subtle anesthetizing currents of thought of the beginning of the twentieth century. The "flesh" interested Chernishevsky very little. It did interest Merezhkovsky later on, just as freedom and uprightness also interested him. I repeat, the morality of the novel *What is to be done?* is a high morality, and it is characteristic of Russian thought. Russian morality in regard to sex and love is very distinct from the morality of the West. In this connection we have always been more free than the Western peoples, and we have thought that the question of love between a man and a woman is a question of personality and does not concern society. If you speak of free love to a Frenchman he thinks first of all of sexual relations, but the Russian, who is less sensual by nature, pictures to himself something entirely different—the value of a feeling which is not dependent upon social law; he thinks of freedom and sincerity. Intelligent Russians regard the serious and profound connection between a man and a woman based upon genuine love, as constituting the genuine marriage even if it has not been blessed by the Church, by ecclesiastical law or by civil; and, on the other hand, the connection which has been blessed by ecclesiastical law, given the absence of love in the case of compulsion on the part of parents or based upon financial considerations, they consider immoral. It may be concealed depravity. The Russians are less legally minded than the Western peoples; to them the content is more important than the form. On this account freedom of love in the deep and pure sense of the word is a Russian dogma, a dogma of the Russian Intelligentsia; it enters into the Russian idea in the same way as the rejection of capital punishment enters into it. In this respect we shall never reach agreement with the Western European peoples who are shackled by a legalistic civilization. In particular we do not agree with official Roman Catholicism which has distorted Christianity into a religion of law. To us it is man who is the important thing; to them it is society, civilization. Chernishevsky had a most wretched philosophy with which the surface of his mind was filled, but the depth of his moral nature inspired him with very true and pure values in life. There was great humaneness in him and he fought for the liberation of man; he fought for man against the power of society over human feelings. But his thinking remained social; he had no psychology and in his anthropology there was no metaphysical depth in man. His essay on "Anthropological principles in Philosophy" which was suggested by Feuerbach, was weak and superficial.

Pisarev and the paper *The Russian Word* put forward other tendencies in the sixties than those of Chernishevsky and the paper *The Contemporary*. If Chernishevsky was regarded as a typical socialist, Pisarev was viewed as an individualist, but even in Pisarev there were to be found characteristically Russian social motifs. Free human personality was to him the highest value and he naively connected this with a materialist and utilitarian philosophy. We shall see that therein lay the principal inner contradiction of Russian nihilism. Pisarev was interested not only in society but also in the equality of man; he wanted the free man to make his appearance; he considered that only a man belonging to the Intelligentsia, a man of intellectual labor, was such a free man—"a thinking reality". In him there breaks out an arrogant attitude towards the representatives of physical labor, such as it would be impossible to meet with in Chernishevsky. But this does not prevent him from identifying the interests of personality with the interests of labor, a subject which N. Mikhailovsky was to develop later on. He demands useful labor; he preaches the idea of the economy of forces. In an essay entitled "Realists" he writes: "The final purpose of all our thinking and all the activity of every honest man, all the same consists in this, in deciding once and for all the inescapable problem of hungry and naked men and women. Outside the question there is most decidedly nothing whatever about which it would be worthwhile to worry, to ponder or to fuss." It is expressed in an extreme form, but here the "nihilist" Pisarev was nearer to the Gospel than the "imperialist" who considers that the might of the State is the final end. Pisarev is deserving of separate consideration in connection with the question of Russian nihilism and the Russian attitude to culture. He is interesting because of the attention he paid to theme of personality. He represented Russian radical enlightenment; he was not a *narodnik*.

3

The seventies were preeminently the time when *Narodnichestvo* flourished among us. The Intelligentsia went to the people in order to pay their debt to them, in order to redeem their own guilt. This was not primarily a revolutionary movement. The political struggle for freedom retired into the background. Even the "black re-deal," which had fought for a reapportionment of the land and the leasing of it to the peasants, was opposed to political conflict. The *narodnik* Intelligentsia went to the people in order to mingle with their lives and bring them enlightenment and to improve their economic position. The *narodnik* movement only took on a revolutionary character after the Government began to persecute the activity of the *narodniks*, an activity which was essentially cultural in character. The fate of the *narodniks* of the forties was tragic because they not only met with persecution from the authorities but they were not even welcomed by the people themselves, who had a different outlook upon life from that of the Intelligentsia, and different beliefs. At times the peasants handed over *narodniks* to the representatives of authority, those *narodniks* who were ready to give their lives for the people. The outcome of this was that the Intelligentsia went over to a terrorist struggle. But in the period when the *narodnik* movement and *narodnik* illusions were flourishing, N. Mikhailovsky, the controlling spirit of the left Intelligentsia at that time, repudiated freedom in the name of social truth and right, in the name of the interests of the people. He demanded social and not political reform.

"For man in general; for the citoyen," writes Mikhailovsky, "for the man who has tasted of the fruits of the human tree of the knowledge of good and evil, which is open to all, there cannot be anything more seductive than to engage in politics, freedom of conscience, freedom of the spoken and printed word, freedom of exchange of thought, and so on; and we desire this, of course, but if all the rights associated with this freedom must come to us only like a bright sweet-smelling flower, we do not desire these rights or this freedom. Let them be accursed if they not only give us no possibility of settling with our duties, of settling our debts, but even increase them." This passage is very characteristic of the psychology of the *narodniks* of the seventies. And in connection with it it must be said that Mikhailovsky did not make an idol of the people; he was a representative of the Intelligentsia and to him the interests of the people were binding. The opinions of the people were not binding. He certainly made no effort towards simplification; he distinguishes the labor of honor which belongs especially to the working people and which ought to elevate, and the labor of conscience which ought to belong especially to the privileged and educated classes; they ought to have redeemed their guilt before the people. The work of conscience is an act of repentance for social sin and it engrossed Mikhailovsky. During the seventies the intellectual atmosphere changed. The extremes of nihilism were mitigated. A transition took place from materialism to positivism; the exclusive dominant position of natural science came to an end. Büchner and Moleshott ceased to occupy attention. Comte, John Stuart Mill and Herbert Spencer were the influences which played upon the left Intelligentsia. But the attitude towards the tendencies of Western thought became more independent and more critical. The flower of Dostoyevsky's and Tolstoy's creative work was already with us in the seventies and Vladimir Solovyov had made his appearance; but the left *narodnik* Intelligentsia remained shut up within itself in its own world and had its own potentates of thought. The most interesting is N. Mikhailovsky, a man of great intellectual gifts, an admirable sociologist who stated interesting problems, but with a not very high philosophical culture, and familiar principally with the philosophy of positivism. In contrast with the people of the forties, he was almost entirely unacquainted with German idealistic philosophy, which might have been of assistance to him in solving more successfully the problems which disturbed him, problems concerning "a subjective method" in sociology and "the struggle for individuality."[4] There was to be found in him the very true and very Russian idea of the fusion of right in the sense of truth, and right in the sense of justice, of integral knowledge by the whole being of man. Both Khomyakov and Ivan Kireevsky—and later on Vladimir Solovyov—also had always thought this, although their philosophical and religious outlook was entirely different. Mikhailovsky was entirely right when he rebelled against the transference of the methods of natural science to the social sciences and insisted that values are inescapable in sociology. In his studies *The Hero and the Crowd* and *Pathological Magic* he made use of a method of psychological association which it is necessary to distinguish sharply from the moral values of social phenomena. There was in the subjective method of sociology no recognition of the truth of personalism. Like Comte, Mikhailovsky establishes three periods of human thought which he calls objectively anthropocentric, eccentric, and subjectively anthropocentric. His view of the world in general he calls subjectively anthropocentric and he sets it in antithesis to the metaphysical (eccentric) world outlook. Existential philosophy may in another way be regarded as subjectively anthropocentric. Christianity is anthropocentric; it liberates man from the power of the objective world and of cosmic forces. But in the seventies all intellectual life stood under the banner of skepticism and positivism. Mikhailovsky's theme broke through the mass of positivism with difficulty. The theme already stated by Belinsky and Herzen of the conflict between human personality, the individual, and the natural and historical process, acquires an original character in the psychological works of Mikhailovsky.

All the sociological thought of an upholder of the subjective method is defined by the struggle against naturalism in sociology, against the organic theory of society and the application of Darwinism to the social process. But he did not understand that to naturalism in socialism, one must oppose spiritual truths, which he did not want to acknowledge, and he does not see that he must remain a naturalist

---

4. See an early book of mine, *Subjectivism and the Individual in Objective Philosophy.*

in sociology. Mikhailovsky affirms the conflict between the individual as a differentiated organism and society, into a function. One must strive for the sort of organism of society in which the individual will be not an organ or a function but the highest end. Such a society appeared to Mikhailovsky to be a socialistic society. Capitalist society turned the individual into an organ and a function to the maximum degree. Therefore Mikhailovsky, like Herzen, is a defender of individualistic socialism. He makes no philosophical distinction between the individual and the person, and he interprets the individual too biologically. The integral individual with him has an entirely biological character. He desires the maximum physiological distribution of labor and is hostile to public distribution of labor. Given public distribution of labor, given the organic type of society, the individual is only "a toe on the foot of the common organism." He sharply criticizes Darwinism in sociology, and his criticism is very successful. It is difficult to reconcile with Mikhailovsky's positivism his true idea that the ways of nature and the ways of man are opposed to each other. He is an enemy of "the natural march of things"; he demands the active intervention of man, and changes in "the natural march." He displays very great perspicacity when he exposes the reactionary character of naturalism in sociology, and revolts against the application of Darwin's idea of the struggle for existence, to the life of society. German racialism is naturalism in sociology. Mikhailovsky defended the Russian idea and exposed all the falsity of this naturalism. I have developed the same idea philosophically in another form. There are two interpretations of society; either society is to be understood as nature, or society is to be understood as spirit. If society is nature, then the violence of the strong upon the weak, the selection of the strong and the fittest, the will to power, the domination of man over man, slavery and inequality, man being a wolf to his fellow man, are justified. If society is spirit then the highest value of man and the rights of man, freedom, equality and brotherhood are asserted. Mikhailovsky has this distinction in view, but he expresses it very inadequately and within a biological framework. Here is the difference between the Russian and the German, between Dostoyevsky and Hegel, between Tolstoy and Nietzsche.

Mikhailovsky draws an important distinction between types of development and degrees of development. In his view there is a high *type* of development in Russia but on a lower *degree* of development. The high *degree* of development among the European capitalist societies is linked with a low *type* of development. The Slavophils put forward the same idea in another form, and it was an idea of Herzen's also. Mikhailovsky was a social-minded person and he thought socially as did all the left wing of the Russian Intelligentsia, but sometimes he gives the impression of being the enemy of society. In society, in completely formed society, he sees an enemy to personality. "Personality," he says, "ought never to be offered as a sacrifice; it is wholly inviolable." The *narodnik* standpoint of Mikhailovsky found expression in the fact that he asserted the coincidence of the interests of personality and the interests of the people, of personality and of labor. But this did not prevent him from envisaging the possibility of a tragic conflict between personality and the masses of the people. It was as though he foresaw the conflict which was to occur when the Russian Revolution flamed up. "In my house there is a table and upon it stands a bust of Belinsky which is very precious to me, and there is a cupboard full of books with which I have spent many hours of the night. If Russian life, with all its own special way of living, breaks into my room and smashes the bust of Belinsky and burns my books, I shall not take it submissively even from the people of the village. I shall resist, unless, of course, my hands are tied." That is to say, there may be a duty which lies upon personality to wage war against society as an organism, and even against the people. Mikhailovsky everywhere puts forward the idea of the struggle for individuality. "Human personality is to be regarded as one of the degrees of individuality." Subjectively he selects it as the supreme degree.

P. L. Lavrov was also a defender of personality and an upholder of individualistic socialism. He was a man of wide scholarship; he was more learned than Mikhailovsky, but less gifted. He wrote in a very tedious manner. At the outset a professor in the School of Artillery, he spent a considerable part of his life as an émigré, and in the realm of ideas he was a leader of the revolutionary movement of the seventies. The wits said of him that he viewed the foundation of revolutionary socialism as part of the cosmogenic process and dated it from the movement of the nebulous masses. His greatest claim to interest rests on the ground of his book *Historical Letters* which as printed under the pseudonym of "Mitrov." Lavrov maintained the anthropological principle in philosophy and regarded critically thinking persons as the fundamental motive power in the historical process. He preached the obligation of personality to develop itself. But the moral values of personality are according to him realized in a group, in a party. Lavrov's personalism is limited. In his view, in fact, man as a separate person does not exist; he is formed by society. In Lavrov there is already an element of Marxism, but like all social *narodniks*, he was an opponent of the liberal fight for the constitution, and wanted to rely upon the commune and the guild. Socialism linked with positivism gives no possibility of providing a basis for the value of the independence of personality. But the real problem of personality is stated by Dostoyevsky. Lavrov's adherence to the *narodnik* point of view is shown chiefly by the fact that he recognizes the guilt of the Intelligentsia before the people, and demands that the debts to the people be repaid. But in the seventies there were forms of *Narodnichestvo* which required of the Intelligentsia the complete repudiation of cultural values, not only for the sake of the well-being of the people but even for the sake of the people's opinions. These forms of *Narodnichestvo* did not defend personality. Sometimes *Narodnichestvo* took on a religious and mystical color. There were religious brotherhoods in the seventies, and they also represented one of the forms of *Narodnichestvo*. The people lived under the "power of the soil" and the Intelligentsia, divorced as it was from the soil, was ready to submit to that power.

The Intelligentsia was disillusioned by finding no revolutionary spirit among the peasantry. There still existed among the people powerful ancient beliefs in the religious sanctity of the autocratic monarchy; they were more hostile to the landowners and minor State officials than to the Tsar, and the people had a poor understanding of the enlightenment which the Intelligentsia, itself a stranger to the religious beliefs of the people, offered. All this was a blow to *Narodnichestvo* and explains the transition to political conflict and to terror. In the end disillusionment with the peasantry led to the rise of Russian Marxism. But there were in Russia revolutionaries who were more extreme both in the end they set before themselves, and especially in the means and methods they adopted in the struggle, than the predominant currents of thought of *narodnik* socialism. Such were Nechaev and Tkachev. Nechaev was a zealot and a fanatic, but by nature a hero. As a means of realizing social revolution he preached deceit and pillage and pitiless terror. He was so strong a man that at the time when he was in Alexeevsky Ravelin he subjected the prison staff to such propaganda that through it he issued his directions to the revolutionary movement. He was in the grip of a single idea and in the name of that idea he demanded the sacrifice of everything. His *Revolutionary's Catechism* is a book which is unique in its asceticism. It is a sort of instruction in the spiritual life of a revolutionary, and the demands which it makes are harsher than the requirements of Syrian asceticism. The revolutionary must have no interests, no business, no personal feelings and connections; he must have nothing of his own, not even a name. Everything is to be swallowed up by the single exclusive interest, by the one idea, the one passion—revolution. Everything which serves the cause of revolution is moral. Revolution is the one criterion of good and evil. The many must be sacrificed for the one. But this is also the principle of asceticism. In such a case the living human person is crushed; it is deprived of all the richness of the content of life for the sake of the Revolution-God. Nechaev demanded an iron discipline and the extreme centralization of groups, and in this respect he was a predecessor of bolshevism. The revolutionary tactics of Nechaev which permitted the most non-moral methods repelled the greater part of the Russian revolutionaries of *narodnik* persuasion; he even alarmed Bakunin, whose anarchism I shall treat in another chapter. The greatest interest attaches to P. Tkachev as a theoretician of revolution, whom one must regard as a predecessor of Lenin.[5] Tkachev was an opponent of Lavrov and Bakunin. He was very hostile to any anarchic tendency, which was so characteristic of the social *narodniks*. He was the only one of the old revolutionaries who wanted political power and devoted attention to the means of attaining it. He was a politician, a supporter of the dictatorship of power, an enemy of democracy and anarchism. In his view revolution is an act of violence by a minority upon a majority. The rule of the majority is evolution, not revolution. Civilized people do not make a revolution. The State must not be allowed to turn into a

---

5. See P.N. Tkachev, *Selected Writings*, 4 volumes, Moscow, 1933.

constitutional and bourgeois State. According to Tkachev also, with all the difference there is between him and *Narodnichestvo*, Russia should avoid the bourgeois capitalist period of development. He is opposed to propaganda and preparation for revolution, a thing upon which Lavrov was specially insistent. The revolutionary ought always to consider the people ready for revolution. The Russian people is socialist by instinct; the absence of a real bourgeoisie is Russia's advantageous opportunity for the social revolution, a theme which is traditionally *narodnik*. It is an interesting fact that Tkachev considers the destruction of the State to be absurd. He is a Jacobin. The anarchist desires revolution through the agency of the people; the Jacobin, on the other hand, looks for it through the agency of the State. Like the bolsheviks Tkachev preaches the seizure of power by the revolutionary minority and the exploitation of the machinery of government for the revolutionaries' own purposes. He is an upholder of a strong organization. Tkachev was one of the first in Russia to talk about Marx. In 1875 he wrote a letter to Engels in which he says that the path to be followed by the Russian Revolution is a peculiar one and that the principles of Marxism cannot be applied to Russia. Marx and Engels spoke of the bourgeois character of revolution in Russia and they were rather "mensheviks" than "bolsheviks." In this connection a letter which Marx wrote to N. Mikhailovsky is of interest. Tkachev is more of a predecessor of bolshevism than Marx and Engels were. His interest lies in the fact that he is a theoretician of Russian revolution and a forerunner of bolshevism. His ideas were acute, but his level of culture was not very high. He was also a literary critic—a very bad one—and he considered *War and Peace* a book without talent and a harmful production. This gives some evidence of the gulf which existed between the revolutionary movement and the cultural movement.

4

We now pass into another atmosphere, one in which Russian genius flourished. The theme of social revolution, when men surrendered to it completely, overwhelmed the mind and aroused a conflict with creative richness of thought, with the flowering of culture. There was mped upon Russian social revolutionary thought the imprint of a peculiar sort of asceticism. In the same way as the Christian ascetics of the past thought it was above all things necessary to struggle against individual sin, so the Russian revolutionaries thought it is above all things necessary to fight against social sin. All the rest can be dealt with later on. But there were people who had a strong sense of sin, who were no strangers to the Russian social theme and who displayed the creativity of genius. In the front rank of such men were Tolstoy, Dostoyevsky and Solovyov. These great Russian writers, who provided so vivid a contrast in type, were representatives of religious *Narodnichestvo*. They believed in the rightness of simple working people. The Russian genius, in contrast to the Western European, when it has reached a summit throws itself down and wants to mingle with the earth and the people. There is no desire to be a privileged race. The idea of the super-man is alien to it. It is enough to compare Tolstoy with Nietzsche. Both Tolstoy and Dostoyevsky in the basic principles of their view of life were hostile to the revolutionary Intelligentsia, but Dostoyevsky was even unjust to it and his attack upon it was reminiscent of the pamphleteer. But both of them strove after social truth and justice, or—to put it better— both of them strove after the Kingdom of God into which social truth and justice also entered. With them the social theme assumed a religious character. Tolstoy, with unprecedented radicalism, revolted against the injustice and falsity of history and civilization, the bases of the State and society. He accused historical Christianity, and the historical Church, of making the covenants of Christ conform to the law of this world, of replacing the Kingdom of God by the Kingdom of Caesar, of betraying the law of God. He had a quivering sense of guilt, of guilt which was not only personal but also belonged to that class of which he himself was a member. By birth an aristocrat of ancient lineage and actually a *grand seigneur* he could not endure his privileged position and all his life he struggled against it. The West knows no such repudiation of one's own aristocracy, one's own wealth, and finally of all one's own fame. Certainly Tolstoy was not consistent; he could not give effective expression to his faith in life, and he achieved this only at the end of his life by the genius of his withdrawal. Family life crushed him and dragged him down. He was a passionate man; much of the elemental strength of the soil was in him and he was by instinct attached to the life of that same soil, from the wrongnesses of which he suffered so much. He was certainly not a person of vegetarian temperament. He was wholly the scene of a struggle between conflicting principles. He was a proud man, inclined to anger; he was a pacifist with fighting instincts; he was fond of hunting, was a great card player; he lost a million at cards; he was a preacher of non-resistance and he was essentially inclined to resistance and could be submissive to nothing and to nobody; he felt the seductive attraction of women and he wrote *The Kreutzer Sonata.* When a search was made in his house at one time during his absence at his country estate—a thing which happened not rarely in Russia—he arrived in such a fury that he demanded an apology from the government and asked his aunt, who had close connections with the court, to speak about it to Alexander III, and he threatened to leave Russia for good. And again, when some Tolstoyans were arrested and exiled he demanded that they should arrest and exile him too. He had to gain the mastery over his attraction to the soil, over his earthly nature, and he preached a spiritual religion which was akin to Buddhism. In this lies the interest of Tolstoy and his unique destiny. He stood for the belief that the truth and meaning of life are to be found among the common people and in labor. In order to mingle with the people and their belief he at one time forced himself to regard himself as Orthodox; he kept all the injunctions of the Orthodox Church, but it was not within his power to humble himself; he rebelled and began to preach his own faith, his own Christianity, his own Gospel. He demanded a return from civilization to nature, which was to him divine. Most radically of all he repudiated large landed property and saw in it the source of all evils. In so doing he repudiated his own position as a landowner. Among Western social thinkers Proudhon and Henry George had a certain influence upon him. Marxism was utterly alien to him. Of Tolstoy's relation to Rousseau I shall have something to say in connection with his doctrine of non-resistance to evil by violence, and with his anarchism. Tolstoyism, which stands on a lower level than Tolstoy himself, is chiefly interesting on the ground of its criticism and of its positive teaching. Tolstoy was a great lover of truth. In that extraordinarily truthful Russian literature of the nineteenth century he was the most truthful writer. Tolstoy enters into the Russian idea as a very important element. It would be impossible to think about the Russian vocation and to leave him out of account. If to repudiate social inequality and to convict the ruling classes of wrongness is a most essential Russian motif, in Tolstoy it reaches the limit of its religious expression.

Dostoyevsky expresses more than anyone all the contradictions of the Russian nature and the passionate intensity of Russian problems. In his youth he belonged to Petrashevsky's circle and served a term of penal servitude for it. He experienced a spiritual shock and, to adopt the usual phraseology, from a revolutionary he became a reactionary, and attacked the wrongness of the revolutionary point of view—atheistic socialism. But in his case the question is immeasurably more complex. Much of the revolutionary was left in Dostoyevsky; he was a revolutionary of the spirit. *The Legend of the Grand Inquisitor* is one of the most revolutionary—one might almost say one of the most anarchistic—productions in the literature of the world. He did not become indifferent to the Russian social theme; he had his own social utopia—a theocratic utopia—in which the Church swallows up the State as a whole and gives effect to a kingdom of freedom and love. He might be called an Orthodox socialist; he was an enemy of the bourgeois world, of the capitalist order, and the like. He believes that right exists within the Russian people and he professes religious *Narodnichestvo*. Theocracy, in which there will be no force applied by the State, will arise from the East and will come out of Russia. It is interesting to note that Dostoyevsky became an enemy of revolution and of the revolutionaries as the result of his love for freedom. He saw in the spirit of revolutionary socialism the denial of freedom and personality. In revolution freedom degenerates into slavery. If what he says about the revolutionary socialists is true with reference to Nechaev and Tkachev, it is certainly not true as regards Herzen or Mikhailovsky. He foresaw Russian communism, and in antithesis to it he put the Christian answer to the social question. He does not yield to the temptation to turn stones into bread, nor accept the solution of the problem of bread through the denial of the freedom of the spirit. In his view the denial of freedom of the spirit is the principle of antichrist. He sees this alike in authoritarian Christianity and in authoritarian socialism. He does not desire a worldwide unit achieved by force; the prospect of turning human society into an ant heap fills him with horror. "To level the hills is a good idea." Thus Shigalev and Peter Verkhovensky. It is the compulsory organization of human happiness. "The attainment of unlimited freedom," says Shigalev, "I take to be unlimited despotism." No sort of democratic freedom will be left. In the prophetic *Legend of the Grand Inquisitor* there is genius which foresees not only authoritarian catholicism but also authoritarian communism and fascism, and all totalitarian regimes; and it is true in relation to the historical theocracies of the past. *The Legend of the Grand Inquisitor*, like many passages in *The Possessed*, may be interpreted chiefly as directed against Roman Catholicism and revolutionary socialism. But in actual fact the subject is broader and deeper. It is the theme of the kingdom of Caesar, of the rejection of the temptation of the kingdoms of this world. All the kingdoms of this world, all the kingdoms of Caesar, the ancient monarchies and the new socialist and fascist kingdoms, are founded upon compulsion and upon the denial of freedom of the spirit. Dostoyevsky is in essence a religious anarchist and in this respect he is very Russian. The question of socialism, the Russian question of the organization of mankind in terms of a new personnel is a religious question; it is a question of God and immortality. In Russia the social theme remains a religious theme, even given atheistic thought. "Russian boys," atheists, socialists and anarchists are a phenomenon of the Russian spirit. Dostoyevsky understood this most profoundly and it is, therefore, all the more strange that at times he wrote so unjustly, almost spitefully, about these "Russian boys," especially in *The Possessed*. There was much which he understood and perceived very profoundly. He saw the spiritual subsoil of phenomena which on the surface appeared to be only social. But at times he went off the lines. In *The Diary of a Writer* he put forward some very banal conservative political views. There is much in *The Diary of a Writer* which is completely out of correspondence with the spiritual depths of his novels. The utopia of an earthly paradise greatly disturbed Dostoyevsky. *Versilov's Dream* and *The Dream of the Ridiculous Man*, which displays even greater genius, are dedicated to this theme. There are three possible answers to the question of world harmony, of paradise, of the final triumph of good. First: Harmony, paradise, life in the good, without freedom of choice, without world tragedy, without suffering, but also without creative work. Second: Harmony, paradise, life in the good, on the heights of earthly history, purchased at the price of innumerable sufferings and the tears of all human generations doomed to death and turned into a means for the happiness of those who are to come. Third: Harmony, paradise, life in the good, at which man will arrive through freedom and suffering, in an economy into which all who at any time lived and suffered enter, that is to say, in the Kingdom of God. Dostoyevsky rejects the first two answers to the question of world harmony and paradise and accepts only the third. The argument of Ivan Karamazov is complex and it is not always easy to understand on which side Dostoyevsky himself is. In my opinion he was half on the side of Ivan Karamazov. In Dostoyevsky there was a complex attitude to evil. To a large extent it may look as though he was led astray. On the one hand evil is evil and ought to be exposed and must be burned away. On the other hand, evil is a spiritual experience of man. It is man's part. As he goes on his way man may be enriched by the experience of evil, but it is necessary to understand this in the right way. It is not the evil itself that enriches him; he is enriched by that spiritual strength which is aroused in him for the overcoming of evil. The man who says "I will give myself up to evil for the sake of the enrichment" never is enriched; he perishes. But it is evil that puts man's freedom to the test. In history and in social life we see the same thing. There is a sort of law of dialectic development in accordance with which what is base and evil is within a certain time not destroyed but overcome (*aufheben*) and all the positive good of the preceding period enters into the overcoming of it. Dostoyevsky brings us to this thought; he reveals the metaphysical depths of the Russian theme of social right. In his view it is linked with Russian messianism. The Russian people, as a people, are God-bearers; they ought to solve the social problem better than the West. But great temptations lie in wait for this people.

Vladimir Solovyov, who belongs particularly to the theme of Russian philosophy, was certainly no stranger to the social theme. The question of the possibility of a Christian society disturbed him all his life, and he exposed the lie of a society which has falsely called itself Christian. He has a primary intuition of the spiritual oneness of the world. There enters also the effectual realization of social right, the creation of the perfect society. Solovyov has his own utopia which he calls a free theocracy. He believed that the

Kingdom of God would be established even upon earth and he sought for the realization of it. Only towards the end of his life did he become disillusioned in theocracy and the possibility of the Kingdom of God on earth. His theocracy was a real religious utopia and constructed on very rationalistic lines, according to the threefold scheme of tsar, high priest and prophet. It is a most interesting point that he affirms a prophetic principle and prophetic function in Christianity. He is most Russian in this respect. He said that in order to conquer what is wrong in socialism it is necessary to acknowledge what is right in socialism and put it into effect. But Solovyov was not a *narodnik*, and in contrast with other representatives of Russian thought he recognized the positive mission of the State, only demanding that the State should be subjected to Christian principles. The transfiguration of the whole cosmos was his dream. The social problem took a second place with him. His great service was his exposure of the wrongness of nationalism, which during the eighties took a zoological form among us. Solovyov was a representative of Russian universalism and in a purer form than that of Dostoyevsky who was so closely related to him. Very Russian and very Christian was his protest against capital punishment, as the result of which he was obliged to resign his professorial chair at the university. But the role of Solovyov in the history of Russian social ideas and tendencies remains secondary; he enters into the Russian idea from other sides of his creative work as the most distinguished representative of Russian religious philosophy in the nineteenth century. We shall see that the personality of Solovyov was very complex and even enigmatic. It was in any case bent upon the effective realization of Christian truth not only in the individual life but in the life of society, and he rebelled sharply against that dualism which acknowledges the morality of the Gospel for the individual while admitting an animal morality for society. In this respect he is very different from K. Leontyev who frankly asserted such a moral dualism in an extreme form, and who by no means desired an effective realization of Christian Gospel truth in society. In his case aesthetic values predominated decisively over moral values. With the radicalism of thought and sincerity which were characteristic of him he recognized that the effectual realization of Christian truth and love in society would lead to ugliness and in reality he did not want that realization. Freedom and equality give rise to bourgeois philistinism. In actual fact "the liberal egalitarian process" which he hated corresponds to Christian morality more than does the power of the State, of aristocracy and monarchy which have not stopped short at the cruelties which Leontyev defended. His whole thought is an aesthetic reaction against Russian *Narodnichestvo*, the Russian liberating movement, the Russian search for social right, the Russian search for the Kingdom of God. He was a politician, an aristocrat, but before all, more than anything, he was a romantic, and he shows absolutely no similarity to the reactionary conservatives as they expressed themselves in practical life. Leontyev's hatred of philistinism, of the bourgeois, was the hatred of a romantic for the empirical reactionaries and conservatives, the philistines and bourgeois. Towards the end of his life, disillusioned about the possibility of an organic flower culture in Russia, and partly under the influence of Solovyov, Leontyev even projected something in the nature of monarchical socialism, and made a stand for social reform and the solution of the labor question, not so much out of love of justice and the will to give effect to what is right, as from a desire to preserve even something of the beauty of the past. Leontyev is one of our most distinguished people; the boldness, the sincerity and forthrightness of his thought act as a driving force, and his religious fate is very moving. But he stands apart. A much more central figure and one which is more characteristic of the Russian ideal, of the Russian striving after the effective realization, is N. Fedorov; but he belongs more to the beginning of the twentieth century than to the nineteenth. The social theme played a large part with him and his view of it often shows affinity with communist collectivism; it is an ideology of labor, a control of nature and a planned outlook. Such ideas as these of his were for the first time to come into contact with religious thought. The murder of Alexander II by the party of "The People's Will" set a sharply defined line of demarcation in our social currents of thought. The eighties were a period of political reaction against the pseudo-Russian style of Alexander III. These years saw the rise of nationalism, which had not existed before, not even among the Slavophils. The old *narodnik* socialism was on the decrease. The party of "The People's Will" was the last vigorous manifestation of the old revolutionary tendency. It was chiefly in the person of Zhelabov that it found expression. He was a heroic figure and the words which he uttered during the trial of the 1st March are of great interest. "I was baptized in the Orthodox Church but I reject Orthodoxy, although I acknowledge the essential teaching of Jesus Christ. This essential teaching occupies an honored place among my moral incentives. I believe in the truth and the righteousness of that teaching and I solemnly declare that faith without works is dead and that every true Christian ought to fight for the truth and for the rights of the oppressed and the weak, and even if need be, to suffer for them. Such is my creed."[6] During the eighties the way was prepared for Russian Marxist socialism. In 1883 the group known as "The Liberation of Labor" was founded abroad with G. V. Plekhanov at its head, the chief exponent of the theory of Russian Marxism. This opened a new era in Russian socialist movements. It was at the same time to bring about a serious crisis in the thought of the Russian Intelligentsia. The Marxist type, as I have already said, was to be harsher than the *narodnik* but less emotional. But on the soil of Marxism there developed among our left wing Intelligentsia a higher and more complex form of culture, which prepared the way for Russian idealism at the beginning of the twentieth century. I shall say something about this later on. To sum up and view as a whole Russian nineteenth century thought upon the social theme, which arose out of the Russian search for social right, it may be said that the Russian idea of the brotherhood of man and of peoples was worn out. It was a Russian idea, but insofar as this idea was asserted in the atmosphere of a breakaway from Christianity which was its source, poison entered into it, and this showed itself in the duality of communism, in the intertwining of truth and falsehood in it. This duality was already to be seen in Belinsky. With Nechaev and Tkachev there began the predominance of the negative over the positive, while the currents of spiritual thought became more indifferent to the social theme. Thus division and schism all the while grew stronger in Russia.

6. See A. Voronsky, *Zhelabov*, 1934.

6

1

THE THEME of the justification of culture occupied a larger place in Russian thought than it did in the thought of the West. The people of the West rarely had any doubts about the justification of culture. They considered themselves the heirs of Mediterranean Greco-Roman culture and they were believers in the sanctity of its traditions. At the same time that culture presented itself to them as universal and unique while all the rest of the world was barbarian. This point of view was particularly clear-cut among the French. It is true that J. J. Rousseau had doubts about the good of civilization. But that was the exception, almost a scandal, and the question was posed in another way than among the Russians. We shall see the difference in the case of Tolstoy. There was among the Russians none of that veneration of culture which is so characteristic of Western people. Dostoyevsky said we are all nihilists. I should say we Russians are either apocalyptists or nihilists. We are apocalyptists or nihilists because our energies are bent upon the end, and we have but a poor understanding of the gradualness of the historical process. We react

against pure form. Spengler had this in view when he said that Russia
is an apocalyptic revolt against antiquity, that is to say against perfect form, perfect culture.[1] But Father George Florovsky's opinion
that Russian nihilism was anti-historical utopianism is entirely mistaken.[2] Nihilism belongs to the Russian historical destiny, as revolution does also. One must not recognize as historical only what
pleases conservative taste. Revolt is also an historical phenomenon.
It is one of the ways in which historical destiny is realized. The Russian cannot realize his historical destiny without revolt; that is the
sort of people we are. Nihilism is a typically Russian phenomenon
and it grew out of the spiritual soil of Orthodoxy. It contains the
experience of a powerful element belonging to Orthodox asceticism.
Orthodoxy, and especially Russian Orthodoxy, does not have its
own justification of culture. There was in it a nihilistic element in
relation to everything which man creates in this world. Roman
Catholicism assimilated the ancient humanisms to itself. In Orthodoxy the expression of the eschatological side of Christianity was
stronger than anything, and in Russian nihilism it is possible to distinguish ascetic and eschatological elements. The Russian people are
a people of the end, and not of the intervening historical process,
whereas humanistic culture does belong to the intervening historical
process. Russian literature of the nineteenth century, which in common parlance was the greatest manifestation of Russian culture, was
not culture in the Western classical sense of the word, and had
always passed beyond the frontiers of culture. The great Russian
writers felt the conflict between a perfect culture and a perfect life
and they bent their energies towards the perfect transfigured life.
Although they did not always express it with success they were well
aware of the fact that the Russian idea is not an idea of culture.
Gogol, Tolstoy and Dostoyevsky are very significant in this connection. I have already said that Russian literature was not of the Renaissance, that it was penetrated by the pain and sufferings of man and
of the people and that the Russian genius wanted to plunge down to
earth, to the elemental people. But an obscurantist reaction to culture
is also a property of the Russians and this obscurantist element is to

1. See O. Spengler, *Der Untergand des Abendlandes*, vol. II.
2. See G. Florovsky, *The Ways of Russian Theology*.

be found also in official Orthodoxy. The Russians when they become ultra-Orthodox readily fall into obscurantism, but the opinions about culture held by people who are uncultured or at a very low level of culture, are not interesting; they present no problem at all. The interest is provided when the problem of the justification of culture is stated by those very great Russians who have created Russian culture, or when it is stated by the Intelligentsia who received their intellectual training in the sphere of Western scientific enlightenment. It was precisely in the second half of the nineteenth century that the awakening of Russian thought posed the problem of the value of culture. It was stated, for instance, by Lavrov (Mitrov) in *Historical Letters*; and he faces the question frankly, whether or not culture is a sin. Russian nihilism was a moral reflection upon the culture created by a privileged class and designed for itself only. The nihilists were not skeptics about culture; they were believing people. It was a movement of youth with a faith. When the nihilists protested against morality they did so in the name of the good; they accused idealist principles of falsity, but they did this in the name of love, of unembellished truth; they rebelled against the conventional lie of civilization. Thus Dostoyevsky also, who was an enemy of the nihilists, revolted against "the high and the beautiful." He broke with the "Schillers" and with the idealists of the forties. The exposure of an exalted lie is one of the essentially Russian motifs. Russian literature and Russian thought exhibited to a remarkable degree a polemical and accusatory character. Hatred for the conventional lie of civilization led to the search for truth in the life of the people. Hence a process of simplification—the casting off from the self of the conventional garments of culture, the desire to attain to the real authentic kernel of life. This is displayed most of all in Tolstoy. In "nature" there is greater truth and right, there is more of the divine, than in "culture." It is to be noted that long before Spengler, the Russians drew the distinction between "culture" and "civilization," that they attacked "civilization" even when they remained supporters of "culture." This distinction in actual fact, although expressed in a different phraseology, was to be found among the Slavophils. It is found in Herzen and Leontyev and in many others. It may be that here there was some influence from German romanticism. It may be said that it was easy for the Russians to feel doubts about culture and to rebel against it, because they were less permeated by the traditions of Greco-Roman culture, and that they were called upon to sacrifice few treasures. This argument, which is connected with the fact that in Russian thought and consciousness of the nineteenth century there was less association with the burden of history and tradition, proves nothing. It was precisely this which led to the greater freedom of Russian thought; and it must not be said, by the way, that in Russia there was no link at all with Greece. Such a link existed through Greek patristics, although it was interrupted. It is a curious thing that classical education in that form in which it was instituted by the Minister of Public Education Count D. Tolstoy had a clearly reactionary character at the time when in the West it bore a progressive character and upheld the humanist tradition, whereas among us it was the natural sciences which were an inspiration of emancipating significance.

2

Russian nihilism is a radical form of Russian enlightenment. It is a dialectic moment in the development of the Russian soul and Russian consciousness. Russian nihilism has little in common with what is called nihilism in the West. They called Nietzsche a nihilist. Such people as Maurice Barres may be called nihilists. A nihilism of that sort may be associated with refinement, and certainly does not belong to the epoch of enlightenment. In Russian nihilism there is no refinement whatever and it quite frankly casts doubt upon all refinement and culture and demands that it should justify itself. Dobrolyubov, Chernishevsky, Pisarev were Russians of the enlightenment; they bore little resemblance to Western men of the Enlightenment, to Voltaire or Diderot, who did not proclaim a revolt against world civilization and were themselves a product of that civilization. Dobrolyubov's diary is of great interest in arriving at an understanding of the spiritual sources of nihilism. As a boy Dobrolyubov was of a very ascetic frame of mind. The formation of his soul was Christian and Orthodox. Even in the most insignificant satisfaction of his desires he saw sin, for example, if he ate too much jam. There was something stern in him. He lost his faith after the death of his mother, for whom he had an ardent love. The low spiritual level of the life of the Orthodox Church from which he sprang perturbed him. He could not reconcile belief in God and divine providence with the existence of evil and unjust suffering. Dobrolyubov's atheism—and this is the case with Russian atheism in general—was akin to Marxism in its primary sources, but it found expression in a period of enlightenment which was concerned mainly with negations.[3] There was in Russian nihilism a great love of truth and a revulsion from falsity and from embellishments and all elevated rhetoric. Chernishevsky had an extreme love for truth. We have noted this already in his attitude to love and his demand for sincerity and freedom of feeling. Pisarev is regarded as a leader of Russian nihilism and in personality he appeared to many to be like Turgeniev's Bazarov. In actual fact there was no similarity at all. In the first place, as contrasted with Chernishevsky, Dobrolyubov and the other nihilists of the sixties, who came of other classes, he was of gentle birth; he was a typical child of a gentlefolk's house and his mother's darling.[4] His upbringing was such that he was received as *jeune homme correcte et bien elevé*. He was a very obedient little boy; he often cried. His truthfulness and uprightness were so marked that they called him "the little crystal box." This nihilist, this destroyer of aesthetics, was a very well brought up young man who spoke French well, was irreproachably elegant and aesthetic in his tastes. There was something gentle about him; he had not the moral sternness of Dobrolyubov; there was no similarity to Bazarov with the exception of an inclination for the natural sciences. Pisarev's desire was the naked truth; he hated phrases and embellishments; he had no love for enthusiasm; he belongs to the realistically disposed epoch of the sixties, when there was a conflict with the generation of the idealists of the forties; it was an epoch that made a demand for useful activity and had no fondness for dreaming. In another epoch he would have been different and would have waged his fight for personality in some other way. The violent reaction of Pisarev, the born aesthete, against Pushkin and against aesthetics, was a struggle against the generation of "idealists," against the luxuries which the privileged circle of cultured people allowed themselves. Reality stands higher than art. This

---

3. See my *Psychology of Russian Nihilism and Atheism.*
4. See E. Solovyov, *Pisarev.*

is Chernishevsky's thesis, but reality is there interpreted in another way than the way in which Belinsky and Bakunin understood it in the Hegelian period. The concept of "reality" did not bear the stamp of conservatism but of revolution. As a typical fighting man of the enlightenment Pisarev thought that the enlightened mind is the principal instrument for the alteration of reality. His fight is above all on behalf of personality and the individual; he poses the personal moral problem. It is characteristic that in his early youth Pisarev belonged to a Christian ascetic "society of thinking people." This ascetic leaven continued to work in Russian nihilism. During the forties there was worked out the ideal of the harmonious development of personality. The ideal of the "thinking realist" of the sixties which Pisarev preached was a narrowing of the idea of personality, a lessening of its scope and depth. With this is connected a fundamental inconsistency of nihilism in its fight for the emancipation of personality. But there was evidence of a wildness of temperament in the aptitude which the nihilists displayed for sacrifice, in the refusal by these utilitarians and materialists of every sort of felicity which life offered. Pisarev's preaching of egoism indicates anything but the preaching of egoism; it points to a protest against the subjection of the individual to the general; it was an unconscious personalism and a personalism which had but a poor philosophical basis. Pisarev's desire is to fight for individuality, for the rights of personality. In that respect there is in him something which is his own, something original. But his philosophy was certainly not his own, nor was it original. He was not indifferent to the social question, but it receded into a second place in comparison with the fight for personality, for intellectual emancipation. But all this took place in the atmosphere of the intellectual enlightenment of the sixties, that is, under the dictatorship of the natural sciences. The nihilists adopted an attitude of suspicion towards high culture but there existed a cult of science, that is to say of the natural sciences, from which they looked for the solution of all problems. The nihilists themselves made no scientific discoveries at all; they popularized the philosophy of the natural sciences, that is to say, at that time, materialist philosophy. So far as philosophy was concerned this was such a wretched time of decline that they considered a serious argument against the existence of the soul could be derived from the fact that in the course of the dissection of bodies they did not come across a soul. There would be more foundation for saying that if they had found a soul it would have been an argument to the advantage of materialism. In the vulgar and half-literate materialism of Büchner and Moleshott they found support for the liberation of man and the people, and that in spite of the fact that spirit alone can liberate, while matter, on the other hand, can only enslave. There were admirable and first-class scholars in the field of natural science in Russia, for example Mendeleev, but they had no relation to nihilism. This passing through a period of an idolatrous attitude towards the natural sciences was a fateful moment in the life of the Intelligentsia which had been searching for the truth; and connected with this was the fact that the science of the spirit was turned into an instrument for the enslavement of man and people. Such is human fate. This madness about the natural sciences partly explains the scientific backwardness of Russia in spite of the existence of individual men who were admirable scholars. The provincial backwardness and low level of culture made themselves felt in Russian militant rationalism, and especially in materialism. The historian of the intellectual development of Russia, Shchapov, whose ideas were near akin to Pisarev's, regarded idealistic philosophy and aesthetics as aristocratic, while recognizing the natural sciences as democratic.[5] This was also Pisarev's idea. Shchapov thought that the Russian people were realist, not idealist, and that they had an innate disposition for natural philosophy and technical knowledge and for the sciences which have useful results in the sphere of practical life. Only he forgot the predominantly moral structure of Russian thinking and the religious restlessness of the Russian people who are disposed constantly to pose problems of a religious character. It is a curiosity in the depressing history of Russian enlightenment that the Minister of Public Education Prince Shirinsky Shakhmatov, after having suppressed the teaching of philosophy in the fifties, administered a fillip to the natural sciences which appeared to him to be neutral from a political point of view. The philosophical sciences, on the other hand, appeared to him to be a source of disturbance to the mind. In the sixties the position changed and the natural sciences

5. A. Shchapov, *The Social and Educational Conditions of the Intellectual Development of the Russian People.*

were recognized as a source of mental agitation while philosophy
was a source of reaction. But in either case both philosophy and science were not taken into consideration on their own merits, but simply as tools, and the same thing must be said with regard to morality.
Nihilism was accused of rejecting morality, of being amoral. In
actual fact there is a strong moral feeling of indignation in face of the
evil and injustice which held sway in the world, a feeling which was
bent upon striving for a better life, one in which there would be a
greater element of right. Russian maximalism showed itself in nihilism. In this maximalism there was Russian eschatology, unconscious, and expressed in a pitiable philosophy, a striving towards the
end, a reaching out towards the ultimate state, nihilistic nakedness, a
stripping off of fraudulent coverings, a refusal to accept the world
which "lies in evil." This refusal to accept the evil of the world
existed in Orthodox asceticism and eschatology and in the Russian
schism. There is no need to assign too great a significance to the considered formulae of thought; it is all defined at a deeper level. But
Russian nihilism sinned in its fundamental inconsistency and this is
seen with special clearness in Pisarev. Pisarev fought for the liberation of personality; he preached freedom of personality and its right
to the fullness of life; he demanded that personality should be raised
above the social environment, above the traditions of the past. But
from whence is personality to get strength for such a conflict?
Pisarev and the nihilists were materialists and in morality they were
utilitarians. The same is to be said of Chernishevsky. One can understand the assertion of materialism and utilitarianism as instruments
for the repudiation of the prejudices of the past and of the traditional
general view of things, which had been used as a means to bring personality into servitude. Only in this way is it even possible to explain
the attraction of such primitive theories, of theories which are incapable of surviving any sort of philosophical criticism. But positively
speaking were these theories able to provide anything for the defense
of personality from the enslaving power of nature and the social
environment or for the attainment of the fullness of life? Materialism
is an extreme form of determinism. It is the determining of human
personality by the external environment; it does not see any principle
within human personality which it might be able to set in opposition
to the action of the external environment by which it is surrounded.

Such a principle could only be a spiritual principle, an interior support of the freedom of man, a principle which is not derivable from them, from nature or society. The utilitarian basis of morality which the nihilists found so alluring is certainly not favorable to the freedom of personality and certainly does not justify striving after the fullness of life, towards the increase of the breadth and depth of life. Utilitarianism is a principle of adaptation for the safeguarding of life and the attainment of happiness, but the safeguarding of life and happiness may be inconsistent with the freedom and dignity of personality. Utilitarianism is anti-personalist. John Stuart Mill was obliged to say that it is better to be a discontented Socrates than a contented pig, and the Russian nihilists had not the least desire to be like a contented pig. The principle of development which the nihilists recognized was better—personality is realized in a process of development; but development was understood in the spirit of a naturalistic evolutionary theory. Vigorous champion of personality as he was, Pisarev denied the creative fullness of personality, the fullness of its spiritual and even psychic life; he denied the right of creativity in philosophy, in art, and in the highest spiritual culture, and he maintained an extremely restricted and impoverished idea of man. It seemed that man was doomed exclusively to the natural sciences and it was even proposed that popular essays in natural philosophy should be written instead of novels. This pointed to an impoverishment of personality and the crushing of its freedom. Such was the reverse side of the Russian fight for liberation and for social right. The effects were seen in the Russian Revolution and in the persecution of the spirit in which it indulged. But it would be unjust to assign all the responsibility in this respect to the nihilists alone and those who were their followers. In the same way it would be unjust to saddle the French enlightened philosophy of the eighteenth century with exclusive responsibility for European godlessness and the decline from Christianity. A very heavy measure of guilt lies also upon historical Christianity and in part upon Orthodoxy. Militant godlessness is a repayment for a servile conception of God, for the adaptation of historical Christianity to the ruling powers. Atheism can be an existential dialectic moment, purifying the conception of God; the denial of the spirit may be a cleansing of the spirit from the part it has played in serving the ruling interests of the world. There cannot be a class truth but there can be a class lie, and it plays no small role in history. The nihilists were men who were led astray by the Christianity and spirituality of history. Their philosophical outlook was false in its very foundations, but they were men with a love of truth. Nihilism is a characteristically Russian phenomenon.

3

During the seventies the subject of culture was presented in another way than by the nihilism of the sixties. It was in the first place a theme of the duty of the section of society which had profited by culture, of the Intelligentsia. The culture of the privileged classes was made possible thanks to the sweat and blood poured out by the laboring people. This debt must be paid. P. Lavrov especially insisted upon such a statement of the case during the seventies. But there was no hostility to culture in itself in him. Leo Tolstoy was much more interesting and radical. He expressed with genius a religiously founded nihilism in relation to culture. In him the consciousness of guilt in respect of the people, and repentance, went to the utmost limit of expression. The usually accepted view makes a sharp opposition between Tolstoy, the artist, and Tolstoy, the thinker and preacher, and greatly exaggerates the abruptness of the revolution that took place in him. But the fundamental motifs and ideas in Tolstoy may already be found in the early stories—in *The Cossacks*, in *War and Peace* and *Anna Karenina*. In them there is already affirmed the rightness of the primitive life of the people and the falsity of civilization, the lie upon which the life of our society rests. The charm and the fascination of Tolstoy's artistic creativity are due to the fact that he depicted a twofold life—on the one hand the life of his heroes in society with its conventions in civilization, with its obligatory falsehood, and on the other hand the matter of his heroes' thoughts when they are not faced by society, when they are placed face to face with the mystery of existence, face to face with God and nature. This is the difference between Prince Andrew in Anna Karenina's St. Petersburg drawingroom and Prince Andrew facing the starry heavens when he is lying wounded on the field. Everywhere and always Tolstoy depicts the truth of the life which is near to nature, the truth of labor, the profundity of birth and death, in comparison with the falsity and lack of genuineness of the so-called "historical" life in civilization. In his view truth is to be found in the natural and unconscious, the lie in the civilized and conscious. We shall see that here there is an inconsistency in Tolstoy, for he desired to base his religion upon reason. Levin is all the while rebelling against the falsity of the life of civilized society and goes off to the country, to nature, to the people and to work. Attention has more than once been drawn to the affinity of Tolstoy's ideas with J. J. Rousseau. Tolstoy loved Rousseau, but we must not, therefore, exaggerate the influence that Rousseau had upon him. Tolstoy is more profound and more radical. There was in him the Russian consciousness of guilt, and that is not to be found in Rousseau. He was very far from regarding his own nature as good; his was a nature full of passions and the love of life, and he had also an inclination to asceticism and he always retained something of Orthodoxy. Rousseau did not experience such an intense search for the meaning of life and such a painful consciousness of his sinfulness and guilt, such a quest for the perfection of life. Rousseau demanded a return from the drawingrooms of eighteenth-century Paris to nature, but he had not that very Russian love of simplicity which was Tolstoy's, nor the demand for cleansing. There is further an enormous difference in the fact that while Rousseau did not rest content with the truth of the life of nature, and was demanding a social contract (after which a most despotic state was created, which denied the freedom of conscience), Tolstoy had no desire for any social contract and wanted to remain in the truth and divine nature which is also a fulfillment of the Law of God. Both Rousseau and Tolstoy confuse fallen nature, in which the pitiless struggle for existence reigns supreme, egoism, violence and cruelty, with transfigured nature, that nature which is noumenal or belongs to paradise. Both were bent upon a life of paradise. Both were critics of progress and saw in it a movement which was the reverse of the movement towards paradise, towards the Kingdom of God. It is interesting to compare the suffering of Job with the suffering of Tolstoy, who came near to suicide. The cry of Job is the cry of the sufferer from whom everything in life has been taken, who became the most unhappy of men; the cry of Tolstoy is the cry of the sufferer who was established in a fortunate position, who had everything but who could not endure his privileged position. Men strive for fame, riches, learning, family happiness; in all these they see the blessedness of life. Tolstoy had all these things and bent all his energies upon repudiating them. His desire was to become simplified and to fuse his life with that of the laboring people. In the suffering which he endured in this connection he was very Russian; he wanted a final defined and completed state of life. The religious drama of Tolstoy himself was infinitely more profound than his religious and philosophical ideas. Solovyov, who did not like Tolstoy, said that his religious philosophy is nothing but the phenomenology of his great spirit. Tolstoy was far from being a nationalist, but he saw the great truth which is in the Russian people; he believed that "the revolution will begin not just anywhere but precisely in Russia, and that, because nowhere is the Christian outlook upon the world held with such strength and purity as it is among the Russian people." "The Russian people have always reacted towards power in a different way from that of the European peoples; they always looked upon power not as a blessing but as an evil. To solve the problem of the land by the abolition of landed proprietorship and to show other peoples the way to a rational, free and happy life outside the sphere of commerce, industry and capitalist violence and slavery, that is the historical vocation of the Russian people." Both Tolstoy and Dostoyevsky in their different ways rejected the European world, civilized and bourgeois, and they were precursors of the revolution. But the revolution did not recognize them, just as they would not have acknowledged it. Tolstoy perhaps is most akin to Orthodoxy in his idea of the unjustifiability of the creative work of man and of the sin of that creativity. But here there is also a very great danger for Tolstoyism. He passed through a stage of repudiating his own great creativity, but this is the very last respect in which we should follow him. He was striving not for perfection of form but for the wisdom which nature bestows. He had a reverence for Confucius, Buddha, Solomon, Socrates, and he added the name of Jesus Christ to the sages; but in his view the sages were not propagators of culture but teachers of life and he himself wanted to be a teacher of life. He connected wisdom with simplicity, whereas culture is complex, and in truth everything great is simple. Proust is such a product of complex culture, a man who combined within his own person subtlety and simplicity. For this reason he might be called a writer of genius, France's only writer of genius.

The attitude of K. Leontyev to culture was the polar opposite of Tolstoyism and *Narodnichestvo*. In him the Russian stratum of the gentry, as it were, defends its right to its privileged position and had no wish to repent of social sin. It is an astonishing thing that at a time when people who were not Christians, and in any case not Orthodox Christians, were repenting and suffering, Orthodox Christians had no desire to repent. This has an interesting bearing upon the historical fate of Christianity. K. Leontyev, who had secretly assumed the monastic tonsure, has no doubts about the justification of a flourishing culture, although it might be bought at the price of great suffering, terrible inequalities and injustice. He says that all the sufferings of the people are justified if thanks to them the phenomenon of Pushkin was made possible. Pushkin himself was not so sure about this, if his poem *The Village* is remembered. Leontyev did not share in the Russian pricking of conscience, in the acknowledgment of the primacy of the moral criterion. The scientific criterion was to him universal and it coincided with the biological criterion. He was a predecessor of those present-day currents of thought which assert the will to power as the pathos of life. At one time he believed that Russia might exhibit a completely original culture and take its place at the head of mankind. Beauty and the flowering of culture were in his view associated with variety and inequality. The equalizing process destroys culture and tends to ugliness. With all the falsity of his moral position he succeeded in revealing something essential in the fated process of the decline and collapse of cultures. There was a great fearlessness of thought in Leontyev and he was decided in his exposure of what others cover up and suppress. He alone decided to acknowledge that he does not want truth and righteousness in social life because it means the ruin of the beauty of life. He emphasized the inconsistency of historical Christianity to the very highest degree. There is a conflict between the evangelical precepts and pagan attitude to life and the world, to the life of societies. He got out of the embarrassment by postulating an extreme dualism between the morality of the individual and the morality of society. A monastic asceticism he applied to one sphere and power and beauty to the other. But the Russian Idea is not an idea of flowering culture and a powerful monarchy. The Russian Idea is an eschatological idea of the Kingdom of God. This is not a humanistic idea in the

158 ❖ THE RUSSIAN IDEA

European sense of the word, but the Russian people are exposed to danger on the one side from an obscurantist rejection of culture instead of an eschatological criticism of it, and on the other side from a mechanical collectivist civilization. Only a culture of the end can overcome both dangers. N. Fedorov came very near to this. He also exposed the falsity of culture and desired a complete change of the world, and that the attainment of kinship and brotherhood should be not only social but also cosmic.

7

*Authority and the State · Russian attitude to authority · The with-
drawal from the State to free self-expression · The Intelligentsia
seeks freedom and justice, it struggles against the Empire, and
professes a Stateless ideal · The Anarchism of K. Aksakov · The
anarchist element in the Slavophil conception of the basis of
autocratic monarchy · Bakunin · Passion for destruction is a creative passion · God and the State · Slav Messianism · Kropotkin
· The religious anarchism of L. Tolstoy · The doctrine of non-
resistance · The twofold nature of Russian consciousness · The
anarchist element in Dostoyevsky · The anarchist ideal enters
into the Russian Idea*

1

ANARCHISM is in the main a creation of the Russians. It is an
interesting point that anarchist theories were created preeminently
by the highest stratum of the Russian gentry. Of such was the chief
and the most extreme anarchist, Bakunin; such was Prince Kropotkin, and the religious anarchist, Count Tolstoy. The subject of the
authority and the justification of the State is a very Russian theme.
The Russians have a particular attitude towards authority. Leontyev
was right when he said that the Russian theory of the State with its
powerful authority came into being thanks to Tartar and German elements in it. According to his opinion the Russian people and in general the Slavonic world would not be able to create anything except
anarchy. This is an exaggerated expression of opinion. There is in
the Russian people a greater aptitude for organization than is generally supposed; their aptitude for colonizing was in any case greater
than that of the Germans, who are hampered by the will to power and
a disposition to violence. But it is true that the Russians do not like
the State and are not inclined to regard it as their own; they either

revolt against the State or they meekly submit to its pressure. The evil and the sin of all authority is felt strongly by the Russians, more strongly than by the peoples of the West. But one may well be struck by the contradiction between Russian anarchism and love for free self-expression, and Russian submission to the State and the consent of the people to lend themselves to the building up of a vast empire. I have already said that the Slavophil conception of Russian history does not explain the building up of a vast empire. The growth of the power of the State which sucks all the juices out of the people had, as its reverse side, Russian desire to resist a withdrawal from the State either physically or in spirit. Russian schism is a fundamental thing in Russian history. Anarchist tendencies grow out of the soil of schism; there was the same attitude in Russian sectarianism; withdrawal from the State was justified by the fact that there was no truth and right in it; it was not Christ but antichrist which triumphed in it; the State was the Kingdom of Caesar, established in opposition to the Kingdom of God, the Kingdom of Christ. Christians have here no abiding city; they seek one to come. This is a very Russian idea. But dualism, schism, runs right through Russian history. Official State Orthodoxy has always provided a religious basis and support for autocratic monarchy and the might of the State. Only the Slavophils endeavored to combine the idea of an absolute monarchy with that of essential Russian anarchism. But this attempt was not successful. Among their children and grandchildren the monarchic idea of the State was victorious over anarchist truth. The Russian Intelligentsia, from the end of the eighteenth century, from Radishchev, were stifled in the atmosphere of the autocratic sovereignty of the State over freedom and truth in social life. Throughout the nineteenth century the Intelligentsia fought against the Empire and professed a stateless non-authoritarian ideal, and created extreme forms of anarchist ideology. Even the revolutionary socialist line of thought, which was not anarchist, did not visualize the seizure of power into its own hands and the organization of a new State after the triumph of the Revolution. The single exception was Tkachev. Everything was expressed in terms of opposition: "we," the Intelligentsia, society, the people, the liberation movement; and "they," the State, the Empire, authority. Western Europe has had no experience of so sharp a contradiction. Russian literature of the nineteenth century could not endure the Empire; the accusatory element was strong in it. Russian literature, like Russian culture in general, corresponded to the immensity of Russia; it could arise only in a vast country with unlimited horizons. But it did not associate this with the Empire, with the power of the State. There was the immense land of Russia; there was the vast elemental power of the Russian people, but a vast State and Empire seemed like treachery to the soil and the people and a perversion of the Russian idea. An original anarchic element may be discerned in all social tendencies of the Russian nineteenth century, both religious and anti-religious; in the great Russian writers, in the very make-up of the Russian character, a makeup which certainly did not lend itself to being organized. The reverse side of Russian pilgrimage which was always essentially anarchist, of Russian love of freedom of action, is Russian bourgeois philistinism which made its appearance in the manner of life of our merchants, minor officials and townsfolk. This is again that same polarization of the Russian soul. Among a people who were anarchist in their fundamental bent, there existed a State that developed to a monstrous degree, and an all-powerful bureaucracy surrounding an autocratic Tsar and separating him from the people. Such was the peculiarity of Russian destiny. It is characteristic that there never existed a liberal ideology in Russia which might have been an inspiration and have had some influence. The active people of the sixties who brought in the reforms might be called liberals, but this was not linked up with a definite ideology and an integrated world view. What interests me at the moment is not the history of Russia in the nineteenth century but the history of Russian nineteenth-century thought in which the Russian idea was reflected. The Russian feeling for freedom was connected with anarchism rather than with the strict principle of liberalism. P. Chicherin might be called the one philosopher of the liberals, and even he was rather a liberal-conservative or a conservative-liberal than a pure liberal. His was a powerful mind, but preeminently the mind of an administrator, as Solovyov said of him. A forthright Hegelian and a dry rationalist, he had very little influence. He was a hater of socialism, which reflected the Russian quest for truth. He was that rare thing in Russia, a statesman, very much of a contrast in this respect to both the Slavophils and the Westernizers of the left. In his view the State is a higher value than human personality. One might call him a Westernizer of the right; he accepted the Empire; he wanted it to be cultured and to absorb liberal elements of the right. In Chicherin there can be studied a spirit which was opposed to the Russian Idea, as it was expressed in the prevailing tendencies of Russian thought in the nineteenth century.

2

It has already been said that there was a powerful anarchist element in the ideology of the Slavophils. The Slavophils had no love for the State and authority; they saw evil in all authority. Their idea that the cult of power and glory which is attained by the might of the State is foreign to the makeup of the soul of the Russian people was a very Russian idea. Of the Slavophils K. Aksakov was the most of an anarchist. "The State as a principle is an evil"; "The State in its idea is a lie," he wrote. In another passage he writes: "The work of Orthodoxy ought to be accomplished by taking a moral line without help from outside, without the aid of compulsory force. There is only one wholly worthy path for man to tread, the path of free persuasion, that path which the divine Savior revealed to us and the path which His Apostles took." In his view "the West is the triumph of external law." At the basis of the Russian State lie spontaneous goodwill, freedom and peace. In actual historical fact there was nothing of the kind. This was a romantic utopian embellishment, but reality lies in the fact that Aksakov desired spontaneous goodwill, freedom and peace. Khomyakov says that the West does not understand the incompatibility between the State and Christianity. In reality he refuses to acknowledge the possibility of the existence of a Christian State. And at the same time the Slavophils were supporters of the autocratic monarchy. How is this to be reconciled? The monarchical doctrine of the Slavophils fundamentally and in its inward pathos was anarchist and was a product of their revulsion from authority. In his interpretation of the sources of authority Khomyakov was a democrat and an upholder of the sovereignty of the people.[1] Primarily the fullness of power belongs to the people, but the people have no love

---

1. See my book, *A. C. Khomyakov.*

for power; they reject it; they choose the Tsar and instruct him to bear the burden of power. Khomyakov sets great store by the fact that the Tsar was chosen by the people. In his view, as in the view of the Slavophils in general, there was absolutely no religious foundation for the autocratic monarchy; there was no mysticism of autocracy; the Tsar reigns not in the strength of divine right, but in the strength of his election by the people, as an indication of the people's will. The Slavophil basis of monarchy takes a very peculiar form of its own. The autocratic monarchy based upon election by the people and the confidence of the people, is the State at a minimum, authority at a minimum; such, at least, it ought to be. The idea of the Tsar is not a State idea but a people's idea; it ought to have nothing in common with imperialism. And the Slavophils sharply contrast their autocracy with Western absolutism. The authority of the State is evil and vile. Authority belongs to the people, but the people refuse to have it and transfer the power in its plenitude to the Tsar. It is better that one man should be besmirched with power than that the whole people should. Power is not a right but a load and a burden. No one has the right to exercise authority, but there is one man who is obliged to bear the heavy burden of authority. Juridical guarantees are not necessary; they will lure the people away into an atmosphere of domination into politics, which are always evil. All the people need is freedom of the spirit, freedom of thought, of conscience and of speech. The Slavophils set in sharp relief the contrast between the *zemstvo*, society, and the State. They were convinced that the Russian people does not like power and rule and does not wish to be concerned with it, that it wishes to be left in the freedom of the spirit. The actual fact was that Russian autocracy, and especially the autocracy of Nicholas I, was absolutism and imperialism, which things the Slavophils did not want. It was a monstrous development of an all-powerful bureaucracy which the Slavophils could not endure. Behind their anarchist ideology of monarchy which was nothing but a utopia, the Slavophils concealed their love of freedom and their sympathy with the ideal of absence of power. In contrast to the Slavophils Herzen concealed nothing; he did not attempt to reconcile the irreconcilable. The anarchist and stateless tendency of his thought is clear. Leontyev is the very antithesis of the Slavophils in his attitude to the State. He recognizes that there is in the Russian people a disposition to anarchy, but he regards that as a great evil. He says that Russian statecraft is the creation of Byzantine principles and the Tartar and German elements. He also emphatically does not share the patriarchal family ideology of the Slavophils and thinks that in Russia the State is stronger than the family. Leontyev was much truer in his interpretation of reality than the Slavophils. He had a keener vision. But the Slavophils were immeasurably higher and more right than he in their actual sense of values and in their ideals. But let us return to the real Russian anarchism.

3

Bakunin passed from Hegelianism to a philosophy of action, to revolutionary anarchism in the most extreme form. He is a characteristically Russian phenomenon, a Russian gentleman who proclaimed revolt. He became known all over the world and chiefly in the West. At the time of the revolutionary uprising in Dresden, he proposed that they should set up Raphael's *Madonna* in front of the struggling revolutionaries, in the belief that the army would not bring itself to fire upon it. Bakunin's anarchism is also Russian messianism. There was a strong Slavophil element in it. In his view light comes from the East. From Russia there will issue a worldwide conflagration which will embrace the whole world. Something of Bakunin entered into the communist revolution in spite of his hostility to Marxism. Bakunin thought that the Slavs themselves would never create a state; only fighting peoples establish a state; the Slavs lived in brotherhoods and communes. He much disliked the Germans and his book bears the words "The cat-o-nine-tails German Empire" on its title page. At one time in Paris he was associated with Marx, but later on he separated from him sharply and carried on a quarrel about the First International in which Marx was victorious. In Bakunin's view Marx was a man of the State, a Pan-Germanist and a Jacobin, and he greatly disliked the Jacobins. Anarchists want revolution brought about by the people; the Jacobins want it to come through the State. Like all Russian anarchists he was an opponent of democracy. He reacted in a completely negative way to the right of universal suffrage. In his opinion governmental despotism is most powerful when it relies upon the so-called representation of the people. He also took up a very hostile attitude to allowing the control of life to get into the hands of scientists and scholars. Marx's socialism is a learned socialism. To this Bakunin opposes his own revolutionary dionysism. He makes the grim prediction that if any people attempts to realize Marxism in its own country, it will be the most terrible tyranny which the world has ever seen. In opposition to Marxism he asserted his belief in the elemental nature of the people, and above all of the Russian people. There is no need to get the people ready for revolution by means of propaganda. It is only necessary to rouse them to revolt. As his own spiritual predecessors he recognizes Stenka Razin and Pugachëv. To Bakunin belong the remarkable words—"the passion for destruction is a creative passion." What is needed is to set fire to a worldwide blaze; it is necessary to destroy the old world; upon the ashes of the old world, on its ruins, there will spring up a new and better world of its own accord. Bakunin's anarchism is not individualist as was Max Stirner's. He collectivized it. Collectivism or communism will not be an affair of organization; it will spring out of the freedom which will arrive after the destruction of the old world. A free and brotherly society of producing associations will arise of its own accord. Bakunin's anarchism is an extreme form of *Narodnichestvo*. Like the Slavophils he believes in truth hidden away in the elemental mass of the people, but he wants to arouse the very lowest strata of the laboring people to revolt and he is prepared to associate the criminal classes with them. Above all he believes in elemental nature and not in conscious thought. Bakunin has an original anthropology. Man became man through plucking the fruit of the tree of the knowledge of good and evil. There are three signs of human development: (1) human animality; (2) thought; (3) revolt. Revolt is the only sign that man is rising to a higher level. He assigns an almost mystical significance to revolt. Bakunin was also a militant atheist. He put this in his book *God and the State*. In his opinion the State finds its support principally in the idea of God; the idea of God is the rejection of human reason, of justice and of freedom. "If there is a God then man is a slave." God is vindictive; all religions are cruel. In militant godlessness Bakunin goes further than the communists. The social revolution alone, says he, is the thing, "the one thing which will get the power to shut all the pubs and all the churches at the same time." He is entirely incapable of stating the problem about God in its essence by cutting himself free from those social influences which have distorted the human idea of God. He saw and he knew only distortions. To him the idea of God was very reminiscent of an evil God, Marcion's creator of the world.[2] Sincere godlessness always sees only that sort of God, and the blame for this rests not only upon the godless but to an even greater extent upon those who make use of belief in God for base and interested earthly ends, for the support of evil forms of the State. Bakunin was an interesting, almost a fantastic, Russian figure and with all the falsity that existed in the basis of his outlook upon the world he frequently comes near to the authentic Russian idea. The principal weakness of his world outlook lay in the absence of any idea of personality which was at all thought out. He proclaimed revolt against the State and all authority, but this revolt was not made for the sake of human personality. Personality is left in subjection to the collective body and it is drowned in the elemental mass of the people. Herzen stood on a higher level in his feeling for human personality. Bakunin's anarchism is inconsistent in this respect, that he makes no thoroughgoing rejection of violence and power over man. The anarchist revolution is to be achieved by way of bloody violence and it presupposes the power of the insurgent people over personality, even if it is an unorganized power. The anarchism of Kropotkin was to some extent of another type; he is less extreme and more idyllic; he rests upon a foundation of naturalism and presupposes a very optimistic view of nature and of man. Kropotkin believes in a natural disposition to cooperation. A metaphysical sense of evil is lacking in the anarchists. There was an anarchist element in all Russian *Narodnichestvo*, but in the Russian revolutionary movement the anarchists in the proper sense of the word played a secondary part. Anarchism must be appraised otherwise than as just the Russian rejection of the temptation of the kingdom of this world. Aksakov and Bakunin agree in this, but as a doctrine it assumed forms which cannot survive criticism and are frequently absurd.

---

2. A. Harnack, *Marcion das Evangelium von Fremden Gott*. Harnack asserts that there is among the Russians a disposition to Marcionism.

4

The religious anarchism of Leo Tolstoy is a most thoroughgoing and radical form of anarchism, that is to say it is a rejection of the principle of authority and force. It is entirely mistaken to regard as more radical that form of anarchism which requires violence for its realization like, for example, Bakunin's anarchism. In the same way it is a mistake to consider as the most revolutionary that tendency which leads to the shedding of the greatest amount of blood. The real spirit of revolution demands a spiritual change in the primary foundations of life. It is usual to regard Tolstoy as a rationalist. This is untrue of Tolstoy not only as an artist but also as a thinker. It is very easy to discover in Tolstoy's religious philosophy a naive reverence for the reasonable; he confuses reason in the sense of wisdom, the divine wisdom, with the reason of the enlightened, with the reason of Voltaire, with natural judgment. But it was precisely Tolstoy who demanded foolishness in life, precisely he who would not admit any sort of compromise between God and the world, he who proposed to venture everything. Tolstoy demanded an absolute likeness between means and ends at a time when historical life was based on an absolute lack of likeness between means and ends. Vladimir Solovyov, with all his mysticism, constructed very reasonable, considered and safe plans for the theocratic ordering of human life, with rulers, with an army, with property, with everything which the world regards as a blessing. It is very easy to criticize Tolstoy's doctrine of non-resistance to evil by force; it is easy to show that in that case evil and evil men must triumph. But the actual depth of the problem before us is not commonly understood. Tolstoy draws an antithesis between the law of the world and the law of God, but proposes to adventure the world for the fulfillment of the law of God. Christians ordinarily arrange and organize their practical life in every instance in such a way that it may be profitable and expedient and that their affairs may go well, independently of whether there is a God or not. There is almost no difference in practical life, in individual life, or in the life of society, between a man who believes in God and a man who does not believe in God. Nobody, with the exception of individual saints or queer people, even attempts to order his life upon the Gospel principles, and all are in practice convinced that this would lead to the

ruin of life, individual life and social, although this does not prevent
them from recognizing in theory that there is an absolute significance behind the Gospel principles; but it is taken as a significance
which in spite of its absoluteness lies outside life. Does God exist or
does He not? And are the forces of the world organized according to
the law of the world and not according to the law of God? That was
what Tolstoy could not come to terms with, and the fact does him
great honor, even although his religious philosophy was feeble and
his teaching not realizable in practice. The meaning of Tolstoy's
non-resistance by force was much deeper than is commonly thought.
If a man ceases to oppose evil by force, that is, ceases to follow the
law of this world, then there will be an immediate intervention of
God; then divine nature will enter upon its rights. The good conquers
only upon the condition of action by the Divine itself. Tolstoy's doctrine is transferred to the life of society and history. For all the importance of Tolstoy's ideas there was a mistake in this respect, that
Tolstoy was not, so to speak, interested in those against whom violence is exercised and whom it is necessary to defend from violence.
He is right in saying that one ought not to fight evil with force in
order to win, to bring good into effect by force, but he does not recognize that it is necessary to set an external limit to force. There is a
force which enslaves and there is a force which liberates. The moral
maximalism of Tolstoy does not see that good is compelled to act in
a world which provides a dark evil environment and, therefore, its
action does not move in a straight line. But he did see that in the conflict good is affected by evil and begins to avail itself of evil methods. He wanted to take into his heart the Sermon on the Mount to the
extreme limit. The case of Tolstoy leads to a very serious thought,
that truth is dangerous and gives no guarantees, and the whole social
life of man is based upon a useful lie. There is a pragmatism of falsehood. This is a very Russian theme and it is foreign to the more
socialized peoples of Western civilization.

It is a great mistake to identify anarchism with anarchy. Anarchism is opposed not to order, concrete harmony, but to authority,
force and the Kingdom of Caesar; anarchy is chaos and disharmony,
that is to say it is ugliness. Anarchism is an ideal of freedom, of harmony and of order which arises from within, that is to say, it is the
victory of the Kingdom of God over the kingdom of Caesar. Behind

the violence and the despotism of the State there is usually concealed an inward anarchy and disharmony. Anarchism, which has in principle a spiritual foundation, is combined with a recognition of the function and the significance of the State, with the necessity of the functions of the State, but it is not bound to the supremacy of the State, to its absolutism, to its encroachment upon the spiritual freedom of man, to its will to power. Tolstoy justly considered that crime was a condition of the life of the State, as it develops in history. He was shocked by capital punishment, as were Dostoyevsky, Turgeniev and Solovyov, and as all the best Russians were. The Western peoples are not shocked, and capital punishment arouses no doubts in their minds; they even see in it the outcome of social instinct. We, on the other hand, have not been so socialized, thank God! The Russians have even had their doubts about the righteousness of punishment in general. Dostoyevsky defended punishment only on the ground that he saw in the criminal himself the need for punishment to assuage the torments of conscience, but not because of its usefulness to society. Tolstoy entirely rejects law courts and punishment, taking his ground upon the Gospel.

The external conservative political views put forward by Dostoyevsky in his *Diary of a Writer* hindered the consideration of his essential anarchism. Dostoyevsky's monarchism belongs to the anarchist type, just as much as the monarchism of the Slavophils. The theocratic utopia disclosed in *The Brothers Karamazov* was entirely outside the sphere of the State. It should overcome the State and in it the State must finally give place to the Church. A kingdom must be revealed in the Church, that is, the Kingdom of God, but not the kingdom of Caesar. This is an apocalyptic expectation. Dostoyevsky's theocracy is opposed to bourgeois civilization; it is opposed to every sort of State. Within it the wrongness of external law is exposed (a very Russian motif which was also to be found in K. Leontyev) and into it there enters a Russian Christian anarchism, a Russian Christian socialism (Dostoyevsky speaks outright of Orthodox socialism). The State is replaced by the Church and disappears. "Out of the East of the land the light arises," says Father Paisiy, "and let there be light, let there be light even if it be but at the end of the ages." The frame of mind is clearly eschatological. But the real religious and metaphysical basis of anarchism is given in *The*

Legend of the Grand Inquisitor. The anarchist character of the *Legend* has not been sufficiently noted; it led many people astray, for instance, Pobedonostzev who was very much pleased with it. Apparently the exposure of Christianity in its Catholic form in the *Legend* put him off the track. In actual fact *The Legend of the Grand Inquisitor* strikes a terrible blow at all authority and all power; it lashes out at the kingdom of Caesar not only in Roman Catholicism but also in Orthodoxy and in every religion, just as in communism and socialism. Religious anarchism in Dostoyevsky has a special character and has a different basis from the one it has in Tolstoy. It penetrates to a greater depth. To him the problem of freedom of the spirit is of central importance and it is not so in Tolstoy. But Tolstoy was freer from the external attack of traditional ideas and he has less confusion of thought. A very original feature in Dostoyevsky is that freedom is to him not a right of man but an obligation, a duty. Freedom is not ease, it is a burden. I have formulated this idea in this way, that it is not man who demands freedom from God, but God who demands it from man, and in this freedom He sees the worth and dignity of the God-likeness of man. On this account the Grand Inquisitor reproaches Christ on the ground that He has proceeded as though He did not love man, by laying upon him the burden of freedom. The Grand Inquisitor himself desires to bestow upon millions of millions of people the happiness of feeble infants, by withdrawing from them the burden of freedom which is beyond their strength, taking from them freedom of spirit.[3] The whole Legend is constructed upon the acceptance or rejection of the three Temptations of Christ in the Wilderness. The Grand Inquisitor yields to all three temptations: Roman Catholicism yields to them, as every authoritarian religion yields to them, and every form of imperialism and atheistic socialism and communism. Religious anarchism is based upon the rejection by Christ of the temptation of the kingdom of this world. In Dostoyevsky's view compulsive power in the ordering of the earthly kingdom is a Roman idea which atheistic socialism also follows. To the Roman idea which is founded upon compulsion he opposes the Russian Idea, which is founded upon freedom of the spirit. He exposes the false

---

3. See my book, *The World Outlook of Dostoyevsky*, the basis of which is an exposition of *The Legend of the Grand Inquisitor*.

theocracies in the name of true free theocracies (an expression of Solovyov's). False theocracy, and the godlessness which is similar to it, is that thing which is now called the totalitarian system, the totalitarian State. The denial of freedom of the spirit is to Dostoyevsky the temptation of antichrist. Authoritarianism is the principle of antichrist. This is the most extreme form of the rejection of authority and compulsion which the history of Christianity knows, and Dostoyevsky here passes beyond the frontiers of historical Orthodoxy and historical Christianity in general and enters upon an eschatological Christianity and a Christianity of the spirit, and discloses the prophetic side of Christianity. A compromising, opportunist and conforming attitude to the State, to the kingdom of Caesar in historical Christianity is commonly justified by the fact that it is said that we should render Caesar's things unto Caesar and God's things to God, but in principle the attitude of the Gospel to the kingdom of Caesar is defined by the rejection of the temptation of the kingdom of this world. Caesar is certainly not a neutral figure; he is the prince of this world, that is to say the principle which is the reverse of Christ, the principle of antichrist. In the history of Christianity God's things have been constantly rendered to Caesar. This has taken place every time that the principle of authority and power has been asserted in the spiritual life, every time that compulsion and violence have been exercised. It would seem that Dostoyevsky himself had but an inadequate understanding of the anarchist issues of the Legend. Such was the audacity of Russian thought in the nineteenth century. Already at the end of that century and at the beginning of the next, that strange thinker N. Fedorov, a Russian of the Russians, will likewise found his own original form of anarchism, one which is hostile to the State and combined, as in the case of the Slavophils, with a patriarchal monarchy which is not a State, and reveals the most grandiose and the most radical utopia which is known to the history of human thought. But in his case the thought ultimately passes on into the eschatological sphere, to which a separate chapter will be devoted. Anarchism in Russian forms remains a subject of Russian thought and Russian research.

8

The determining significance of the religious theme • Russian Philosophy is of a religious character • The religiousness of non-religious tendencies • The totalitarian character of thought • Apprehension is a coordination of spiritual forces and not merely reason • The problem of theodicy • Criticism of Western rationalism • The philosophical ideas of I. Kireevsky and Khomyakov • Criticism of Hegel • Voluntarism • Love as the organ of apprehension • Criticism of the abstract principles of Solovyov • Theosophy, theocracy and theurgy • The divine and the existent • The idea of God-manhood • The doctrine of Sophia • Freedom as a theme in Dostoyevsky • Dostoyevsky as a metaphysician • The religious philosophy of L. Tolstoy • Archbishop Innocent • Bukharev • The religious anthropology of Nesmelov • German idealism and Russian religious thought • Philosophical spiritualism in Russia • Basic trends of Russian religious philosophy • The official theology of scholasticism, the monastic-ascetic tradition • The Dobrotolubie • Russian theology, based upon freedom and sobornost • Christian Platonism • Schelling • Sophiology (the problem of the cosmos) • Anthropologism and eschatology (the problem of man, history, culture and society) • A new problem concerning man and the cosmos • Expectation of a new era of the Holy Spirit

1

IN RUSSIAN CULTURE during the nineteenth century, the religious theme was of decisive importance, and this was the case not only in specifically religious fields of thought but also in those currents of thought which lay outside religion and were fighting against God, although perhaps not consciously so. There were no philosophers in Russia of such stature as that of our writers, like Dostoyevsky and Tolstoy. Russian academic philosophy was not distinguished by any particular originality. Russian thought was by its very intensity too totalitarian; it was incapable of remaining abstract philosophy; it wanted to be at the same time religious and social, and there was a strong ethical feeling in it. For a long while no cultured philosophical environment was formed in Russia; it began to take shape only in the eighties when the journal *Questions of Philosophy and Psychology* began to be published. In connection with the establishment of philosophical culture among us importance attaches to the work of N. Grote, who was himself a philosopher of little interest. Conditions were unfavorable for the development of philosophy among us. Philosophy was subject to persecution from the side of the authorities and from the side of the general public both of the right and of the left. But an original religious philosophy was created in Russia and it grew; this fact constitutes one of the riddles of Russian thought. I am definitely talking about religious philosophy and not about theology. In the West thought and learning are very much differentiated; everything is distributed according to categories. Official Catholicism and official Protestantism have brought an enormous theological literature into being. Theology has become a professional affair. It has been the concern of specialists of the clerical class, of the professors in theological faculties and institutes. Professors of theology have never had any love for religious philosophy, which has seemed to them to be too liberal and has been suspected of a tendency to gnosticism. As defenders of orthodoxy they have jealously guarded the exclusive rights of theology. In Russia, in Russian Orthodoxy, there existed no theology at all for a long while, for there existed only an imitation of Western scholasticism. The one and only tradition of Orthodox thought, the tradition of Platonism and Greek patristics, had been interrupted and forgotten. In the eighteenth century it was even considered that the philosophy of the rationalist and enlightened Voltaire corresponded closely with Orthodoxy. Originally it was not a professor of theology, not a hierarch of the church, but a retired officer of the Horse Guards and a landowner, Khomyakov, who exercised himself in Orthodox theology. Thereafter the most remarkable ideas of religious philosophy were to be evolved among us, not by specialist theologians but by writers, by liberal-minded people. The same movement of free expression found scope in the religious and philosophical spheres in Russia, and it remained under suspicion in official ecclesiastical circles. Vladimir Solovyov was a philosopher and not a theologian. He was a *privat docent*, and he was expelled from the university after a speech of his against capital punishment. He was not in the least like a specialist in theology. It is interesting to note that philosophy, after it had been driven out from the universities, found a refuge in the academies. But the theological academies had created no original Russian philosophy, with very few exceptions. Russian religious philosophy awoke from its long intellectual sleep as the result of the jolt which it received from German philosophy and chiefly from Schelling and Hegel. The one hierarch of the Church who provides a certain interest in the field of thought, Archbishop Innocent, belongs rather to religious philosophy than to theology. Of the professors of the clerical academies the most original and notable thinker was Nesmelov, a spiritual and religious philosopher, not a theologian, and he makes a valuable contribution to the creation of Russian religious philosophy. The pure theologian is concerned with the nature of the Church and relies chiefly upon Holy Scripture and tradition; he is dogmatic in principle, and not open to doubts; his science is socially organized. Religious philosophy is free, is not bound to any set ways of apprehension, although at its basis there lies spiritual experience and faith. To the religious philosopher revelation is spiritual experience and spiritual fact, but not authority; his method is intuitive. Religious philosophy presupposes the union of theoretical and practical reason and the attainment of integrality in apprehension; its apprehension operates by a combination of the powers of the spirit and not by reason alone. Russian religious philosophy especially insists upon the truth that philosophical apprehension is an apprehension by the integral spirit, in which reason is combined with will and feeling and in which there is no rationalist disruption. On this account a criticism of rationalism is the first problem. They regarded rationalism as the original sin of Western thought, which is wrong because it is almost entirely colored by rationalism. There always existed in the West tendencies which were opposed to rationalism, but Russian religious philosophy discovered itself and defined itself in terms of opposition to Western thought. In this connection Schelling, Hegel, and Franz Baader were of great importance to it.[1] Baader fought rationalism no less vigorously than the Slavophil philosophers. But its totalitarian character and its quest for integrality must be considered the peculiar originality of Russian religious thought. We have already seen that the positivist N. Mikhailovsky, no less than I. Kireevsky and Khomyakov, were bent upon an integral view of right, right as truth and right as justice. If we make use of contemporary phraseology, it may be said that Russian philosophy, colored as it was by religion, desires to be existential. In it the apprehending and philosophizing self was existential. In giving expression to spiritual and moral effort it was an integrated and not a disrupted effort. The greatest Russian metaphysician and the most existential was Dostoyevsky. Unamuno said that Spanish philosophy is contained in Don Quixote. In the same way we can say that Russian philosophy is contained in Dostoyevsky. It was characteristic of Russian thought in the nineteenth century that the non-religious tendencies of the Russians, that socialism, *Narodnichestvo*, anarchism, nihilism, and even our atheism, had a religious theme, and that religious pathos entered into their experience. Dostoyevsky understood this admirably. He says that Russian socialism is a question of God and godlessness. Revolution was a religious matter to the revolutionary Intelligentsia; it was totalitarian and one's attitude towards it was totalitarian. The religious character of Russian trends of thought was revealed again in the fact that above all the problem of theodicy was a torment. The problem of the existence of evil had tormented Belinsky and Bakunin just as much as it did Dostoyevsky. With this problem Russian atheism also is connected.

The program of independent Russian philosophy was first sketched out by I. Kireevsky and Khomyakov; they passed through the school of German idealism, but they exerted themselves to adopt a critical attitude to what was the high-water mark of European philosophy in their day, that is Schelling and Hegel. It might be said that Khomyakov derived his thought from Hegel, but he was never a Hegelian and his criticism of Hegel is very remarkable. I. Kireevsky wrote in his essay on a philosophical program: "How necessary philosophy is; every development of our intelligence requires it; our poetry lives and breathes by it alone; it alone gives a soul and integrality to our infant science; our very life itself, it may be, borrows

---

1. See the recently issued very detailed exposition of Baader's philosophy by E. Suisini, *Franz von Baader et le Romanticisme Mystique*, 2 vols.

from it the beauty of its order. But whence does it come? Where are we to look for it? Of course our first step towards it must be a review of the intellectual riches of that country which has outstripped all other peoples in speculation, but thoughts of others are useful only for the development of our own. German philosophy can never take root in us. *Our* philosophy must develop from *our* life. It must be created out of current problems. It is the dominating interest of *our* corporate and individual existence." The fact that I. Kireevsky desires to derive philosophy from life is characteristic. Khomyakov asserts the dependence of philosophy upon religious experience. His philosophy conforms to his own type of character in being a philosophy of action. Unfortunately I. Kireevsky and Khomyakov did not write a single philosophical book; they limited themselves to some philosophical essays only. But they both of them had remarkable powers of intuition. They proclaim the end of abstract philosophy and are striving towards integrated knowledge. Hegelianism was being superseded and a transition was taking place from abstract idealism to concrete idealism. Vladimir Solovyov is to continue along this same path and to write books in which he gave expression to his philosophy. According to the scheme of things as seen by the Slavophils, Catholicism gives birth to Protestantism, Protestantism gives birth to idealist philosophy and Hegelianism, and Hegelianism passes into materialism. Khomyakov foresees with remarkable perspicacity the appearance of dialectic materialism. Above all Khomyakov's criticism exposes the disappearance in Hegel's philosophy of the existent, of the substratum. "The existent," he says, "ought to be set entirely apart by itself. Conception itself as an *abstract par excellence* must have given birth to everything out of itself." "The eternal, which issues from itself is a product of an abstract concept which has in itself no essence." The fundamental idea of Russian philosophy is the idea of the concrete existent, of the underlying real existence which precedes rational thought. The Slavophil philosophy, like the philosophy of Solovyov, came particularly near to Franz Baader and to a certain extent to Schelling in his last period. There is to be noted a very original gnosiology which might be called a corporate Church gnosiology. Love is recognized as the principle of apprehension; it guarantees the apprehension of truth; love is a source and guarantee of religious truth. Corporate experience of love, *sobornost*, is the criterion of apprehension. Here we have a principle which is opposed to authority; it is also a method of apprehension which is opposed to the Cartesian *cogito ergo sum*. It is not *I* think, but *we* think, that is to say, the corporate experience of love thinks, and it is not thought which proves my existence but will and love. Khomyakov is an upholder of the will; he affirms the *willing reason*. "For man the will belongs to the sphere of the pre-objective." It is only the will, only the willing reason, not the reason without will, which decides the difference between "I" and "not-I," between the inward and the outward. Faith lies at the foundation of knowledge. The existent is laid hold upon by faith. Knowledge and faith, in fact, are identified. "It is in this sphere (the sphere of primary faith) which precedes logical thought and is filled with vital consciousness, which stands in no need of proofs and inferences, that man recognizes what belongs to his own intellectual world and what belongs to the external world." The will perceives the existent before rational thought. With Khomyakov the will is not blind and not irrational; it is as with Schopenhauer, willing reason. This is not irrationalism but super-rationalism. Logical thought does not grasp the object in its fullness. The reality of the existent is grasped before logical thought comes into play. With Khomyakov philosophy depends upon religious experience as the primary thing, to such an extent that he even speaks of the dependence of philosophical apprehension upon belief in the Holy Trinity. But Khomyakov makes one mistake in regard to German philosophy. Engulfed as he was in his struggle with Western rationalism he, so to speak, did not notice to how large an extent German metaphysics was permeated by voluntarism, which goes back for its origin to Jacob Boehme and which exists in Kant, Fichte and Schelling. It is true that the voluntarism of Khomyakov himself was to some extent different. With him the will also denotes freedom, but the freedom has not a dark irrational source. The will is united to reason, not cut off from it. It is an integrality, an integrality of the spirit. Khomyakov had remarkable philosophical intuitions and fundamental philosophical ideas, but they were in an undeveloped state and were not worked out. The philosophy of Vladimir Solovyov is to move in this same direction, but in a more rational form; and the same is true in particular of Prince S. Trubetskoy with his doctrine of corporate consciousness, which he did not succeed in developing adequately. The spiritualist philosophy of Golubinsky and Kudryavtsev and others, which arose in the ecclesiastical academies, bore a different character and was akin to Western currents of speculative theism. Of greater interest was Yurkevitch in view of the fact that he maintained the central significance of the heart. In the philosophy of the universities Kozlov and Lopatin are particularly notable. This was a spiritualist philosophy akin to Leibnitz, Maine de Biran, Lotze and Teichmüller. Kozlov and Lopatin are evidence of the fact that independent philosophical thought existed in Russia, but they were not representative of original Russian philosophy, which is always totalitarian in its statement of a problem, always combines the theoretical and practical reason, and is always tinged with religious feeling. The theological thought of Khomyakov, which is as a matter of fact closely connected with his philosophy, is more open to view. But one must not expect systematic work in theology from Khomyakov. Unfortunately he used to set out his positive thought in the form of polemics against Western confessions, against Catholicism and Protestantism, to both of which he was frequently unjust. It is particularly obvious that in speaking of the Orthodox Church Khomyakov has in view an ideal Orthodoxy of a kind that ought to have existed according to his ideas, while in speaking of the Roman Catholic Church he has in view the Catholicism of experience, the sort that existed in historical reality and was frequently very unattractive. At the basis of his theological thought Khomyakov put the idea of freedom—of *sobornost*, the organic union of freedom and love, community. He had a feeling for spiritual freedom; all his thinking was permeated by it; he had a genius's intuition for *sobornost* which he perceived was not in the historical reality of the Orthodox Church, but behind it. *Sobornost* belongs to the image of the Church which is comprehensible to the mind, and in relation to the Church of experience it is an obligation to be discharged. The word *sobornost* is untranslatable into other languages. The spirit of *sobornost* is inherent in Orthodoxy and the idea of *sobornost*, of spiritual community, is a Russian idea. But it is difficult to discover Khomyakov's *sobornost* in historical Orthodoxy. Khomyakov's theological writings were suppressed in Russia by the censor; they were published abroad in French and only after a considerable lapse of time made their appearance in Russian. This is a very characteristic fact. Khomyakov's friend and follower Samarin proposed that Khomyakov should be recognized as a teacher of the Church. The dogmatic theology of the Metropolitan Makari, which Khomyakov called delightfully stupid, and which is the expression of the official mind of the Church, was an imitation of Roman Catholic scholasticism. Khomyakov on the other hand did endeavor to express original Orthodox theological thought. What then does *sobornost* represent to Khomyakov?

Khomyakov's theological work was occupied principally with the doctrine of the Church, which in his view coincided with the doctrine of *sobornost*, and further the spirit of *sobornost* was in his view the spirit of freedom; he was a decided and radical opponent of the principle of authority. I will describe Khomyakov's views in his own words: "We recognize no head of the Church, either spiritual or secular. Christ is the head and the Church knows no other." "The Church is not an authority, for authority is something which is external to ourselves. It is not authority, but truth, and at the same time life, which is the inner life of a Christian." "He who searches outside hope and faith for any sort of guarantees of the spiritual life, that man is already a rationalist." "Infallibility rests solely in the ecumenicity of the Church which is held in unity by mutual love." This again is *sobornost*. "The Church knows brotherhood, but it does not know subjection." "We confess to a Church which is one, which is free." "Christianity is nothing else than freedom in Christ." "I acknowledge a Church which is more free than the Protestants. In the affairs of the Church a compulsory community is a lie, and compulsory obedience is death." "No external mark, no sign limits the freedom of the Christian conscience." "The unity of the Church is nothing else than the agreement of individual freedoms." "Freedom and unity, such are the two powers to which the mystery of human freedom in Christ is worthily committed." "Knowledge of the truth is bestowed only upon mutual love." One might multiply extracts from Khomyakov, from the second volume of his collected works, which is devoted to theology. It would seem that no one hitherto had given expression to such an interpretation of Christianity as the religion of freedom, to such a thoroughgoing rejection of authority in religious life. In antithesis to authority he sets not only freedom but also love. Love is the principal source of the knowledge of Christian truth, and

the Church is a unity of love and freedom. A formal rational definition of the Church is impossible. It is recognized only in the spiritual
experience of the Church. In all this there is a profound difference
from Roman Catholic theology, and it is a characteristic of Russian
theology of the nineteenth century and of the beginning of the twentieth. The subject of freedom was particularly pronounced in
Khomyakov and Dostoyevsky. Western Christians, both Catholic
and Protestant, usually find some difficulty in understanding what
sobornost is. *Sobornost* is opposed both to Catholic authoritarianism
and to Protestant individualism. It indicates a unity which knows of
no external authority over it, but equally knows no individualistic
isolation and seclusion. In Khomyakov's view no ecumenical council was an authority which imposes upon Church people its own
interpretation of Christian truth. The ecumenical character of the
Church Council has no outward formal marks. It is not the case that
the Holy Spirit operates where, in accordance with formal signs,
there is an ecumenical synod, but that there is an ecumenical synod
and council where the Holy Spirit operates. There are no external
formal marks of any sort to define the Holy Spirit; nothing on the low
level of legalism, as in the life of the State, can be a criterion of the
authentic activity of the Holy Spirit. In the same way the rational logical mind cannot be a criterion of the truth of dogmas. The Holy
Spirit knows no other criteria than the Holy Spirit Himself. Where
an authentic ecumenical council has to be recognized and where an
unauthentic—like, for example, the "robber council"—is decided by
the whole body of the faithful, that is, it is decided by the spirit of
sobornost. This view was directed with particular trenchancy against
the Roman Catholic doctrine of the Church. It would be a complete
mistake to set the Catholic doctrine of the infallibility of the Pope,
when he speaks *ex cathedra*, in antithesis to an Orthodox doctrine of
the infallibility of a council of bishops. Khomyakov in like manner
denies even the authority of the episcopate. In his view truth is not in
the Council but in *sobornost*, in the spirit of community which
belongs to the whole body of the faithful. But the calamity was that
official Orthodox theology was inclined to acknowledge the authority of the episcopate in opposition to the authority of the Pope.

For too long a period there have been no councils in the Orthodox
Church; in Russia it needed a terrible revolution to make a Council

possible. Orthodox circles of the right who considered themselves especially orthodox even asserted that *sobornost* was an invention of Khomyakov's, that Orthodox freedom in Khomyakov bears the impress of the teaching of Kant and German idealism about autonomy. There was some measure of truth in this, but it only means that Khomyakov's theology endeavored creatively to give meaning to the whole spiritual experience of the unfolding history of his time. In a certain sense it is possible to call Khomyakov an Orthodox modernist. There is in him a certain kinship with Roman Catholic modernism, a struggle against scholasticism and the intellectualist interpretation of dogma, and a strong modernist element in his defense of free critical thought. In his time there was no Roman Catholic modernism, but he had a special affinity with Möhler—a remarkable Roman Catholic theologian of the first half of the nineteenth century, who defended an idea which came very near to Khomyakov's *sobornost*.[2] Khomyakov read the Swiss Protestant Vinet and certainly sympathized with his defense of religious freedom, but Khomyakov's combination of the spirit of freedom with the spirit of community remains a very Russian idea. Khomyakov felt considerable sympathy with the Anglican Church and corresponded with Palmer, whom he wanted to convert to Orthodoxy. He adopted a skeptical attitude to synodal government as did the Slavophils in general. Khomyakov thought there was evidence that in Orthodoxy great freedom of thought was possible, speaking, that is, of inward not outward freedom. This is explained in part by the fact that the Orthodox Church has no binding system and separates dogmas from theology more definitely than Roman Catholicism. And this, by the way, has even deeper causes. But Khomyakov's theological thought had its limits. Many questions which were later on raised by Russian philosophical thought he does not touch upon, for example the cosmological problem. The direction of his thought had very little eschatological element in it. The expectation of a new revelation of the Holy Spirit (paracletism) finds no place in his writings. The religious philosophical thought of Solovyov had a wider sweep, but Khomyakov thought more truly about the Church. It is

---

2. See J. A. Möhler, *Die Einheit in der Kirche* and a book by E. Wermeil, *J.A. Möhler et l'Ecole catholique de Tubingue*. Wermeil regarded Möhler as an originator of modernism.

interesting to note that in Russian religious, philosophical and theological thought there was absolutely no idea of the natural theology
which played a great part in Western thought. Russian thought does
not make a distinction between revealed theology and natural theology; Russian thinking is too integral for that, and at the foundation
of knowledge it sees the essay of faith.

2

Vladimir Solovyov is recognized as the most outstanding Russian
philosopher of the nineteenth century. In contrast to the Slavophils
he wrote a series of philosophical books and created a complete system. The figure of the man himself, if we take him as a whole, is
more interesting and original than his philosophy in the proper sense
of the word.[3] He was an enigmatic self-contradictory man. The most
varied judgments upon him are possible and the most varied tendencies sprang from him. Two Procurators of the Holy Synod acknowledged themselves as his friends and pupils. The brothers Trubetskoy
were intellectually descended from him and so was S. Bulgakov,
who provided such a contrast to them; they associated themselves
with him and revered him as their spiritual forebear. The Russian
symbolists, A. Blok, A. Bely and Vyacheslav Ivanov were ready to
acknowledge him as their teacher, and the anthroposophists regarded
him as one of themselves. Right and left, Orthodox and Roman Catholic alike appealed to him and sought for support in him. But at the
same time Vladimir Solovyov was a very lonely figure, but little
understood and very tardily appreciated. Only at the beginning of the
twentieth century the myth about him took shape, and it contributed
to the formation of this myth that there was a Solovyov of the day
and a Solovyov of the night, outwardly revealing himself and in that
very revelation concealing himself, and in the most important
respect not revealing himself at all. Only in his poetry has he
revealed what was hidden, what was veiled and overwhelmed by the
rational schemes of his philosophy. Like the Slavophils he criticized
rationalism but his own philosophy was too rationalist, and the

---

3. For the personal character of Solovyov, Mochulsky's book *Vladimir Solovyov* is particularly
interesting. For the exposition and criticism of Vladimir Solovyov's philosophy the greatest
interest attaches to Prince E. Trubetskoy's *Vladimir Solovyov's World Outlook*, 2 volumes.

schemes of which he was very fond played too great a part in it. He
was a mystic; he had a mystical experience. All who knew him bore
witness to this. He had occult gifts which certainly did not belong to
the Slavophils, but his mode of thought was very rationalist. He
belonged to the number of those who hide themselves in their intellectual creation and do not reveal themselves, as, for example, Dostoyevsky revealed himself, with all his inconsistencies. In this
respect he is like Gogol. Gogol and Solovyov are the most enigmatic
figures in the Russian literature of the nineteenth century. Our very
greatest Christian philosopher of the last century was certainly not a
man who bore the stamp of the life of his own day as the Slavophils
did; he was a man of the air, not of the earth; he was a wanderer in
this world, not a settled person. He belonged to the period of Dostoyevsky, with whom he had direct links. He did not like Leo Tolstoy. But this enigmatic wanderer always wanted to find principles
and strength for the life of man and societies, in stable objective
truths, and always expressed this foundation in rationalist schemes.
It is a striking point about Solovyov that he always strove for integrality, but there was no integrality in him himself. He was an erotic
philosopher in the platonic sense of the word. *Eros* of the highest
order played an immense part in his life and was his existential
theme; and at the same time there was a strong ethical element in
him; he demanded the effective realization of Christian morality in
the whole of life. This moral element makes itself specially felt in his
essays on Christian politics and in his struggle with the nationalists.
He was not only a rationalist philosopher who acknowledged the
rights of reason, but also a theosophist. He had affinities not only
with Plato, Kant, Hegel and Schopenhauer, but also with the Christian theosophists, Jacob Boehme, Pordage, Franz Baader and Schelling in his later period. He wanted to build up a system of free
Christian theosophy and to combine it with free theocracy and theurgy. Vladimir Solovyov had his own primary intuition, as every
notable philosopher has; it was the intuition of an all-embracing
unity. He had a vision of the integrality, the all-embracing unity of
the world, of the divine cosmos, in which there is no separation of
the parts from the whole, no enmity and discord, in which there is
nothing abstract and self-assertive. It was a vision of Beauty; it was
an intellectual and erotic intuition; it was a quest for the transfigura-

tion of the world, and for the Kingdom of God. The vision of all-embracing unity makes Solovyov a universalist in the fundamental tendency of his thought, and his Roman Catholic sympathies were to be connected with this. It is a very interesting point that behind this universalism, behind this striving after the all-embracing unity, there was hidden an erotic and ecstatic element; there was hidden an ardent love for the beauty of the divine cosmos, to which he gives the name of Sophia. Vladimir Solovyov was a romantic, and as such he was given to an illusive association and identification of love for the beauty of eternal femininity, of the divine wisdom, with that love of beauty which we find in the search for the concrete idea of woman, a thing which he was always so unable to discover. The intuition of the all-embracing unity, of concrete universalism, makes him above all a critic of concrete universalism, makes him above all a critic of "abstract principles," and to that his chief book is devoted. Solovyov was an intellectualist not a voluntarist. For that reason freedom does not play such a part with him as it does with the voluntarist Khomyakov. His world outlook belongs rather to the type of universal determinism, but the determinism is spiritual. He belongs also to the type of evolutionary outlook, but evolutionism is accepted not on the ground of naturalist doctrines about evolution, but on the basis of German idealist metaphysics. The attainment of the all-embracing unity, both social and cosmic, is for him of an intellectual character. There is no irrational freedom with him. The falling away of the world from God is the acceptance of principles which are hostile to God. Egoistic self-assertion and alienation are the chief signs of the fall of man and of the world. But every one of the principles which have separated themselves from the highest center includes in itself a partial truth. The reunion of these principles, together with the renewed subjection of them to the highest divine principle, is the attainment of the all-embracing unity. This all-embracing unity is thought of not in an abstract way but concretely, with the inclusion in it of all the individual grades. Thus, in his theory of apprehension, empiricism, rationalism and mysticism are abstract principles which are false in their exclusive self-assertion, but do contain partial truths which enter into the integral apprehension of a free theosophy. Thus also, in the practical sphere a free theocracy is attained by the combination of the principles of Church, State and *zemshchina*, as they then designated society in Slavophil terminology. Vladimir Solovyov was at one time too much convinced that the intellectual conception of free theosophy and free theocracy is able to contribute greatly to the attainment of the concrete all-embracing unity. Later on he was himself disillusioned in this respect; but his idea was absolutely true that what he called "abstract principles" must not be regarded as evil, as sin and delusions. Thus empiricism is in itself a delusion but there is a partial truth contained in it which ought to enter into the theory of knowledge, knowledge of a higher type. Thus humanism in its exclusive self-assertion is an error and untruth, but there is in it a great truth which belongs to the divine-human life. The overcoming of "abstract principles" is also what Hegel calls *aufhebung*. What there was of truth in that which precedes enters into the process of overcoming. Solovyov says that in order to overcome the wrong in socialism it is necessary to recognize what is right in socialism. But all the while he strives for integrality; he wants knowledge which is integrated, and in his mind not only truth and goodness but also beauty was always connected with integrality. He remains in line with Hegel and the German romantics from whom he had accepted universalism and the idea of the organic. The problem of freedom, personality and conflict was not an acute experience with him; but he felt the problem of unity, of integrality and harmony, very powerfully. His triple utopia of theosophy, theocracy and theurgy is all the while the same thing as the Russian quest for the Kingdom of God and the perfect life. In this utopia there is a social element, his social Christianity. In Solovyov's opinion there are two negative principles, death and sin, and two positive desires, the desire for immortality and the desire for right. The life of nature is concealed corruption. Matter which holds sway in the natural world, being separated from God, is a repellent infinity. Belief in God is belief in the truth that good exists, that it is a real existent, while temptation lies in the fact that evil takes the form of good. The victory over death and corruption is the attainment of the all-embracing unity, a transfiguration not only of man but also of the whole cosmos. But the most interesting and original idea of Solovyov's is the distinction he draws between being and existence. He was, of course, strongly under the influence of Hegel, but all the same he solved the question of being in a different way.

Being is only the predicate of the subject, which is existence; it is not the subject itself, it is not the existence itself. Being tells us that something is, but it does not tell us what is. It cannot be said that being is, only the existent, the underlying existence, is. The concept of being is logically and grammatically ambiguous. Two meanings are confused in it. Being means that something is and being also means that which is. But the second meaning of being ought to be set aside. Being appears as subject and as predicate, as the underlying substance and as the attribute; but it is truer to regard being as predicate only. The words are used, "this creature is" and "this feeling is" and so there takes place a "gnosticization" of the predicate.[4] In reality the subject of philosophy ought not to be being in general but that to which and to whom being belongs, that is to say, the existent.[5] This distinction between being and existence, which is important for the understanding of Solovyov, cannot be expressed in every language. Here he, so to speak, approaches existential philosophy, but his own philosophical thought does not belong to the existential type. At the basis of his philosophy there lies the living intuition of the concrete existent, and his philosophy was the work of his life. But his philosophy itself remains abstract and rationalist. In it the existent is overwhelmed by his schemes. He all the while insists upon the necessity of the mystical element in philosophy. His criticism of abstract principles and his search for integral knowledge are permeated with this. At the basis of knowledge, at the basis of philosophy, there lies belief. The very recognition of the reality of the external world presupposes belief. But as a philosopher Solovyov was certainly not an existentialist. He did not give expression to his inward nature, he used to cover it up. He tried to find compensation in poetry, but even in poetry he would shelter himself behind some joke and this sometimes produced an impression which does not correspond with the seriousness of his theme. The peculiarities of Solovyov both as a thinker and as a writer gave Tareev grounds for writing of him: "It is terrible to reflect that Solovyov who has written so much about Christianity, has not in one single word shown the

---

4. See Vladimir Solovyov, *A Critique of Abstract Principles* and *The Philosophical Sources of Integral Knowledge.*
5. I have dealt with this in my *Creation and Objectivization. An Essay in Eschatological Metaphysics.*

spirit of Christ."[6] In saying this Tareev had in view that Solovyov in speaking about Christ usually spoke as though he were thinking of the Logos of Neoplatonism and not of Jesus of Nazareth. But his intimate spiritual life has remained hidden from us and it is not fitting that we should pass judgment upon him. It must be remembered that he was distinguished by extraordinary kindliness, that he distributed his clothes among the poor and on one occasion was obliged to appear in a blanket. He belonged to the number of those who are divided inwardly, but he strove after integrality, after the existent, after the all-embracing unity, after concrete knowledge. Hegel also was bent upon concrete knowledge but he attained this only partially and chiefly in the "phenomenology of the spirit."

As was to be expected in a Russian philosopher the historico-sophiological theme occupied a central position with Solovyov. There is a sense in which the whole of his philosophy is a philosophy of history, the doctrine of the path of humanity towards God-manhood, and towards the all-embracing unity, towards the Kingdom of God. His theocracy is built up on a philosophy of history. The philosophy of history is in his case linked with the doctrine of God-manhood and this is also the chief service he rendered to Russian religious philosophical thought. In this connection his lectures on God-manhood have an immense importance. The idea of God-manhood, fostered by Russian thought and but little understood by Western Catholic and Protestant thought, indicates an original interpretation of Christianity. This idea must not be identified with Solovyov's evolutionism in which both God-man and God-manhood are, as it were, the product of world evolution. But in Solovyov's evolutionism, which was fundamentally mistaken and not combined with freedom, there is a measure of undoubted truth. Thus humanist experience of the new history enters into God-manhood and has a powerful influence upon the evolution of Christianity. Solovyov wants to give a Christian meaning to this experience and expresses it in his admirable teaching about God-manhood.

Christianity is not only belief in God; it is also belief in man, and in the possibility of a revelation of the divine in man. There exists a commensurability between God and man and on that account only is

---

6. See Tareev, *Foundations of Christianity*, vol. IV, "Christian Freedom."

a revelation of God to man possible. Pure abstract transcendentalism makes revelation impossible; it cannot open out pathways to God, and excludes the possibility of communion between man and God. Even Judaism and Mohammedanism are not transcendental in such an extreme form as that. In Jesus Christ the God-man, there is in an individual Person a perfect union of two natures—divine and human. This ought to take place collectively in mankind, in human society. For Solovyov's very idea of the Church is connected with this. The Church is a divine-human organism; the history of the Church is a divine-human process, and, therefore, it is a development. A free union of the divine and the human ought to take place. Such is the ideal set before Christian humanity, which has but badly fulfilled it. The evil and suffering of the world did not hinder Solovyov in this period from seeing the divine-human process of development. There was a preparation for God-manhood already in the pagan world and in pagan religions. Before the coming of Christ history was struggling towards the God-man. After the coming of Christ history struggles towards God-manhood. The humanist period of history, which lies outside Christianity and which is opposed to it, enters into this divine-human process. God-manhood is a possibility because human nature is consubstantial with the human nature of Christ. Upon the idea of God-manhood there lies the impress of the social and cosmic utopia by which Solovyov was inspired. He wanted Christianity to be made actual in history, in human society and not in the individual soul only. He sought for the Kingdom of God which is to make its appearance even on this earth. I do not use the word "utopia" in a depreciatory sense. On the contrary I see the great service which Vladimir Solovyov rendered by the fact that he desired a social and cosmic transfiguration. Utopia means only a whole totalitarian ideal, a perfection within limits. But utopianism is usually connected with optimism. Here we come upon a fundamental inconsistency; the union of manhood and deity, the attainment of God-manhood can only be thought of freely, it cannot be a matter of compulsion, it cannot be the result of necessity. This Solovyov recognizes, and at the same time the divine-human process which leads to God-manhood is to him, as it were, a necessary determined process of evolution. The problem of freedom is not thought out to its final end. Freedom presupposes not uninterruptedness but interruption. Freedom can even be opposition to the realization of God-manhood; it can even be a distortion, as we have seen in the history of the Church. The paradox of freedom lies in this that it can pass into slavery. With Solovyov the divine-human process is non-tragic, whereas in actual fact it is tragic. Freedom gives rise to tragedy. Upon his lectures on God-manhood there lies the undoubted stamp of the influence of Schelling in his last period, but none the less Solovyov's doctrine of God-manhood is an original product of Russian thought. There is nothing of this doctrine in such a form either in Schelling or in other representatives of Western thought. The idea of God-manhood means the overcoming of the self-sufficiency of man in humanism and at the same time the affirmation of the activity of man, of his highest dignity, of the divine in man. The interpretation of Christianity as the religion of God-manhood is radically opposed to the juridical interpretation of the relation between God and man, and the juridical theory of redemption which is widespread in theology both Catholic and Protestant.

The appearance of the God-man and the coming appearance of God-manhood denote the continuation of the creation of the world. Russian religious philosophical thought in its best representatives makes war upon every juridical interpretation of the mystery of Christianity, and this enters into the Russian Idea. At the same time the idea of God-manhood tends towards cosmic transfiguration. It is almost entirely alien to official Catholicism and Protestantism. In the West affinity with the cosmology of Russian religious philosophy is to be found only in German Christian theosophy, in Jacob Boehme, Franz Baader and in Schelling. This brings us to be subject of Sophia, with which Solovyov connects his doctrine of God-manhood. The doctrine of Sophia, which became popular in religious philosophical and poetic trends of thought at the beginning of the twentieth century, is connected with the platonic doctrine of ideas. "Sophia is the expressed actualized idea," says Solovyov; "Sophia is the body of God, the substance of the divine permeated by the principle of the divine unity." The doctrine of Sophia asserts the principle of the divine wisdom in the created world, in the cosmos and in mankind. It does not allow of an absolute breach between the Creator and creation. To Solovyov Sophia is also the ideal humanity and he brings the cult of Sophia near to the cult of humanity, as found in Auguste Comte. In order to endow Sophia with an Orthodox character he points to the icons of St. Sophia, "The Wisdom of God," in the cathedrals of St. Sophia in Novgorod and Kiev. In Orthodox circles the chief attacks upon this doctrine were due to the interpretation of Sophia as the eternal feminine principle and to the introduction of the feminine principle into the Godhead. But to be just, the same objections ought to be raised by the introduction of the male principle into the Godhead. The most intimate mystical experiences of Solovyov are connected with Sophia and they find expression chiefly in his verse. Having heard the inward call he makes a secret journey to Egypt for a meeting with Sophia, the eternal feminine. He describes this in a poem called "Three Meetings" and in other verses:

> With no trust in this cheating world of sight
> I sensed beneath its coarse material husk
> Th'imperishable raiment, purple-bright
> And knew the gleam God gives amid the dusk.

> I saw the all; all is but one, I thought,
> Of woman's grace, one only image known
> Within its scope the immeasurable is brought
> Before me and within, there is but thou alone.

> Unwilling still in this vain world's duress,
> I saw within its coarse material husk
> Th'imperishable glory of its crimson dress
> And sensed the gleam God gives amid the dusk.

and again:

> Know then, eternal womanhood, all bright
> With body incorruptible to earth now leaps,
> New goddess of undying flashing light,
> And heaven is mingled with the watery deeps.

> All fairness of the Aphrodite of this earth
> All homes, and woods and seas with joy replete
> All this, unearthly beauty holds within its girth
> But purer, stronger, more alive, complete.

The vision of Sophia is the vision of the beauty of the divine cosmos, of the transfigured world. If Sophia is Aphrodite, then Aphrodite is of heaven and no common birth. Solovyov's doctrine of Sophia, the eternal feminine and his verses devoted to it, had an enormous influence upon the symbolist poets of the beginning of the twentieth century, Alexander Blok and Andrei Byelii, who believed in Sophia and had little belief in Christ, a fact which constituted an enormous difference between them and Solovyov. In the West the doctrine of Sophia was to be found expressed with genius in Jacob Boehme, but it bore rather a different character from that which it had in Solovyov and in Russian sophiology.[7] Boehme's doctrine of Sophia is a doctrine of eternal virginity and not of eternal femininity. Sophia is virginity, the completeness of man, the androgynous image of man. It was man's fall into sin which was his loss of his virgin-Sophia. After the Fall Sophia flew away to heaven and upon earth Eve appeared. Man yearned for his virgin-Sophia, for integrality. Sex is a sign of dividedness and fall. It is possible to discover an affinity between Boehme's doctrine of Sophia and Plato (The Doctrine of Androgyny) and also between it and the Kabbala. Sophiology in Boehme is chiefly of an anthropological character. In Solovyov it is mainly cosmological. Boehme's doctrine is purer than Solovyov's which might open the way for turbidity in minds which dwell upon sophiology. Undoubtedly the lure of the cosmos is to be found in Solovyov; but there was great truth in his expectation of the beauty of the transfigured cosmos. In this respect he passes beyond the frontiers of historical Christianity as did all the original currents of Russian religious thought. Solovyov's essay on *The Meaning of Love* is the most remarkable of all that he wrote. It is even the one and only original word which has been spoken on the subject of love as *Eros* in the history of Christian thought. But there may be found in it a contradiction of the doctrine of Sophia. The doctrine of love is higher than the doctrine of Sophia. Solovyov was the first Christian thinker who really acknowledged a personal and not merely a family meaning of love between man and woman. Traditional Christian thought has not acknowledged the meaning of love and even not noticed it. The only justification of the union of man

---

7. See my essay, "The Doctrine of Jacob Boehme on Sophia" in *Put*.

and woman that exists is for the procreation of children, that is to say a family justification. What St. Augustine wrote about this reminds one of a treatise on cattle-breeding, but such was the prevailing ecclesiastical point of view, and to him the begetting of children was the sole justification for the union of man and woman. Solovyov insists upon a contradiction between the completion of personality and the begetting of children. This is a biological truth. But the metaphysical truth lies in this that there is a contradiction between the view which is concerned with personal immortality and that which takes into consideration the replacement of the generations as they are born anew. Personality, as it were, disintegrates in the process of begetting children. The impersonal species triumphs over personality. Solovyov combines the mystical *Eros* with asceticism. An anthropological problem is posed with the perspicacity of genius in *The Meaning of Love*. There is in it less of that synthesizing adjustment which often exasperates in Solovyov, exasperates most of all in his *Justification of the Good*, a system of moral philosophy. He thinks radically in this essay. We may regard Franz Baader as his only predecessor in this field, but his point of view was, nevertheless, somewhat different.[8]

Solovyov was but little appreciated and understood in his own day. It was his idea of theocracy which was chiefly valued, that is to say, quite the weakest point about him. His liberal journalism obtained a wider recognition. Later on he had an enormous influence upon the spiritual renaissance at the beginning of the twentieth century when there occurred a spiritual crisis among part of the Russian Intelligentsia. How is the work of Vladimir Solovyov to be appraised? His style of philosophical thinking belongs to the past; it is more out of date than Hegel's philosophy which is beginning to make its influence felt afresh in our time. Unfortunately Solovyov's construction of a worldwide theocracy, with the threefold services of Tsar, High Priest and Prophet, he himself destroyed, and is less than anything capable of being retained. In the same way the plan which he proposed for the union of the Churches, which is concerned with Church government, seems naive and out of touch with our present

---

8. See *Schriften Franz Baaders*, Insel-Verlag: "Sätze aus der erotischen Philosophie." "Vierzig Sätze aus einer religiösen Erotik."

way of thinking, which attaches greater importance to types of spirituality and mysticism. Yet, nevertheless, the importance of Solovyov is very great. In the first place his assertion of the prophetic side of Christianity has an immense significance in his work, and it is in this respect most of all that he enters into the Russian idea. His prophetism has no necessary connection with his theocratic scheme and it even overthrows it. Solovyov believed in the possibility of innovation in Christianity; he was permeated with the messianic idea; he was orientated to the future and in this respect he has the closest affinities with us. The currents of Russian religious thought, of Russian religious quests belonging to the beginning of the twentieth century were to continue the prophetic work of Solovyov. He was an enemy of all monophysite tendencies in the interpretation of Christianity; he asserted the activity of man in the task of establishing Christian God-manhood. He brought the truth of humanism and humanitarianism into Christianity. The question of Solovyov's Roman Catholicism usually has a false light thrown upon it both by his Roman Catholic friends and by his Orthodox opponents. He was never converted to Roman Catholicism; that would have been too simple, and would not have been in accord with the importance of the theme he propounded. He wanted to be both a Roman Catholic and an Orthodox at the same time. He wanted to belong to the Ecumenical Church in which there would be fullness of a sort which does not yet exist either in Roman Catholicism or in Orthodoxy taken in their isolation and self-assertion. He allowed the possibility of inter-communion. This means that Solovyov was a supra-confessionalist; he believed in the possibility of a new era in the history of Christianity. His Roman Catholic sympathies and inclinations came particularly to the fore at the time when he was writing his book *Russia and the Ecumenical Church*. They were an expression of his universalism. But he never broke with Orthodoxy, and at his death he made his confession to an Orthodox priest and received communion at his hands. In *Stories of Antichrist*, the Orthodox *starets* Johann is the first to recognize antichrist and in this way the mystical calling of Orthodoxy is affirmed. Like Dostoyevsky Solovyov went beyond the limits of historical Christianity and in this lies his religious significance. I shall speak in the next chapter about his eschatological frame of mind towards the end of his life.

The optimism of his theocratic and theosophic schemes was followed by disillusionment; he saw the power of evil in history. But this was only a moment in his inner destiny; he belonged to the type of messianic religious thinkers who are akin to the Polish messianist Cieszkowski. It must further be said that the conflict which Solovyov waged against nationalism, which was triumphant in the eighties, may from an external point of view appear to be out of date, but it remains a living issue even for our own day. This was a great service that he rendered. The same thing must be said of his fight for freedom of conscience, of thought and of expression. In the twentieth century there have already arisen from the rich, variegated and often inconsistent thought of Solovyov, various currents of thought: the religious philosophy of Bulgakov and Prince E. Trubetskoy, S. Frank's philosophy of the all-embracing unity, the symbolism of A. Blok, A. Byelii and V. Ivanov. The current problems of the beginning of the century were closely connected with him, although perhaps there cannot be and has not been any "Solovyovism" in the narrow sense among us.

3

But the chief figures in Russian religious thought and the religious quest of the nineteenth century were not philosophers, but the novelists Dostoyevsky and L. Tolstoy. Dostoyevsky is the greatest Russian metaphysician or rather anthropologist; he revealed many important things about man and from him there dates a new era in the inner history of man. After Dostoyevsky man was no longer what he had been before. Only Nietzsche and Kierkegaard can share with Dostoyevsky the glory of this new era which has been inaugurated. This new anthropology treats of man as a self-contradictory tragic creature, in the highest degree unhappy, not only suffering but in love with suffering. Dostoyevsky is more of a pneumatologist than a psychologist; he poses problems of the spirit, and he wrote his novels on the same theme—the problems of the spirit. He depicts man as moving forward through a twofold experience; it is people of a divided mind who appear in his books. In the human world of Dostoyevsky there is revealed polarity in the very depth of being, a polarity of beauty itself. Dostoyevsky begins to be interested in man when an inward revolution of the spirit begins, and he depicts the existential dialectic of the human twofold experience. Suffering is not only profoundly inherent in man, but it is the sole cause of the awakening of conscious thought. Suffering redeems evil. Freedom, which is the mark of the highest dignity of man, of his likeness to God, passes into willfulness, and willfulness gives rise to evil. Evil is a sign of the inward depth of man. Dostoyevsky reveals the substratum and the underlying deeps of man's nature and the depths of the subconscious. Out of these deeps man cries out that he wants "to live according to his own stupid will" and that "twice two are four" is a principle of death. The fundamental theme in Dostoyevsky is the question of freedom, a metaphysical theme which had never yet been so profoundly stated; and with freedom is linked suffering also. A refusal of freedom would mitigate suffering. There is a contradiction between freedom and happiness. Dostoyevsky sees the dualism of an evil freedom and a compulsory good. This subject of freedom is the basic theme in *The Legend of the Grand Inquisitor*, which is the summit of Dostoyevsky's creation. The acceptance of freedom indicates belief in man, belief in spirit. The refusal of freedom is disbelief in man. The repudiation of freedom is the spirit of antichrist. The mystery of the Crucifix is the mystery of freedom. The Crucified God is freely chosen as the object of love. Christ does not impose His own example by force. If the Son of God had become a Tsar and organized an earthly kingdom, freedom would have been taken away from man. The Grand Inquisitor says to Christ: "You have desired the free love of man." But freedom is aristocratic; for millions and millions of people it is an unbearable burden. In imposing upon men the burden of freedom "you proceeded as though you did not love them at all." The Grand Inquisitor yields to the three temptations which Christ rejected in the Wilderness. He repudiates freedom of the spirit and wants to bestow happiness upon millions of millions of infants. Millions will be happy through rejecting personality and freedom. The Grand Inquisitor wants to make an ant heap, a paradise without freedom. The "Euclidean mind" does not understand the mystery of freedom which is unattainable by rational methods. It might have been possible to escape evil and suffering but the price would have been the renunciation of freedom. Evil which is brought to birth by freedom in the form of self-will must be consumed, but the process takes place through the experience of temptation. Dostoyevsky discloses the deeps of crime and the deeps of conscience. Ivan Karamazov proclaims a revolt. He does not accept God's world and returns to God the ticket of entrance into world harmony. But this is only the way of man. The whole of Dostoyevsky's world outlook was linked with the idea of personal immortality. Without belief in immortality not a single question is capable of solution, and if there were no immortality the Grand Inquisitor would be right. In the *Legend* Dostoyevsky had in view, of course, not only Roman Catholicism, not only every religion of authority, but also the religion of communism which disowns immortality and freedom of the spirit. Dostoyevsky probably would have accepted a specifically Christian communism and would certainly have preferred it to the bourgeois capitalist order; but the communism which rejects freedom and the dignity of man as an immortal being, he regarded as the offspring of the spirit of antichrist.

The religious metaphysics of Leo Tolstoy are less profound and less Christian than the religious metaphysics of Dostoyevsky. But Tolstoy was of immense importance to Russian religious thought in the second half of the nineteenth century. He was an awakener of the religious conscience in a society which was religiously indifferent or hostile to Christianity. He called for a search into the meaning of life. Dostoyevsky as a religious thinker influenced a comparatively small circle of the Intelligentsia, those of them who were of a more complex structure of spirit. Tolstoy, as a religious moral preacher, had an influence upon a wider circle; he laid his hold upon the masses of the people; his influence was felt in the sectarian movements. Groups of Tolstoyans in the proper sense were not numerous, but the Tolstoyan ethic had great influence upon the moral values of very wide circles of the Russian Intelligentsia. Doubts about the justification of holding private property, especially of the private ownership of land, doubts about the right to judge and to punish, the exposure of the evil and wrong of all forms of state and authority, repentance for his privileged position, the consciousness of guilt before the working people, a revolution from war and violence, and dreams of the brotherhood of man—all these elements were very much part of the makeup of the central body of the Russian Intelligentsia. They penetrated even into the highest stratum of Russian society and seized upon even part of the Russian subordinate officials in the State services. This was platonic Tolstoyism. The Tolstoyan ethic was considered unrealizable, but yet the most lofty which one could imagine. The same attitude was adopted, by the way, towards the ethics of the Gospel in general. In Tolstoy there developed a consciousness of his share of the guilt as a member of the ruling class in Russian society. It was above all an aristocratic repentance. There was in Tolstoy an extraordinary eagerness for the perfect life; it oppressed him through a large part of his life; it was an acute consciousness of his own imperfection.[9] He derived the consciousness of his own sinfulness and a tendency to unceasing repentance from Orthodoxy. The idea that the first and foremost necessity is to reform oneself, rather than to ameliorate the lives of others, is a traditional Orthodox idea. The Orthodox foundation in him was stronger than is generally supposed. Even his very nihilism in regard to culture is derived from Orthodoxy. At one time he made violent efforts to be most traditionally Orthodox in order to be at spiritual unity with the working people. But he could not stand the test. His indignation was aroused by the sins and evils of the historical Church, by the wrong in the lives of those who considered themselves Orthodox, and he became one who used his genius to expose the wrongs of which ecclesiasticalism was guilty in history. In his criticism, in which there was a great deal of truth, he went so far that he began to deny the very primary foundations of Christianity and arrived at a religion which was more akin to Buddhism. Tolstoy was excommunicated by the Holy Synod a body which was not very authoritative. And it must be said that the Orthodox Church had no love for excommunication. It might be said that Tolstoy excommunicated himself. But the excommunication was really shocking in that it was pronounced upon a man who had done so much to awaken religious interests in a godless society, and a society in which people who were dead so far as Christianity was concerned were not excommunicated. Tolstoy was above all a fighter against idolaters. It was in this that he was right. But the limitation of Tolstoy's spiritual type is due to the fact that his religion was so exclusively moralistic. The only thing he never had doubts about was the good. Tolstoy's view of life at times creates a stifling

---

9. Much material is given in P. Biryukov's *L.N. Tolstoy—A Life*.

atmosphere and in his followers it becomes really unbearable. From this moralistic conception of religion Tolstoy's dislike of ceremony is derived. But behind Tolstoy's moralism lay hidden a quest for the Kingdom of God as something which ought to be effectively realized here upon earth and now. One must make a start, and at once; but the ideal of the Kingdom of God is, in his own words, infinite. He was fond of expressing himself with deliberate coarseness of speech and with almost nihilistic cynicism. He did not like embellishments of any kind; in this respect he shows a great likeness to Lenin. Sometimes Tolstoy says: Christ teaches that we should not behave foolishly. But at the same time he says: that which is, is irrational; the rational is that which is not; the rationality of the world is evil, the absurdity of the world is good. He strives after wisdom and in this respect wants to be in the company of Confucius, Lao Tse, Buddha, Solomon, Socrates, the Stoics and Schopenhauer, for the last of whom he had a great respect. He reverenced Jesus Christ as the greatest of the sages, but he stood nearer to Buddhism and Stoicism than to Christianity.

Tolstoy's metaphysics, which find their best expression in his book *Concerning Life*, are sharply anti-personalist. Only the rejection of individual consciousness will conquer the fear of death. In personality, in the individual consciousness, which to him is animal consciousness, he sees the greatest hindrance to the realization of the perfect life and to union with God. And to him God is the true life. The true life is love. It is the anti-personalism of Tolstoy which in particular separates him from Christianity and it is the same thing which brings him near to Indian religious thought. He had a great reverence for Nirvana. To Dostoyevsky man stood at the center. To Tolstoy man is only a part of the cosmic life and he ought to be merged in nature, which is divine. His very artistry is cosmic; it is as though cosmic life itself expresses itself in it. Very great importance attaches to Tolstoy's own destiny in life and to his withdrawal in the face of death. The personality of Tolstoy is unusually distinguished and bears the stamp of genius, even in its very inconsistencies. He belonged essentially to this earth; he took upon himself the whole burden of the soil, and yet he was struggling towards a purely spiritual religion. In this lies his fundamental tragic contradiction, and he could not come to close quarters with the Tolstoyan colonies, not on account of his weakness but on account of his genius. With this proud, passionate man, this gentleman of consequence, this real *grand seigneur*, the remembrance of death was present all through life and all the while he desired to humble himself before the Will of God. He wanted to give effect to the law of the Householder of Life, as he liked to put it. He suffered a great deal and his was a religion without joy. It will be said of him that he desired to realize the perfect life in his own strength. But according to his own idea of God, the realization of the perfect life is the presence of God in man. There was something in Christianity which to the end he could not understand, but the blame for this is not his or not only his. But in virtue of his search for right, for the meaning of life, in virtue of his search for the Kingdom of God, in virtue of his penitence, and his anarchistic revolt in the name of religion against the wrong of history and civilization, he belongs to the Russian Idea. He is the Russian antithesis of Hegel and Nietzsche.

Russian religious problems had very little connection with clerical circles, with the theological academies and the hierarchy of the Church. A notable spiritual writer belonging to the eighteenth century was St. Tikhon Zadonsky, whom Dostoyevsky regarded as of such significance. In him there was the breath of a new spirit; Western Christian humanism, Arndt and others, had an influence upon him. In the nineteenth century one can name a few people who came of clerical circles, and who afford some interest, although they remain outside the strictly clerical trends of thought. Such are Bukharev (the Archimandrite Fedor), Archbishop Innocent, Nesmelov and in particular Tareev. Bukharev's life was very dramatic. He was a monk and an archimandrite but passed through a spiritual crisis, and came to have doubts about his monastic vocation and about the traditional forms of *askesis*. He abandoned the monastic life but remained an ardent Orthodox believer. Later on he married, and he attached a special religious significance to marriage. He continued to be a spiritual writer all his life, and in his case novelty broke through the inertia of traditional Orthodoxy; he posed problems of which traditional Orthodoxy had taken no cognizance. He was, of course, subjected to persecution and his position was tragic and painful. Official Orthodoxy did not acknowledge him as one of its own, while the wider circles of the Intelligentsia did not read him or know him. But later on by the beginning of the twentieth century more interest was being taken in him. He wrote in a very archaic style, in phraseology which was not normal to Russian literature, and he does not make very enjoyable reading. His book on the Apocalypse, which he was writing during a large part of his life and to which he attached particular importance, is the weakest of his productions, very out of date and now impossible to read. The only thing of interest is his own attitude towards the Apocalypse. What was new in him was the exceptional interest he showed in the question of the relation of Orthodoxy to contemporary life, and this is the title of one of his books.[10] Bukharev's understanding of Christianity might be called pan-Christism; he desires the attainment and the assimilation of Christ by the individual self, of Christ Himself, not of His commandments. He brings everything back to Christ, to the Person of Christ. In this respect he is sharply distinguished from Tolstoy, who had but a weak feeling for the Person of Christ. The spirit of Christ is not shown by indifference to people, but by the love of man and by self-sacrifice. Bukharev is particularly insistent that the great sacrifice is the sacrifice of Christ for the world and for man, and not the sacrifice of man and the world for God. This stands in opposition to the juridical interpretation of Christianity. For the sake of every man the Son of God became Man; the Lamb was sacrificed before the creation of the world; God created the world and surrendered Himself for immolation. "The world appears to me," says Bukharev, "not only as a realm which is lying in iniquity, but also as the great sphere of the revelation of the grace of the God-Man, Who has taken upon Himself the evil of the world." "We make use of the idea that the Kingdom of Christ is not of this world, only in the interests of our own lack of love for men, our slothful and mean-spirited unconcern for the laboring and heavy-laden of this world." Bukharev asserts not the despotism of God but the self-sacrifice of the Lamb. The spirit finds its strength in freedom and not in the slavery of fear. What is most precious of all to him is "the condescension of Christ's coming down to earth." Nothing essentially human is repudiated except sin. Christ is placed in contrast to sin, not to nature; powers of man are a

---

10. See his books *On the Relation of Orthodoxy to Contemporary Life* and *On Contemporary Needs of Thought and Life, especially of Russian Thought and Life.*

reflection of God the Word. "Will that spiritual transformation take place among us? and when will it take place? in virtue of which we should begin to understand all earthly things in terms of Christ. All the dispositions of the State we should find understandable and to be consciously supported, on the ground that they were the expressions of a beneficent order." The idea of the Kingdom of God ought to be applied to the judgments and affairs of the kingdom of this world. Bukharev says that Christ Himself operates in the Church and does not hand over His authority to the hierarchy. His originality lies in the fact that he does not so much desire the realization of Christian principles in the whole of life as the attainment of Christ Himself by the fullness of life, as a sort of continuation of the Incarnation of Christ in the whole of life. He maintained the idea of "Divine Service outside the Church," as N. Fedorov did later on. The idea of the prolonged Incarnation of God belongs to Russian religious thought in general, and so does that of the prolongation of the creation of the world in the manifestation of Christ. It is a contrast between Russian religious thought and that of the West. The relation between Creator and creature evokes no sort of idea like that of a judicial process. Bukharev was distinguished by his extreme humaneness. The whole of his Christianity was permeated with the spirit of humaneness. It is his desire to give actual effect to this Christian humaneness, but he, like the Slavophils, still held by monarchy, but in a form, of course, which bore no resemblance to absolutism and imperialism. It appears at times as though monarchism was an umbrella under which Russian Christian thought of the nineteenth century found shelter, but there was in it an element of historical romanticism which had not been overcome.

There is one hierarch of the Church whom it is worthwhile to call to mind when speaking of Russian religious philosophy; this was the Archbishop Innocent.[11] The Metropolitan Philaret was a very gifted man, but he is entirely without interest so far as religious philosophy is concerned; in this field he had no interesting ideas of his own. Bishop Theophan Zatvornik wrote nothing but books on the spiritual life and on asceticism in the spirit of the *Dobrotolubie*. Archbishop Innocent is rather to be called a philosopher than a theologian. Like

11. See the collected works of Archbishop Innocent.

the Slavophils and Solovyov he passed through German philosophy
and he thought very freely. Those who were jealous for Orthodoxy
probably regarded many of his ideas as insufficiently Orthodox. He
says the fear of God is a fit thing for Jewish religion, but it is not
becoming in Christianity. And again he says, "If there were not in
man, in the heart of man, a germ of religion, then God Himself would
never teach it to him. Man is free and God cannot compel me to
desire the thing which I do not desire. Religion loves life and freedom." "He who feels his dependence upon God stands high above all
fear and above despotism." God desires to see His other, His friend.
Revelation ought not to degrade a man. The sources of religion are
the enlightenment of the Holy Spirit, the elect people, tradition and
Holy Scripture, and as a fifth source, the pastors. All revelation is an
inward action of God upon man. The existence of God cannot be
proved. God is apprehended both by feeling and by reason, but not
by reason or understanding alone; religion is accepted only by the
heart. "No science, no good action, no pure pleasure is unwanted by
religion." Jesus Christ gave only the plan of the Church; the organization of it He left to time. Members of the hierarchy are not infalli-
ble. Corruption is present within the Church. Like Solovyov
Archbishop Innocent thinks that all knowledge is based upon belief.
Imagination could not have invented Christianity. There are some
ideas of his which did not correspond with prevailing theological
opinions. Thus, he rightly considers that the soul must be pre-exis-
tent, that it was eternally in God, that the world was created not in
time but in eternity. He looked upon the Middle Ages as a time of
superstition and rapine, which was an exaggeration. There are elements of modernism in the religious philosophy of Archbishop Innocent. The breezes of Western liberal thought touched even our
spiritual life which was very fusty. Many professors at the theological academies found themselves firmly under the influence of German Protestant theology and philosophy, and this was a very good
thing. But unfortunately it led to insincerity and hypocrisy, and some
were obliged to give themselves out as Orthodox who were so no
longer. Among the professors at the theological academies there
were even some who had no religious belief at all, but there were also
those who succeeded in combining complete freedom of thought
with a sincere Orthodox faith. One of them was the remarkable

Church historian Bolotov, a man of immense learning. But in Russian theological literature, there was no work whatever done on Biblical criticism and the scientific exegesis of the Scriptures. This finds its explanation in part in the existence of the censorship. Biblical criticism remained a closed field, and but very few critical ideas succeeded in emerging from it. The one notable work in this field, which stands on a level with the highest European science and free philosophical thought was Prince S. Trubetskoy's book *The Doctrine of the Logos*. But there were many valuable works on patristics. The religious censorship raged with fury. Thus, for example, Nesmelov's book *The Dogmatic System of St. Gregory of Nyssa* was mutilated by the religious censorship. They made him change the end of the book in a way unfavorable to the doctrine of St. Gregory of Nyssa on universal salvation.

Nesmelov was the most substantial figure in Russian religious philosophy. He was a product of the theological academies and in general one of the most remarkable of religious thinkers. In his religious and philosophical anthropology he is of greater interest than Solovyov, but of course he had not the universalism of the latter, nor as wide a range of thought, nor was he such a complex personality. Nesmelov, a modest professor of the Kazan theological academy, indicates the possibility of an original and in many respects new Christian philosophy.[12] His chief work was called *The Science of Man*. The second volume of this work is of enormous interest. It bears the title of *The Metaphysics of the Christian Life*. Nesmelov wants to construct a Christian anthropology, but this anthropology turns into an interpretation of Christianity as a whole, as a result of the particular significance which he attaches to man. The riddle of man, that is the problem which he poses very trenchantly. To him man is the one and only riddle in the life of the world. This enigmatic character of man is expressed in the fact that he is on the one hand a natural creature, while on the other hand, he does not find a place in the natural world and passes beyond its frontiers. Among the doctors of the Church St. Gregory of Nyssa undoubtedly had an influence upon Nesmelov. St. Gregory of Nyssa's doctrine of man

12. I think I was the first to draw attention to Nesmelov in my paper entitled *"An Essay in the Philosophical Justification of Christianity,"* printed in *Russian Thought* thirty-five years ago.

204 ❖ THE RUSSIAN IDEA

rises above the general level of patristic anthropology; he desires to raise the dignity and worth of man. To him man was not only a sinful creature but also in actual fact the image and likeness of God and a microcosm.[13] To Nesmelov man is a twofold being. He is a religious psychologist and he wishes to deal not with logical concepts but with the real facts of human existence. He is much more concrete than Solovyov. He puts forward a new anthropological proof of the existence of God. "The idea of God is in actual fact given to man, only it is given to him not from somewhere or other outside him in the quality of thought about God, but as something factually realized in him, by the nature of his personality as a new image of God. If human personality were not ideal in relation to the real condition of its own existence man could not only have no idea of God but also no revelation could ever communicate the idea to him, because he would not be in a condition to understand it.... Human personality is real in its being and ideal in its nature and by the very fact of its ideal reality it directly affirms the objective existence of God as true personality." Nesmelov is particularly insistent upon the fact that human personality is inexplicable in terms of the natural world, that it rises above it and demands a higher order of being than that of the world. It is interesting to note that Nesmelov places a high value upon Feuerbach and wants to turn Feuerbach's thought about the anthropological mystery of religion into a weapon for the defense of Christianity. The mystery of Christianity is above all an anthropological mystery, and Feuerbach's atheism can be understood as a dialectic moment in the Christian apprehension of God. Absract theology with its play of concepts had to arouse the anthropological reaction of Feuerbach. A service which Nesmelov rendered was that he wanted to turn the anthropology of Feuerbach to the use of Christianity. His psychology of the Fall is interesting and original. He sees the essence of the Fall in a superstitious attitude to material things as a source of power and knowledge. "Men have desired that their life and destiny should be decided not by them themselves but by outward material causes." Nesmelov is all the while fighting against pagan idolatrous and magical elements in Christianity. He is the

---

13. Notice that Roman Catholics and especially the Jesuits have interested themselves in St. Gregory of Nyssa. See an interesting book by Hans von Balthasar, *Présence et Pensée. Essai sur la Philosophie Religieuse de Gregoire de Nysse.*

most extreme opponent and keenest critic of the juridical theory of redemption as a bargain with God. In the search for salvation and happiness he sees a pagan, Judaistic, superstitious doctrine of Christianity. In opposition to the concept of salvation he places the concept of the true life. Salvation is admissible only as the attainment of the true and perfect life. He would also like to purge Christianity from the fear of punishment and replace it by the consciousness of imperfection. Like Origen, St. Gregory of Nyssa and many of the Eastern doctors of the Church, he looks for universal salvation. He wages war upon slave-consciousness in Christianity, against the debasement of man in the ascetic and monastic interpretation of Christianity. Nesmelov's Christian philosophy is personalism in a higher degree than Solovyov's Christian philosophy. Russian religious philosophical thought put the problem of religious anthropology in a different way from Catholic and Protestant anthropology, and it goes further than the patristic and scholastic anthropology; there is more humaneness in it. Nesmelov occupies a high place in this religious anthropology.

Tareev, a professor of the Moscow Theological Academy, created an original idea of Christianity, which is a great contrast to traditional Orthodoxy.[14] A hidden Protestantism was discovered in him, but that, of course, is relative terminology. But there is also something characteristically Russian. According to Tareev's opinion the Russian people are humbly believing and meekly loving. In his christology the principal place is occupied by the doctrine of *kenosis*, the humiliation of Christ and His submission to the laws of human existence. The divine Word was united not with human power, but with human abasement. The Divine Sonship of Christ is at the same time the divine sonship of every man. What is individually valuable in the religious sphere can be recognized only immanently, through affinity with the object. True religion is not only sacerdotally-conservative but also prophetically-spiritual, not only elementally of the people but also individually spiritual; it is even preeminently prophetically-spiritual. Tareev is an upholder of spiritual Christianity. Individual spirituality belongs to the Gospel as an absolute. This absoluteness and spirituality cannot be realized in a

14. See Tareev, *Foundations of Christianity*, 4 volumes.

natural historical life which is always relative. The spiritual truth of Christianity cannot be embodied in historical life; it is expressed in it only symbolically. Tareev's conception of Christianity is dualistic and offers a sharp contrast to the monism of the Slavophils and Solovyov. There is much that is true in Tareev; he is a decided foe of theocracy and he is also the foe of all forms of gnosticism. The Kingdom of God is a kingdom of persons who are spiritually free. The fundamental idea of the Gospel is the idea of the divine spiritual life. There are two ways of understanding the Kingdom of God—the eschatological and the theocratic. The eschatological interpretation is the true one. In the Gospel the Church is of secondary importance and the Kingdom of God is everything. There can be no power and authority in the Kingdom of Christ. Tareev desires the liberation of spiritual religion from the symbolism in which it is wrapped. He draws a contrast between the symbolic service of God and the spiritual service of God. Evangelical belief is an absolute form of religion and it is steeped in limitless freedom. Tareev asserts the freedom of an absolute religion of the spirit from historical forms and the freedom of the natural life of history from the pretensions of religious authority. Therefore, for him there can be no Christian people, Christian State or Christian marriage. Eternal life is not life beyond the grave, but the true spiritual life. The truth is not part of human nature but the divine element in man. The insurmountable dualism of Tareev has monism as its reverse side. Nesmelov's religious anthropology is a higher religious anthropology than Tareev's. Tareev's dualism is of great value as a criticism of the falsity of the historical embodiment of Christianity. The dualism rightly draws attention to the mingling of the symbolic with the real, of the relative with the absolute. But it cannot be final. The meaning of the existence of the historical Church with its symbolism remains unexplained. There is no philosophy of history in Tareev, but he is an original religious thinker, acute in the contrasts that he draws, and it is inaccurate to separate him as a whole from German Protestant influences and to place him side by side with Ritschl. Tareev's dualism is in every way the opposite of K. Leontyev's dualism. Tareev was inclined to a certain form of immanentism. Leontyev professed an extreme transcendentalism; his religion is a religion of fear and force, not love and freedom as Tareev's was; it is a religion of transcendent egoism. With all Tareev's decline from traditional Orthodoxy his Christianity is more Russian than Leontyev's Christianity, which, as has already been said, was entirely non-Russian, Byzantine, exclusively monastic and ascetic, and authoritarian. It is necessary to assert the difference between Russian creative religious thought which poses the anthropological and cosmological problem in a new way, and official monastic, ascetic Orthodoxy for which the authority of the *Dobrotolubie* stands higher than the authority of the Gospel. What was new in that creative religious thought, so distinct from deadening scholasticism, was the expectation, not always openly expressed, of a new era in Christianity, an era of the Holy Spirit, and this is above all the Russian Idea. Russian thought is essentially eschatological and this eschatology takes various forms.

9

*The eschatological and prophetic character of Russian thought •
The Russian people are a people of the End • Apocalypsis among
the masses and in the cultured clas • The Reality of Russian Messianism, its distortion by imperialism • The rejection of the bourgeois virtues among the Russian people • The people's searchers
after the Kingdom of God • Distorted eschatology among the revolutionary Intelligentsia • Russian expectation of the revelation
of the Holy Spirit • Eschatology and Messianism in Dostoyevsky
• Outbursts in V. Solovëv and K. Leontyev • The genius of Fedorov's idea about the conditionality of eschatological prophecy •
The problem of birth and death in Solovyov, Rozanov and Fedorov
• Three currents in Orthodoxy*

1

I wrote in my book on Dostoyevsky that the Russians are apoca-
lyptics or nihilists. The Russian is an apocalyptic revolt against
antiquity (Spengler). This means that the Russian people, in accordance with their metaphysical nature and vocation in the world, are
a people of the End. Apocalypse has always played a great part both
among the masses of our people and at the highest cultural level,
among Russian writers and thinkers. In our thought the eschatological problem takes an immeasurably greater place than in the thinking
of the West, and this is connected with the very structure of Russian
consciousness which is but little adapted and little inclined to cling
to finished forms of the intervening culture. Positivist historians may
point out that in order to sketch the character of the Russian people
I make a selection. I select the few, the exceptional, whereas the
many, the usual have been different. But an intellectually attainable
picture of a people can only be sketched by way of selection, which
intuitively penetrates into what is most expressive and significant. I

have laid stress all the while upon the prophetic element in Russian literature and thought of the nineteenth century. I have spoken also of the part which the eschatological mentality has played in the Russian schism and sectarian life. The academic and administrative element has either been very weak among us, almost absent, or it has been horrible and abominable as in the "Domostroi." The books on ethical teaching by Bishop Theophan Zatvornik have also a rather degrading character, but this is connected with the rooted Russian dualism, with the evil powers which organize the earth and earthly life, powers which have abandoned the truth of Christ. The forces of good seek for the city which is to come, the Kingdom of God. The Russian people have many gifts, but the gift of form is comparatively weak among them. A strong elemental force overthrows every kind of form, and it is this which to Western people, and especially to the French, among whom primitive elementalism has almost disappeared, appears to be barbarous. In Western Europe civilization, which has attained great heights, more and more excludes eschatological thought. Roman Catholic thought fears the eschatological interpretation of Christianity since it opens up the possibility of dangerous innovations. The spirit which strives towards the world which is to come, the messianic expectation, is incompatible with the academic socially organized character of Roman Catholicism; it evokes fears that the possibility of the direction of souls might be weakened. In the same way bourgeois society, believing in nothing whatever, fears that eschatological thought might loosen the foundations of that bourgeois society. Leon Bloy, that rarity in France, a writer of the apocalyptic spirit, was hostile to bourgeois society and bourgeois civilization; they had no liking for him and set little value upon him.[1] In years of catastrophe the apocalyptic mentality has made its appearance in European society. Such was the case after the French Revolution and the Napoleonic wars.[2] At that time Jung-Stilling prophesied the near appearance of antichrist. In the most distant past, in the ninth century in the West there was the expectation of antichrist. Nearer to the Russians were the prophecies of Joachim

---

1. See L. Bloy's amazing book, *Exégèse des lieux communs*. It is a terrible exposure of the bourgeois spirit and of bourgeois wisdom.
2. Much interesting material is to be found in A. Wiatte, *Les sources occultes du romantisme*, 2 volumes.

of Floris about a new era of the Holy Spirit, an era of love, friendship and freedom, although all this was too much associated with monarchism. The figure of Saint Francis of Assisi has close affinities with the Russians, Saint Francis who redeemed many of the sins of historical Christianity. But the Christian civilization of the West was organized outside the sphere of eschatological expectation. I must explain what I understand by eschatology. I have in mind not the eschatological section of theological Christianity which one can find in every course on theology, whether Catholic or Protestant; I have in mind the eschatological interpretation of Christianity as a whole, which must be opposed to the historical interpretation of Christianity. The Christian revelation is an eschatological revelation, a revelation of the end of this world, a revelation of the Kingdom of God. The whole of primitive Christianity was eschatological. It expected the second Advent of Christ and the coming of the Kingdom of God.[3] Historical Christianity and the Church of history indicate failure in the sense that the Kingdom of God has not come; they indicate failure, owing to the accommodation of Christian revelation to the kingdom of this world. There remains, therefore, in Christianity the messianic hope, the eschatological expectation, and it is stronger in Russian Christianity than in the Christianity of the West. The Church is not the Kingdom of God; the Church has appeared in history and it has acted in history; it does not mean the transfiguration of the world, the appearance of a new heaven and a new earth. The Kingdom of God is the transfiguration of the world, not only the transfiguration of the individual man, but also the transfiguration of the social and the cosmic; and that is the end of this world, of the world of wrong and ugliness, and it is the principle of a new world, a world of right and beauty. When Dostoyevsky said that beauty would save the world he had in mind the transfiguration of the world and the coming of the Kingdom of God, and this is the eschatological hope; it existed in the great number of representatives of Russian religious thought. But Russian messianic consciousness like Russian eschatology was twofold.

In Russian messianism, which was so characteristic of the Russian people, the pure messianic idea of the Kingdom of God, the

---

3. The eschatological interpretation of Christianity is to be found in Weiss and Loisy.

kingdom of right, was clouded by the imperialistic idea, by the will to power. We have seen this already in relation to the notion of Moscow as the Third Rome. And in Russian communism in which the Russian messianic idea has passed into a non-religious and anti-religious form, there has taken place the same distortion by the will to power, of the Russian quest for the kingdom of right. But the repudiation of the majesty and the glory of this world is very characteristic of the Russians in spite of all the seductive temptations to which they have been exposed; such at least they are in their finest moments. The majesty and glory of the world remain to them a seduction and a sin, and not as among Western peoples, the highest value. It is a characteristic fact that rhetoric is not natural to the Russians; there was absolutely none of it in the Russian Revolution, whereas it played an enormous part in the French Revolution. In that respect, Lenin, with his coarseness, his lack of any sort of embellishment or theatricality, with his simplicity merging into cynicism, was a typical Russian. Around those figures of majesty and glory, Peter the Great and Napoleon, the Russian people created a legend that they were antichrist.

The bourgeois virtues are lacking among the Russians, precisely those virtues which are so highly valued in Western Europe; while the bourgeois vices are to be found among the Russians, just those vices which are recognized as such. The word "bourgeois," both adjective and noun, was a term which expressed disapproval in Russia at the very time when in the West it indicated a social position which commanded respect. Contrary to the opinion of the Slavophils the Russian people are less family-minded than the peoples of the West; they are less shackled to the family and break with it with comparative ease. The authority of parents among the Intelligentsia, the gentry and the middle classes, with the exception perhaps of the merchant class, was weaker than in the West. Generally speaking the feeling for graduation of rank was comparatively weak among the Russians or it existed in the negative form of servility, that is to say as vice and not as a virtue. In the deep manifestations of its spirit the Russian people is the least philistine of all peoples, the least determined by external forces, and the least fettered to limiting forms of life, the least disposed to value the forms of life. Given this fact, the most Russian manner of life, for instance, that of the merchant class, as described by Ostrovsky, became repulsive to a degree which was unknown to the people of Western civilization. But this bourgeois manner of life was not revered as sacred. In the Russian the nihilist readily comes to the surface. "We are all nihilists," says Dostoyevsky. Side by side with servility and selfishness, the rebel, the anarchist comes easily into view; everything flows on into extremes of opposition, and all the while there is a striving after something final. Among the Russians there is always a thirst for another life, another world; there is always discontent with that which is. An eschatological bent is native to the structure of the Russian soul. Pilgrimage is a very characteristic Russian thing, to a degree unknown in the West. A pilgrim walks about the immense Russian land but never settles down or attaches himself to anything. A pilgrim is in search of the truth, in search of the Kingdom of God. He struggles into the distance; the pilgrim has no abiding city upon earth, he moves eagerly towards the city that is to be. The masses of the people have always produced pilgrims from their ranks, but in spirit the most creative representatives of Russian culture were pilgrims; Gogol, Dostoyevsky, Tolstoy, Solovyov and the whole of the revolutionary Intelligentsia were pilgrims. Not only physical but spiritual pilgrimage exists; it is the impossibility of finding rest and peace in anything finite, it is the striving towards infinity. But this too is an eschatological striving which is waiting in the expectation that to everything finite there will come an end, that ultimate truths will be revealed, that in the future there will be something extraordinary. I should call this a messianic sensitiveness which belongs alike to men of the people and men of the highest culture. Russians are Chiliasts in a greater or less degree, consciously or unconsciously. Western people are much more settled, more attached to the perfected forms of their civilization; they assign a greater value to their present experience and pay more attention to the good order of earthly life; they are afraid of infinity as chaos, and in this respect they are like the ancient Greeks. The Russian word for "elemental" is with difficulty translated into foreign languages; it is difficult to give a name when that to which it applies has itself become enfeebled and almost disappeared. But the elemental is the source, the past, the strength of life, while the spirit of eschatology is a turning to the future, to the end of things. In Russia these two threads are united.

2

It was my good fortune to come into personal contact with wandering Russia during approximately ten years of this century, with the Russia which is searching for God and divine truth. I can speak about this phenomenon which is so characteristic of Russia, not from books but as the outcome of personal impressions, and I can say that it is one of the most powerful impressions of my life. In Moscow, in a tavern near the church of Florus and Laurus there used to take place at one time popular religious discussions every Sunday. The tavern was at the time called Yama (The Pit). To these meetings, which acquired a popular tone if only from the admirable Russian which was spoken there, used to come representatives of the most varied sects. There were "immortalists" and Baptists and Tolstoyans and Evangelists of various shades, and *khlysty* who commonly kept themselves hidden and a few individuals who were theosophists from among the people. I used to go to these meetings and take an active part in the discussions. I was struck by the earnestness of the spiritual quest, the grip upon some one idea or other, the search for the truth about life and sometimes by a profoundly thought-out theory. The sectarian always inclined to show a restrictedness of thought, a lack of universalism and a failure to recognize the complex manifoldness of life. But what a reproach to official Orthodoxy those ordinary people seeking after God were. The Orthodox missioner who was present was a pitiable figure and gave the impression of being a police functionary. Those people in search of divine truth wanted Christianity to be given actual effect to in life; they wanted more spirituality in relation to life; they would not acquiesce in its adaptation to the laws of this world. A particular interest was provided by the mystical sect of the immortalists who assert that he who believes in Christ will never die and that people die simply because they believe in death and do not believe in the victory of Christ over death. I talked to the immortalists a great deal; they found me approachable and I am convinced that it is impossible to change their convictions; they were defending a certain part of the truth, not taking it in its fullness but partially. Some of these simple folk had their share of divine wisdom and were in possession of a whole gnostic system which reminded one of Jacob Boehme and other mystics of the gnostic type. The dualist element was usually strong and the difficulty of solving the problem of evil was a torment. But, as is not infrequently the case, the dualism was paradoxically combined with monism. In the government of N., next to an estate where I spent the summer every year, there was a colony founded by a Tolstoyan, a very remarkable man. To this colony there flocked seekers after God and divine Truth from all quarters of Russia. Sometimes they spent a few days in this colony and went on further into the Caucasus. All those who came used to call on me and we had conversations on spiritual matters, which were sometimes of extraordinary interest. There were many *Dobrolyubovsti*. These were followers of Alexander Dobrolyubov, a "decadent" poet who went to the people, adopted the simple life and became a teacher of the spiritual life. Any contact with the *Dobrolyubovsti* was difficult because they had a vow of silence. All these seekers after God had their system of salvation for the world and were heart and soul devoted to it. They all considered this world in which they happened to be living as evil and godless and they were in search of another world, another life. In their attitude to this world, to history, to contemporary civilization, their frame of mind was eschatological. This world is coming to an end and a new world is beginning with them. Their thirst for spiritual things was intense and its presence among the Russian people was highly characteristic. They were Russian pilgrims. I remember a simple peasant, an ordinary laborer, still very young, and the conversation that I had with him. I found it easier to talk on spiritual and mystical subjects with him than with cultured people of the Intelligentsia. He described a mystical experience which he had passed through, which reminded me very much of what Eckhart and Boehme wrote, writers about whom he, of course, had no knowledge whatever. The birth of God out of the darkness had been revealed to him. I cannot imagine Russia and the Russian people without these seekers after divine truth. In Russia there has always been and there always will be spiritual pilgrimage; there has always been striving after a final order of things. Among the Russian revolutionary Intelligentsia, who professed in the majority of cases the most pitiable materialistic ideology, it would seem there could be no eschatology. But they think as they do because they ascribe too exclusive an importance to intellectual ideas which in many cases merely touch the surface of a man. At a deeper level, one which had not found expression in conscious thought, in Russian nihilism and socialism, there did exist an eschatological mentality; there was eschatological tension; there was an orientation towards the end. The talk always turned upon some final perfect state of existence which ought to arrive and take the place of the evil unjust and slavish world. "Shigalev looked as though he was waiting for the destruction of the world, just as though it was coming the day after tomorrow morning, at exactly 25 minutes past 10." Here Dostoyevsky divines something most essential in the Russian revolutionary. Russian revolutionaries, anarchists and socialists were unconscious Chiliasts; they expected the thousand years' reign. The revolutionary myth is a Chiliastic myth. The Russian nature is particularly favorable to the reception of it. It is a Russian idea that individual salvation is impossible, that salvation is corporate, that all are answerable for all. Dostoyevsky's attitude to the Russian revolutionary socialists was complex and two-sided. On the one hand he wrote against it in a way which almost amounted to lampooning, but on the other hand he said that those who revolted against Christianity are all the same Christlike people.

3

It might be thought that there is no eschatology in Tolstoy, that his religious philosophy being monistic and Indian in its affinities takes no cognizance of the problem of the end of the world. But such a judgment would be only superficial. Tolstoy's withdrawal from his family in the face of death is an eschatological withdrawal and full of profound meaning. He was a spiritual pilgrim; throughout his life he had wished to become one but in this he was not successful. But the pilgrim is bent upon the end; he wants to find himself an outlet from history, from civilization, into the natural divine life; and this is a striving towards the end, towards the thousand years' reign. Tolstoy was not an evolutionist who would wish for a gradual movement of history towards the longed-for end, towards the Kingdom of God; he was a maximalist and desired a break with history; he wanted to see the end of history. He does not wish to go on living in history, which rests upon the godless law of the world; he wants to live in nature, and he confuses fallen nature which is subject to the evil laws of the world no less than history is, with nature which is transfigured and illuminated, nature which is divine. But the eschatological striving of Tolstoy is not open to doubt; he was in search of the perfect life. It was precisely because of his search for the perfect life and his exposure of the life which is vile and sinful that the Black Hundred even called for the murder of Tolstoy. This festering sore upon the Russian nation, which dared to call itself the Union of the Russian people, hated everything which is great in the Russians, everything creative, everything which witnessed to the high calling of the Russian people in the world. The extreme Orthodox hate and reject Tolstoy on account of the fact that he was excommunicated by the Holy Synod. The great question is, could the Synod be recognized as an organ of the Church of Christ and was it not rather typical of the kingdom of Caesar. To repudiate Leo Tolstoy means to repudiate the Russian genius. In the last resort it means the repudiation of the Russian vocation in the world. To set a high value upon Tolstoy in the history of the Russian idea certainly does not mean the acceptance of his religious philosophy, which I regard as weak and unacceptable from the point of view of Christian thought. One's appraisal of him must be based rather upon his personality as a whole, upon the path he chose, upon his quest, upon his criticism of the evil reality of history and of the sins of historical Christianity, and upon his ardent craving for the perfect life. Tolstoy put himself in touch with the spiritual movement among the masses of the people, of which I have spoken, and in this respect he is unique among Russian writers. Together with Dostoyevsky who was so entirely unlike him, he represents the Russian genius at its highest. Tolstoy, who all his life was a penitent, said these proud words of himself: "I am the sort of person I am, and what sort of person I am I know and God knows." But it behooves us also to get to know the sort of person he was.

The creative work of Dostoyevsky is eschatological through and through. It is interested only in the ultimate, only in what is orientated to the end. The prophetic element is more powerful in Dostoyevsky than in any other Russian writer. His prophetic art consists in the fact that he revealed the volcanic ground of the spirit; he described the inner revolution of the spirit. He drew attention to inward catastrophe, from which new souls take their beginning. Together with Nietzsche and Kierkegaard he is a revealer of the tragic in the nineteenth century. There is a fourth dimension in man. It is shown by his orientation towards the ultimate, by his getting away from the intervening existence, from the universally obligatory, to which the name of "allness" has been given. It is precisely in Dostoyevsky that the Russian messianic consciousness makes itself most keenly felt, much more so than in the Slavophils. It is to him that the words "The Russian people is a God-bearing people" belong. These words are put into the mouth of Shatov. But in the figure of Shatov there is also revealed the twofold nature of the messianic consciousness, a twofoldness which existed already among the Hebrew people. Shatov began to believe that the Russian people is a God-bearing people when already he no longer believed in God. For him the Russian people became God; he was an idolater. Dostoyevsky exposes this with great power, but the impression remains that there is something of Shatov's point of view in Dostoyevsky himself. In any case he did believe in the great God-bearing mission of the Russian people; he believed that the Russians as a people were bound to say their own word to the world, a new word, at the end of time. The idea of a final perfected condition of mankind, of an earthly paradise, played an immense part in Dostoyevsky, and he displays a complex dialectic which is connected with this idea. It is always that same dialectic of freedom. *The Dream of the Ridiculous Man* and Versilov's dream in *The Youngster* are devoted to this idea. It is one from which Dostoyevsky's thought could never free itself. He understood perfectly well that the messianic consciousness is universal, and he spoke about the universal vocation of the people. Messianism has nothing in common with an exclusive nationalism. Messianism opens out, it does not shut off. For this reason, in his speech on Pushkin, Dostoyevsky says that the Russian is the All-man, that there is in him a sensitiveness which answers the call of all men. The vocation of the Russian people is seen in an eschatological perspective and because of that, this thought of his presents a contrast with that of the idealists of the thirties and forties. Dostoyevsky's eschatological view is expressed in his prediction of the appearance of the Man-God. The figure of Kirillov is in this respect particularly important. In him Nietzsche and the idea of the superman is heralded. He who conquers pain and fear will be God. Time "will be extinct in the mind"; "that man will put an end to the world" to whom the name "Man-God" will be given. The atmosphere of the conversation between Kirillov and Stavrogin is absolutely eschatological. The conversation was about the end of time. Dostoyevsky wrote not about the present but about the future. *The Possessed* was written about the future. It was about our own day rather than about the time in which it was written. Dostoyevsky's prophecy about the Russian Revolution is a penetrating view into the depth of the dialectic of man, of man who reaches out beyond the frontiers of average normal consciousness. It is characteristic that the negative side of the prophecy has shown itself to be more true than the positive. The political predictions were altogether weak. But of greater interest than all else is the fact that the very Christianity of Dostoyevsky was directed towards the future, towards a new crowning epoch in Christianity. Dostoyevsky's prophetic spirit led him beyond the bounds of historical Christianity. The *Starets* Zosima was the prophecy of a new *starchestvo*; he was entirely different from the *Starets* Ambrose of Optina, and the *Startsi* of Optina did not recognize him as one of themselves.[4] Alësha Karamazov was the prophecy of a new type of Christian and he bore little resemblance to the usual Orthodox type. But the *Starets* Zosima and Alësha Karamazov were less successful than Ivan Karamazov and Dmitri Karamazov. This is explained by the difficulty which prophetic art found in creating the characters. But K. Leontyev was right when he said that Dostoyevsky's Orthodoxy was not traditional Orthodoxy, that his was not Byzantine monastic Orthodoxy, but a new Orthodoxy into which humanitarianism entered. But it must by no means be said that it was rose-colored; it was tragic. He thought that rebellion against God might occur in man because of the divine element in him; it might arise from his feeling for righteousness and pity, and from the sense of his own value and dignity. Dostoyevsky preached a Johannine Christianity, the Christianity of a transfigured earth, and above all a religion of resurrection. The traditional *starets* would not have said what the *Starets* Zosima says: "Brothers, do not be afraid of the sin of man, love man even in his sin: love all God's creation, both the whole and every speck of it; love every leaf, love every ray of God, love the ani-

---

4. The figure of St. Tikhon of Zadonsky who was a Christian humanist of the eighteenth century had a very great influence upon Dostoyevsky.

mals, love the plants, love every single thing; we will love every single thing and arrive at the divine mystery in things." "Kiss the earth, and unceasingly, insatiably love. Love all men; seek out the triumph and the ecstasy of it!" In Dostoyevsky there were the beginnings of a new Christian anthropology and cosmology; there was a new orientation to the created world, one which was strange to patristic Orthodoxy. Marks of similarity might be found in the West in Saint Francis of Assisi. It shows a transition already from historical Christianity to eschatological Christianity.

Towards the end of the nineteenth century there developed in Russia an apocalyptic frame of mind which was connected with a sense of the approach of the end of the world and the appearance of antichrist, that is to say it was tinged with pessimism. They were expecting not so much a new Christian era and the coming of the Kingdom of God as the coming of the kingdom of antichrist. It was a profound disillusionment about the ways of history and a disbelief in the continued existence of historical problems. It was a break with the Russian idea. Some are disposed to explain this expectation of the end of the world by a presentiment of the end of the Russian Empire, of the Russian realm, which was considered sacred. The principal writers who expressed this apocalyptic frame of mind were K. Leontyev and Vladimir Solovyov. Leontyev's apocalyptic pessimism had two sources. His philosophy of history and his sociology, which was grounded in biology, taught the inevitable approach of the decrepitude of all societies, states and civilizations. He connected this decrepitude with liberal egalitarian progress. Decrepitude to him meant also ugliness, the ruin of beauty which belonged to the flower of culture of the past. This sociological theory, which laid claim to be scientific, was with him combined with a religious apocalyptic trend of thought. Loss of belief in the possibility that Russia could still produce an original flourishing culture of its own had an immense importance in the growth of this gloomy apocalyptic state of mind. He always thought that everything on earth was precarious and untrustworthy. Leontyev gave too much of a naturalistic turn to his conception of the end of the world; with him spirit is at no time and in no place active; for him there is no freedom. He never believed in the Russian people and certainly did not expect anything original to be produced by the Russian people; that could only come from the Byzantinism which was imposed upon them from above. But the time came when this mistrust of the Russian people became acute and hopeless. He makes this terrible prediction: "Russian society, which even apart from that was egalitarian enough in its customs, is rushing still more swiftly than any other society along the deadly path of universal confusion, and from the womb of our State, which is first of all classless and then Churchless, or at least with but a feeble Church, we shall unexpectedly give birth to antichrist." The Russian people is not capable of anything else. Leontyev foresaw the Russian Revolution and divined many of its characteristics; he foresaw that the Revolution would not be made with gloved hands, that there would be no freedom in it, that freedom will be entirely taken away, and that the age-long instincts of obedience will be required for the Revolution. The Revolution will be socialistic but not liberal and not democratic; the defenders of freedom will be swept away. While predicting a horrible and cruel revolution Leontyev at the same time recognized that the problem of the relations between labor and capital must be solved; he was a reactionary but he acknowledged the hopelessness of reactionary principles, and the inevitability of revolution. He foresaw not only a Russian but also a world revolution. This presentiment of the inevitability of the world revolution takes an apocalyptic form and is represented as the coming of the end of the world. "Antichrist is coming," exclaims Leontyev. In his case the interpretation of the Apocalypse was entirely passive. Man can do nothing at all, he can only save his own soul. This apocalyptic pessimism attracted Leontyev aesthetically; he enjoyed the idea that right would not triumph on earth. He did not share the Russian craving for universal salvation; and any sort of striving after the transfiguration of mankind and of the world was quite lacking in him. The idea of *sobornost* and the idea of theocracy were essentially foreign to him; he accused Dostoyevsky and Tolstoy of taking a rosy view of Christianity and of humanitarianism. The eschatological views of Leontyev are of a negative kind and not in the least characteristic of the Russian eschatological idea. But it cannot be denied that he was an acute and forthright thinker and that he frequently showed perspicacity in his view of history.

Solovyov's cast of mind changed very much towards the end of his life; it becomes gloomily apocalyptic. He writes *Three Conver-*

sations, which contains a veiled controversy with Tolstoy, and to this is added *A Story about Antichrist*. He becomes finally disillusioned about his own theocratic utopia; he no longer believes in humanist progress; he does not believe in his own fundamental idea of God-manhood, or rather his idea of God-manhood becomes terribly restricted. A pessimistic view of the end of history took possession of him and he feels that the end is imminent. In *A Story about Antichrist* Solovyov above all else squares accounts with his own personal past, with his theocratic humanitarian illusions. It represents above all the collapse of his theocratic utopia; he believes no more in the possibility of a Christian State, and his loss of belief is very advantageous, both to himself and to everyone else. But he goes further; he does not believe in historical problems in general. History is coming to an end and super-history is beginning. The union of the Churches which he continued to desire, will take place beyond the frontiers of history. In regard to his theocratic ideas Solovyov belongs to the past; he rejects this outlived past, but he becomes of a pessimistic and apocalyptic frame of mind. A contradiction exists between the theocratic idea and eschatology. Theocracy realized in history excludes the eschatological outlook; it makes the end, as it were, immanent in history itself. The Church, understood as a kingdom, the Christian State, and Christian civilization take the vigor out of the search for the Kingdom of God. In Solovyov's earlier period his sense of evil had been lacking in strength; now the sense of evil becomes predominant. He set himself a very difficult task in drawing the figure of antichrist; he did this not in a theological and philosophical form but in the form of a story. It was possible to carry this through apparently only by adopting a jocular tone, a form in which he was so fond of taking refuge when the matter under discussion was something very secret and intimate. It shocked a great many people, but this jocularity may be understood as shyness. I do not share the opinion of those who place *A Story about Antichrist* almost higher than anything of Solovyov's. It is very interesting, and without it it is impossible to understand the path along which Solovyov moved. But the story belongs to inaccurate and out-of-date interpretations of the Apocalypse, the sort in which too much is assigned to time at the expense of eternity. It is passive, not active and not creative eschatology; there is no expectation of a new era of the Holy

Spirit. In his drawing of the figure of antichrist it is a mistake that he is depicted as a lover of men, as a humanitarian who makes social righteousness an effective reality. This, so to speak, justified the most revolutionary and obscurantist apocalyptic theories. In actual fact if we are talking about antichrist it is truer to say that he will be absolutely inhuman and will be responsible for a stage of extreme dehumanization. Dostoyevsky was more in the right when he describes the spirit of antichrist as above all hostile to freedom and contemptuous of man. *The Legend of the Grand Inquisitor* stands on a higher level than *A Story about Antichrist*. The English Roman Catholic writer Benson wrote a novel which is very reminiscent of *A Story about Antichrist*. All this takes a line which moves in the opposite direction to that of an active creative interpretation of the end of the world. The teaching of Solovyov about God-manhood, if it is finally worked out, ought to result in an active, not a passive, eschatology; it ought to lead to the thought of the creative vocation of man at the end of history, a creative vocation which alone makes possible the coming of the end of the world, and the Second Advent of Christ. The end of history, the end of the world, is a divine-human end; it depends upon man also and upon human activity. In Solovyov it is not clear what is the positive result of the divine-human process in history. In his earlier period he mistakenly regarded it too much as a matter of evolution. Now he truly regards the end of history as catastrophic. But the idea of catastrophe does not mean that there will be no positive result of the creative work of man on behalf of the Kingdom of God. The one positive thing in Solovyov is the union of the Churches in the persons of Pope Peter, *Starets* Ioann and Dr. Paulus. Orthodoxy appears as in the main mystical. Solovyov's eschatology is nevertheless above all an eschatology of judgment. That is one of the aspects of eschatology, but there ought to be another. The attitude of N. Fedorov to the Apocalypse is entirely different.

Fedorov was little known and valued in his lifetime. It was our generation at the beginning of the twentieth century which became specially interested in him.[5] He was just an ordinary librarian at the Rumyantsev Museum and he lived on 17 roubles a month. He was

---

5. One of the first essays on N. Fedorov was my own, "The Religion of the Resurrection" in *Russian Thought*.

an ascetic and slept on a chest, and at the same time was an opponent of the ascetic interpretation of Christianity. Fedorov was a typical Russian, a native genius, an original. He published next to nothing during his lifetime. After his death his friends published his *Philosophy of the Common Task* in two volumes, which they distributed gratis to a small circle of people, since Fedorov considered the sale of books was not to be tolerated. He was a Russian searcher after universal salvation; in him the sense of the responsibility of all for all reached its ultimate and most trenchant expression. Each person is answerable for the whole world and for all men, and every person is bound to strive for the salvation of all men and of everything. Western people are easily reconciled to the idea of the perishing of the many; this is probably due to the part which righteousness plays in Western thought. N. Fedorov was not a writer by nature; the only thing he wrote is this "project" of universal salvation. At times he reminds one of such people as Fourier; there is a combination of fantasy and practical realism in him, of mysticism and rationalism, of daydreaming and sobriety. But here is what some of the most notable of Russians have said about him. Vladimir Solovyov wrote of him: "Your 'project' I accept unreservedly and without any discussion. Since the time of the appearance of Christianity your 'project' is the first forward movement of the human spirit along the way of Christ. For my part I can only regard you as my teacher and spiritual father."[6] Tolstoy said of Fedorov: "I am proud to be living at the same time as such a man." Doystoyevsky too held a very high opinion of Fedorov and wrote of him: "He [Fedorov] aroused my interest more than enough. I am essentially in complete agreement with these ideas, I have accepted them, so to speak, as my own." What then is to be said of Fedorov's "project" and of the extraordinary thoughts which Russians of the greatest genius found so striking? Fedorov was the only man whose life profoundly impressed Tolstoy. At the basis of his whole outlook on life was the compassion Fedorov felt for the sorrows of men; and there was no man on earth who felt such grief at human death and such a craving for their return to life. He regarded sons as to blame for the death of their fathers; he called sons "prodigal sons" because they forgot the tombs of their

6. See V. A. Kozhevnikov's book *Nicolai Fedorovitch Fedorov*, which is very rich in material.

fathers; they were lured away from them by their wives, by capitalism and civilization; civilization was built upon the bones of the fathers. Fedorov's general view of life was as regards its sources akin to slavophilism; there is to be found in him the idealization of the patriarchal structure of society, of the patriarchal monarchy, and hostility to Western culture. But he goes beyond the limits of the Slavophils, and there are entirely revolutionary elements in him, such as the activity of man, collectivism, the determining importance of labor, his ideas of economic management, and the high value he places upon positive science and technical knowledge. During the Soviet period in Russia there have been tendencies which sprang from the followers of Fedorov. And however strange it may be, there was a certain contact between the teaching of Fedorov and communism in spite of his very hostile attitude to Marxism. But Fedorov's hostility to capitalism was still greater than that of the Marxists. His chief idea, his "project" is concerned with the control of the elemental forces of nature, with the subjection of nature to man. With him belief in the might of man goes further than Marxism and it is more audacious. What is absolutely original in him is his combination of the Christian faith with belief in the power of science and technical knowledge; he believed that a return to life for all the dead, an active revivifying and not merely a passive waiting for the resurrection, ought to be not only a Christian task, Divine service outside the Church, but also an undertaking which is positively scientific and technical. There are two sides to the teaching of Fedorov, his interpretation of the Apocalypse—an effort of genius and unique in the history of Christianity—and his "project" of the resuscitation of the dead, in which there is, of course, a fantastic element. But his moral thought is at its height the very loftiest in the history of Christianity.

There was a great breadth of knowledge in Fedorov, but his culture belonged rather to natural science than to philosophy. He had a great dislike of philosophical idealism and so he had of the gnostic tendencies which were to be found in Solovyov. He was a man of a single idea; he was entirely in the grip of one notion, that of victory over death, of the return of the dead to life. And both in his appearance and in the form of his thought there was something austere. The remembrance of death, in connection with which there exists a Christian prayer, was always present with him. He lived and thought in the face of death, not his own death but that of other people, the death of all men who had died throughout history. But the sternness in him, which would not consent to the use of any destructive force, was an outcome of his optimistic belief in the possibility of the final conquest of death, in the possibility not only of resurrection but also of resuscitation, that is to say, of an active part taken by man in the task of the universal renewal of life. Fedorov is to be credited with a completely original exposition of the apocalyptic prophecies, one which may be called active as distinct from the passive interpretation which is usual. He proposed to interpret the apocalyptic prophecy as dependent on certain conditions, a line which had never been taken hitherto; and in fact it is impossible to understand the end of the world with which the prophecies of the Apocalypse are concerned as a fated destiny. That would be to contradict the Christian idea of freedom. The fated end described in the Apocalypse comes as the result of following the path of evil. If the commandments of Christ are not fulfilled by men, such and such a thing will be inevitable, but if Christian mankind is united for the common fraternal task of the conquest of death and the achievement of universal resurrection, it can escape the fatal end of the world, the appearance of antichrist, the Last Judgment and hell. Mankind can in that case pass over directly into eternal life. The Apocalypse is a threat to mankind, steeped as it is in evil, and it faces man with an active problem; a merely passive waiting for the terrible end is unworthy of man. Fedorov's eschatology is sharply distinguished from that of Solovyov and Leontyev, and the right is on his side, the future belongs to him. He is a decided enemy of the traditional understanding of immortality and resurrection. "The Last Judgment is only a threat to mankind in its infancy. The covenant of Christianity consists in the union of the heavenly and the earthly, of the divine and the human; while the universal resuscitation is an immanent resuscitation achieved by the whole heart, by every thought, every act, that is, by all the powers and capacities of all the sons of men; and it is the fulfillment of the law of Christ, the Son of God and at the same time the Son of Man." Resuscitation stands in opposition to progress, which comes to terms with the death of every generation. Resuscitation is a reversal of time, it is an activity of man in relation to the past and not to the future only. Resuscitation

is also opposed to civilization and culture which flourish in cemeteries and are founded upon forgetfulness of the death of our fathers.
Fedorov regarded capitalist civilization as a great evil; he is an
enemy of individualism and a supporter of religious and social collectivism, of the brotherhood of man. The common Christian task
ought to begin in Russia as the country which is least corrupted by
godless civilization. Fedorov professed Russian messianism. But in
what did this mysterious "project" consist, which struck men so,
and aroused the enthusiasm of some and the mockery of others? It
is nothing more nor less than a "project" to escape the Last Judgment. The victory over death, the universal resuscitating is not just
an act of God in regard to which man remains passive; it is the work
of God-manhood, that is, it is also the work of collective human
activity. It must be admitted that in Fedorov's "project" the perspicacity of genius in his exposition of the apocalyptic prophecies, and
the extraordinary loftiness of moral thought in the conception of the
common responsibility of all for all, are combined with utopian fantasy. The author of the "project" believes that science and technical
knowledge can become capable of reanimating the dead and that
man can finally master the elemental forces of nature, that he can
control nature and subordinate it to himself. And, of course, he
brings this all the while into union with the resuscitating power of
religion, with belief in the Resurrection of Christ. But nevertheless
he rationalizes the mystery of death. He has an inadequate sense of
the significance of the Cross; to him Christianity was simply a religion of resurrection. He had no feeling at all for the irrationality of
evil. In Fedorov's teaching there is a very great deal which ought to
be retained, as entering into the Russian Idea. I do not know a more
characteristically Russian thinker. He is one who must appear
strange to the West. He desires the brotherhood of man not only in
space but also in time, and he believes in the possibility of changing
the past. But the materialist methods of resuscitation which he proposes cannot be retained. The problem of the relation of the spirit to
the natural world he did not think out to its final end.

Messianism is a characteristic not only of the Russians but also
of the Poles. Poland's destiny of suffering has made it more acute in
its own case. It is interesting to place Russian messianic and eschatological ideas side by side with those of the greatest philosopher of

Polish messianism, Cieszkowski, who has not hitherto been sufficiently appreciated. His principal writing, the four-volume work
Notre Père is constructed in the form of an exposition of The Lord's
Prayer.[7] It is an original exposition of Christianity as a whole, but in
particular it is a Christian philosophy of history. Like the Slavophils
and Vladimir Solovyov, Cieszkowski passed through German idealism and came under the influence of Hegel, but his thought
remained independent and creative. He wants to remain a Roman
Catholic; he does not break with the Roman Catholic Church, but he
passes over the frontiers of historical Catholicism. He gives expression to a religion of the Holy Spirit more definitely than the Russian
thinkers. He is bent upon what he calls *Révélation de la Révélation.*
The full revelation of God is a revelation of the Holy Spirit. God
even is the Holy Spirit; that is His real Name. Spirit is the highest
entity; everything is Spirit and through Spirit. It is only in the third
revelation of the Spirit, complete and synthetic, that the Holy Trinity
is disclosed. The dogma of the Trinity could not yet be revealed in
Holy Scripture. Only silence on the subject of the Holy Spirit was in
his view orthodox; everything else was to be regarded as heretical,
the Persons of the Holy Trinity, their names, their natures and the
moments of their revelation. Those who are very orthodox will
probably find in Cieszkowski a tendency to Sabellianism. In Cieszkowski's opinion there was a partial truth in the heresies, but not the
full truth; he predicted the coming of the new era of the Holy Spirit.
It is only the era of the Paraclete which will provide a full revelation.
Following German idealism he affirmed, as did Solovyov, spiritual
progress, spiritual development. Mankind could not yet take the
Holy Spirit to itself; it was not yet sufficiently mature. But the time
of the special activity of the Holy Spirit is drawing near; the spiritual
maturity of man will come when he has it within his power to take
the revelation of the Holy Spirit into himself and to profess a religion of the Spirit. The operation of the Spirit spreads through all
mankind. The Spirit will embrace both soul and body. Into the era
of the Spirit social and cultural elements of human progress will also
enter. Cieszkowski lays stress upon the social spirit of Slavdom; he
looks for the revelation of the word in social act. In this he displays

7. Published in French, Cte A. Cieszkowski, *Notre Père*, 4 volumes.

a similarity to Russian thought. He preaches *Communauté de St. Esprit*. Mankind will live in the name of the Paraclete; the Our Father is a prophetic prayer. The Church is not yet the Kingdom of God. Man takes an active part in the creation of the new world. A very interesting idea of Cieszkowski's is that the world acts upon God. The establishment of social harmony among men which will be comfortable to the era of the Holy Spirit will lead to absolute harmony within the Godhead. The suffering of God is a mark of His holiness. Cieszkowski had been a follower of Hegel and, therefore, recognizes dialectic development. The advent of the new era of the Holy Spirit which will embrace the whole social life of mankind, he views in the aspect of development rather than in the aspect of catastrophe. There cannot be a new religion but there can be a creative development of the eternal religion. The religion of the Holy Spirit is also the eternal Christian religion. To Cieszkowski belief is knowledge which is accepted by feeling. He has a great many interesting philosophical ideas which I cannot stay to dwell upon here. Cieszkowski's teaching is not so much about the end of the world as about the end of an age, about the coming of a new aeon. Time is to him part of eternity. Cieszkowski was, of course, a great optimist; he was filled with hope of the speedy coming of the new aeon, although there was little that was consoling in his environment. This optimism was proper to the period in which he lived. We cannot be so optimistic, but this does not prevent us from appreciating the importance of his fundamental ideas. Much of his thought is similar to Russian thought, to the Christian hopes of the Russians. Cieszkowski was entirely unknown among us; no one ever quotes or refers to him, just as he also knew nothing of Russian thought. The similarity is apparently one which is due to the nature of Slav thought in general. In certain respects I am prepared to place the thought of Cieszkowski higher than Solovyov's, although the personality of the latter was more complex and richer, and it contained more inconsistencies. The similarity lay in the opinion they shared that there must come a new era in Christianity, which will be the eve of a new outpouring of the Holy Spirit, and that man will take an active, not merely a passive part in this. The apocalyptic cast of mind awaits the fulfillment of revelation. The Church of the New Testament is only a symbolical figure of the eternal Church.

*

Three notable Russian thinkers, Vladimir Solovyov, N. Fedorov and V. Rozanov, gave expression to some very profound ideas on the subject of death and on the relation which exists between death and birth. Their thoughts are varied and even contradictory. But what interested all of them more than anything else was the victory of eternal life over death. Solovyov postulates a contradiction between the view which dwells upon the prospect of eternal life for the individual person, and that which envisages the family in which the birth of a new life leads on to the death of the preceding generations. The meaning of love lies in victory over death and the attainment of eternal individual life. Fedorov too sees the connection between birth and death; sons are born, and forget the death of their fathers. But victory over death points to a demand for the resuscitation of the fathers, a transmutation of the energy which gives birth into the energy which resuscitates. In contrast to Solovyov, Fedorov is not a philosopher of *Eros*. In Rozanov we have a third point of view. I shall speak about this extraordinary writer in the following chapter. At the moment I will speak only of his solution of the question of death and birth. All Rozanov's creativeness is an apotheosis of birth-giving life. In the generative process which continually gives birth to new life after new life, Solovyov and Fedorov see an element of death and the poisoning pollution of sin. Rozanov, on the contrary, wants to deify generative sex. Birth is even a triumph over death; it is the eternal blooming of life. Sex is holy because it is the source of life; it is the contrary of death. Such a solution of the question is connected with a deficient feeling for and awareness of personality. The birth of an innumerable quantity of new generations cannot reconcile us to the death of one single man. In any case Russian thought had reflected profoundly upon the theme of death, of victory over death, and upon birth and the metaphysics of sex. All three thinkers grasped the fact that the subject of death and birth is one which concerns the metaphysical depth of sex. In Vladimir Solovyov the energy of sex in eros-love ceases to be generative and leads to personal immortality; he is a platonist. In Fedorov the energy of sex is turned into the energy which revivifies dead fathers. In Rozanov, who returns to Judaism and paganism, the energy of sex is sanctified as being that which generates a new life, and in so doing conquers death. It is a very notable fact that in Russian religion it is the Resurrection which is of chief importance. This is an essential difference from the religion of the West in which the Resurrection recedes to a second place. For Roman Catholic and Protestant thought the problem of sex was exclusively a social and moral problem; it was not a metaphysical and cosmic problem as it was to Russian thought. This is explained by the fact that the West has been too exclusively occupied with civilization, too much socialized; its Christianity was too academic. The mystery of the Resurrection itself has not been a cosmic mystery, but a dogma which has lost its living significance. The mystery of cosmic life has been concealed by the organized forms of social life. There was, of course, Jacob Boehme, who did not fall a prey to this spirit of social organization. It is indisputable that, taken as a whole, Western thought is of great importance to the solution of the problem of religious anthropology and religious cosmology. But Roman Catholic and Protestant thought in their official form are very little concerned with these problems in their full depth, as distinct from questions of ecclesiastical organization and academic guidance. In Orthodoxy there was no organically absorbed Greco-Roman humanism; ascetic self-denial was predominant, but for precisely that reason upon the basis of Orthodoxy something new about man and the cosmos could more easily be revealed. Orthodoxy also did not adopt that active attitude towards history which Western Christianity displayed, but it may be just for that reason that it will show a distinctive attitude of its own towards the end of history. In Russian Orthodox religion there has always been hidden eschatological expectation.

*

There are three currents of thought which may be distinguished in Russian Orthodoxy and they may be found intertwined: the traditional monastic ascetic element which is connected with the *Dobrotolubie*; the cosmocentric current which perceives the divine energies in the created world, which devotes its attention to the transfiguration of the world, and with which sociology is connected; and the anthropocentric, historiosophic, eschatological current which is concerned with the activity of man in nature and society. The first of these currents of thought presents no creative problems at all, and in the past it has found its support not so much in Greek patristics as in Syrian ascetic literature. The second and third present problems concerned with the cosmos and with man. But behind all these distinguishable currents lies hidden the common Russian Orthodox religious sense which has worked out the type of Russian man, with his discontent with this world, with his gentleness of soul, with his dislike of the might of this world and with his struggle towards the other world, towards the end, towards the Kingdom of God. The soul of the Russian people has been nourished not so much upon sermons and doctrinal teaching as upon liturgical worship and the tradition of Christian kindliness which has penetrated into the very depth of the soul's structure. The Russians have thought that Russia is a country which is absolutely special and peculiar, with its own special vocation. But the principal thing was not Russia itself but that which Russia brings to the world, above all the brotherhood of man and freedom of the spirit. It is here that we come upon the most difficult question of all. The Russians are not striving for a kingdom which is of this world; they are not moved by the will to power and might. In their spiritual structure the Russians are not an imperialist people; they do not like the State. In this the Slavophils were right. But at the same time they are a colonizing people; they have a gift for colonization, and they have created the greatest State in the world. What does this mean? How is it to be understood? Enough has already been said about the dualistic structure of Russian history. The fact that Russia is so enormous is not only the good fortune and the blessing of the Russian people in history, but it is also the source of the tragic element in the fate of the Russian people. It was necessary to accept responsibility for the immensity of the Russian land and to bear the burden of it. The elemental immensity of the Russian land protected the Russian, but he himself was obliged to protect and organize the Russian land. The unhealthy hypertrophy of the State was accepted and it crushed the people and often tortured them. A substitution took place within the consciousness of the Russian idea, and of the Russian vocation. Both Moscow the Third Rome and Moscow the Third International were connected with the Russian messianic idea; they represented a distorted form of it. Never in history, I think, has there been a people which has combined such opposites in its history. Imperialism was always a distortion of the

232 ✦ THE RUSSIAN IDEA

Russian idea and of the Russian vocation. But it was not by chance that Russia was so enormous. This immensity was providential and it is connected with the idea and the calling of the Russian people. The immensity of Russia is a metaphysical property of it, and does not only belong to its empirical history. The great Russian spiritual culture can only belong to an enormous country and an immense people. The great Russian literature could arise only among a very numerous people who live in an immense country. Russian literature and Russian thought were permeated by hatred of the Empire and they exposed the evil of it. But at the same time they presupposed an Empire, they presupposed the immensity of Russia. This contradiction is inherent in the very spiritual structure of Russia and the Russian people. The immensity of Russia might have been other than it was; it might not have been an Empire with all its evil aspects; it might have been a people's realm. But Russia took shape in grievous historical circumstances; the Russian land was surrounded by enemies; it was made use of by the evil forces of history.

The Russian Idea was recognized in various forms in the nineteenth century, but found itself in profound conflict with Russian history as it was built up by the forces which held sway in it. In this lies the tragic element in the historical destiny of Russia and also the complexity of our subject.

10

Summing-up of Russian Nineteenth-Century Thought • The cultural Renaissance at the beginning of the century • A change in the ideas of the Intelligentsia • A change in aesthetic consciousness • Interest in philosophy • Critical Marxism and Idealism • The break with traditional materialism and positivism • The attention to types of spiritual culture • The outbreak of religious unrest in literature and culture • Merezhkovsky • Russian symbolism and the flowering of poetry • Ivanov, Byelii, Blok • Interest in the mystical and the occult • The religious philosophical gatherings in Petersburg • The subject of the relation of Christianity to the flesh, to culture and to the life of the community • The significance of Rozanov • The expectation of an era of the Holy Spirit • A section of the Marxists go over to Christianity • Flowering of Russian philosophy and the creation of an original religious philosophy • The subject of Sophiology • The subject of man and creativity • The eschatological theme • "Problems of Life" • The people's quests for the Kingdom of God • The breach between the upper cultured stratum and the revolutionary social movement • The meaning of militant atheism • Communism as a distortion of the Russian Messianic idea • The Russian Idea

1

ONLY at the beginning of the twentieth century were the results of Russian thought during the nineteenth century appraised and a summing-up of them reached. But the problem of the thought of the beginning of the twentieth century itself is very complicated, for new currents entered into it, new elements. At the beginning of the century there was in Russia a real cultural renaissance. Only those who themselves lived through that time know what a creative inspiration was experienced among us and how the breath of the spirit took possession of Russian souls. Russia lived through a flowering of poetry and philosophy. Intense religious enquiry formed part of its experience, a mystical and occult frame of mind. As everywhere and always, with the genuine exaltation there went the following of a fashion and there were not a few insincere babblers. There was a cultural renaissance among us but it would not be true to say that there was a religious renaissance. There was not the necessary strength and concentration of will for a religious renaissance. There was too much cultural refinement; there were elements of decadence in the mentality of the cultured class, and this highest cultured class was too much shut up in itself. It is an amazing fact that it was only at the beginning of the twentieth century that criticism really assessed the value of the great Russian literature of the nineteenth century, and above all of Dostoyevsky and Tolstoy. The spiritual problems posed by Russian literature at its highest achievement were made its very own, it was permeated by them; and at the same time a great change was taking place, one which was not always to the good in comparison with the literature of the nineteenth century. The extraordinary sense of right, the extraordinary simplicity of Russian literature disappeared. People of a double mind made their appearance. Such, above all, was Merezhkovsky, who did undoubted service in forming an estimate of Dostoyevsky and Tolstoy, men whom the traditional journalistic criticism was not capable of appraising. But nevertheless one does not find in Merezhkovsky that same extraordinary love of right. In him everything is two-sided; he plays with combinations of words and takes them for reality. The same must be said of Vyacheslav Ivanov, and of them all. But one remarkable fact emerged—a change in the ideas of the Intelligentsia; the traditional world outlook of the left Intelligentsia was shaken. Vladimir Solovyov conquered Chernishevsky. Already in the second half of the eighties and in the nineties the way was being prepared for this. The influence of the philosophy of Schopenhauer and of Tolstoy was felt. An interest began to be taken in philosophy, and a cultural philosophical group was formed. The paper *Questions in Philosophy and Psychology* played its part in this under the editorship of N. Grote. Interesting philosophers of a metaphysical turn of mind, such as Prince S. Trubetskoy and L. Lopatin, made their appearance. Aesthetic consciousness underwent a change and greater importance began to be attached to art. The paper *The*

Northern Messenger, under its editor A. Volynsky, was one of the symptoms of this change. It was at that time also that Merezhkovsky, N. Minsky and K. Balmont began to be published. Later on papers of a cultural and renaissance line of thought, such as *The World of Art, Scales, The New Way, Problems of Life*, made their appearance. There was no integrated form of culture in the imperial Russia of Peter. A highly composite and much-graduated state of affairs took shape; Russians lived, as it were, in different centuries. At the beginning of the century a hard and often bitter conflict was waged by the men of the Renaissance against the narrowness of mind of the traditional Intelligentsia, a conflict waged in the name of freedom for creativeness and in the name of the spirit. Russia's spiritual cultural Renaissance met with very great hostility from the left Intelligentsia who regarded it as treachery to the traditions of the liberation movement, as a betrayal of the people and as reaction. This was unjust if only because many of the representatives of the cultural Renaissance were supporters of the liberation movement and took part in it. There was talk of the liberation of spiritual culture from the oppressive yoke of social utilitarianism. But an alteration of the basis of a world outlook and a new orientation of thought do not take place easily. The struggle was carried on in various fields and along several different lines. Our Renaissance had a number of sources and turned its attention to various sides of culture. But on all sides it was necessary to achieve victory over materialism, positivism, utilitarianism, from which the left-minded Intelligentsia had not been able to free itself. There was at the same time a return to the creative heights of the spiritual culture of the nineteenth century. But the disastrous thing was that the men of the Renaissance, in the heat of battle and from a natural reaction against the outworn world view, often attached insufficient value to that social truth and right which was to be found in the left Intelligentsia and which retained its power. There was always the same dualism; the same cleavage of spirit continued to be characteristic of Russia. This was to have fateful consequences for the character of the Russian Revolution, for its fighting spirit. In our Renaissance the aesthetic element which had earlier been suppressed showed itself stronger than the ethical element which had become much enfeebled. But this meant an enfeeblement of the will, it meant passivity, and this was bound to have a particularly unfavorable effect on the attempts at religious regeneration. There were many gifts bestowed upon the Russians of the beginning of the century. It was a period of extraordinary talent; it was brilliant; it was an era of great hopes which were not realized. The Renaissance upheld the banner not only of the Spirit but also of Dionysus, and in it a Christian renaissance was mingled with a pagan renaissance.

The acute spiritual crisis connected with the Russian Renaissance had a number of sources. Among them, the one which had its origin in Marxism was of the greatest significance for the Intelligentsia. The section of the Marxists who had reached a higher degree of culture went over to idealism, and in the end to Christianity, and to a considerable extent it was from this movement that Russian religious philosophy issued. This fact may seem strange and it requires some explanation. Marxism in Russia involved a crisis among the left Intelligentsia and led to a breach with a certain number of its traditions. It arose among us in the second half of the eighties as a result of the failure of Russian *narodnik* socialism, which was unable to find any support among the peasantry, and of the shock to the party of "The Peoples' Will" caused by the murder of Alexander II. The old forms of the revolutionary socialist movement seemed to be outlived and it was necessary to seek new forms. A group known as "The Emancipation of Labor" took its rise abroad and laid the foundations of Russian Marxism. Among the members of this group were G. V. Plekhanov, B. Axelrod, V. Zasulich. The Marxists gave a different value to the *narodnik* idea that Russia can and should avoid capitalist development. They were in favor of the development of capitalism in Russia, not however on the ground that capitalism is in itself a good thing, but because the development of capitalism would promote the development of the working class, and that would be the one and only revolutionary class in Russia. In carrying out the work of liberation, the working class was more to be relied upon than the peasantry which, according to Marx, is a reactionary class. A strong Marxist movement developed in Russia in the second half of the nineties and it secured its hold upon ever wider circles of the Intelligentsia. At the same time a workers' movement also came into being. Within a large number of groups a conflict was going on between the Marxists and the *narodniks*, and victory inclined more and more to the side of the Marxists; Marxist periodicals made their appearance. The spiritual character of the Intelligentsia underwent a change, the Marxist type was harsher than the *narodnik*. Marxism was originally a Westernizing movement as compared with the old *Narodnichestvo*. Among certain sections of the Marxists in the second half of the nineties, the level of culture was very much raised, and especially of philosophical culture. More complex cultural questions aroused their interest, and they were dissociating themselves from nihilism. To the old *narodnik* Intelligentsia revolution was a religion; their attitude towards revolution was totalitarian. The whole of their intellectual and cultural life was under the sway of the ideal of the liberation of the people and the overthrow of the autocratic monarchy. At the end of the nineteenth century a process of differentiation began, a freeing of the separate spheres of culture from subjection to the revolutionary center. The philosophy of art and the life of the spirit in general were proclaimed to be free and independent spheres. But we shall see that in the last resort Russian totalitarianism was to have its revenge. There was left over from Marxism the wide outlook upon the philosophy of history which was indeed its principal attraction. In any case upon the soil of Marxism—of a critical Marxism, it is true, and not the orthodox Marxism—an intellectual and spiritual movement became possible, a thing which had almost come to an end among the "Old Believers" in the *narodnik* Intelligentsia. A certain number of Marxists, while remaining true to Marxism in the social sphere, had not from the very beginning consented to be materialists in philosophy. They were disciples of Kant or of Fichte, that is to say they were idealists. This opened up new possibilities. Marxists of the more orthodox type, holding on to their materialism, adopted a very suspicious attitude towards philosophical freedom of thought, and predicted a falling away from Marxism. A distinction was accepted between those who adopted Marxism in its entirety and those who accepted it only partially. Within this second group there took place also a transition from Marxism to idealism. This idealistic stage did not continue very long and a movement towards religion was soon to be revealed, towards Christianity, towards Orthodoxy. To the generation of Marxists who came over to idealism belonged S. Bulgakov, who in time became a priest, the present writer, P. Struve and S. Frank , who was the most politically minded of this group. They all turned their attention to the problems of spiritual culture which in the preceding generations had been stifled by the left Intelligentsia. As one who took part in the movement I can bear witness to the fact that this process was carried forward with great enthusiasm. A whole world of new possibilities was revealed: the intellectual and spiritual thirst was prodigious. The wind of the Spirit was blowing; there was a feeling that a new era was beginning; there was a movement towards something new, something which had not been before; but there was also a return to the traditions of Russian thought of the nineteenth century, to the religious content of Russian literature, to Khomyakov and Dostoyevsky and to Vladimir Solovyov. We found ourselves in a period of extraordinarily gifted creativity. Nietzsche was a very real experience although he did not mean the same to all of us. The influence of Nietzsche was fundamental in the Russian Renaissance at the beginning of this century. But Nietzsche, as a subject of thought, came to the Russians as preeminently a religious theme. Ibsen also had his importance for us. But side by side with this, deriving from the first half of the nineteenth century, was German idealism. Kant, Hegel and Schelling were of enormous importance. It was thus that one of the currents of thought which created the Russian Renaissance took shape.

2

The second source of the Renaissance was predominantly literary. At the beginning of the century, Merezhkovsky played a principal part in awakening religious interest and disquietude in literature and culture. He was a man of letters to the very marrow and lived in literature, in the collecting and distributing of words, more than in life. He had great literary talent; he was an extraordinarily prolific writer but he was not a notable artist; his novels make interesting reading and give evidence of much erudition, but they are immensely lacking in artistry; they are a vehicle for his ideological schemes, and it was said of them that they were a mixture of ideology and archeology. His principal novels, *Julian the Apostate, Leonardo da Vinci, Peter the Great,* are devoted to the subject of Christ and antichrist. Merezhkovsky arrived at Christianity, but not in its traditional form

and not the Christianity of the Church, but at a new religious experience. His principal book, the one which makes him of importance
in the history of Russian thought, is *L. Tolstoy and Dostoyevsky*. In
them adequate attention was for the first time devoted to the religious problems associated with the two greatest of Russian
geniuses. It is a brilliant book but it is marred by Merezhkovsky's
usual deficiencies, rhetoric, ideological schematization, muddled
ambiguity, with more attention to words than to reality. It is moral
feeling which is lacking in Merezhkovsky, that moral feeling which
was so strong in the writers and thinkers of the nineteenth century.
He is bent upon a synthesis of Christianity and paganism and mistakenly identifies it with a synthesis of spirit and flesh. Sometimes
he leaves one with the impression that he wants to synthesize Christ
and antichrist. Christ and antichrist is his basic theme. The possibility of a new revelation within Christianity is in his view connected
with the rehabilitation of the flesh and of sex. Merezhkovsky is a
symbolist and the "flesh" seems to be in his view a symbol of all
culture and of the spirit of community. It is impossible to understand him apart from the influence which V. Rozanov had upon
him. Rozanov was a writer of genius; his writing was a real magic
of words, and he loses a great deal if his ideas are expounded apart
from their literary form; he never once reveals himself in all his stature. His sources were conservative, Slavophil and Orthodox, but it
is not in that that his interest lies. His writings achieve a gripping
interest when he begins to retreat from Christianity, when he
becomes a keen critic of Christianity. He becomes a man of a single
idea and says of himself: "Even if I myself am devoid of gifts, still
my subject is full of talent." In actual fact he was very talented, but
his talent spreads itself upon a talented theme. The theme is sex
taken as a religious thing. Rozanov divides religion into religion of
birth and religion of death. Judaism and for the most part pagan religions are religions of birth, the apotheosis of life, whereas Christianity is a religion of death. The shadow of Golgotha has lain upon
the world and poisoned the joy of life. Jesus has bewitched the
world and in the sweetness of Jesus the world has turned bitter.
Birth is linked with sex; sex is the source of life. If a blessing is to
be bestowed upon life and birth and they are regarded as holy, then
sex must be blessed and sanctified also. In this matter Christianity

has been ambiguous. It has not made up its mind to condemn life and birth; it even recognizes the justification of marriage, the union of man and woman and the birth of children, but sex it abominates and it shuts its eyes to it. Rozanov considers this hypocrisy and challenges Christians to give a decisive answer. In the last resort he arrives at the idea that Christianity is the enemy of life and that it is a religion of death. He declines to see that the last word of Christianity is not the Crucifixion but the Resurrection. In his opinion Christianity is not a religion of the Resurrection, but exclusively the religion of Golgotha. The question of sex has never been posed with such forthrightness and such religious depth. Rozanov's solution was untrue. It means either the Judaising of Christianity afresh or a return to paganism. His desire is not so much for the transfiguration of sex, the flesh and the world, as for the consecration of them in the form in which they now are; but it was right to pose the question and it was a great service that Rozanov rendered. A great many of his admirers were members of the clergy who did not understand him very well and thought that the matter in question was the reform of the family. The question of the relation of Christianity to sex was turned into a question of the relation of Christianity to the world in general and to mankind: a problem of religious cosmology and anthropology was stated.

In the year 1903 religious philosophical gatherings were organized in Petersburg at which members of the Russian Intelligentsia of the highest cultured class met representatives of the Orthodox clergy. The meetings were presided over by the rector of the Petersburg Ecclesiastical Academy, Bishop Sergii, the Patriarch of Moscow. Among the hierarchs of the Church an active part was taken also by Bishop Antony, later on an adherent of the living Church, and, representing lay culture, D. Merezhkovsky, V. Rozanov, M. Minsky, A. Kartashov, who had been expelled from the Ecclesiastical Academy and was later on Minister of Cults in the Temporary Government, the apocalyptic Chiliast V. Tarnovtsev, at that time an official in the special commissions under the procurator of the Holy Synod. The meetings were very lively and interesting, and they were novel in that they gathered together different sorts of people of absolutely separate worlds, and they were novel also in regard to the subjects discussed. The principal part was played by D. Merezhkovsky, but the subjects of discussion were connected with Rozanov. His influence was shown in the fact that the subject of sex predominated; there was also the subject of the relation of Christianity to the world and to life. The representatives of culture plied the hierarchy of the Church with questions about whether Christianity is an ascetic religion, a religion hostile to the world and to life, or can it bestow its blessing upon the world and life? Thus the subject of the relation of the Church to culture and to social life became the focal point of discussion. Everything that the representatives of secular culture said presupposed the possibility of a new Christian thought, of a new era in Christianity; this was difficult for the prelates of the Church to admit, difficult even for the most enlightened of them. To the representatives of the clergy Christianity had long become a matter of everyday prose, whereas those who were in search of a new Christianity wanted it to be poetry. These religious and philosophical gatherings were interesting principally for the questions that were asked rather than for the answers that were given. It was true that on the ground of historical Christianity it was difficult, indeed almost impossible, to solve the problems concerned with marriage, with a just order of society, with cultural creativity and with art. A number of those who took part in the gatherings expressed this in the form of the expectation of a new revelation of right in regard to land. Merezhkovsky connected it with the problem of the flesh, and in this connection he made use of the word "flesh" in a philosophically inaccurate sense. In the life of the Church of history there was certainly too much of the flesh, too much fleshliness and a lack of spirituality. Rozanov spurned the figure of Christ in whom he saw an enemy of life and of birth, but he liked the way of life of the Orthodox Church; in that he saw more of the flesh. The new Christianity will be not more fleshly but more spiritual. Spirituality certainly does not stand in opposition to the flesh, to the body, but to the realm of necessity, to the enslavement of man to nature and the social order. At these religious philosophical gatherings the Russian expectation of an era of the Holy Spirit was rejected. This expectation took a variety of forms in Russia, sometimes very imperfectly expressed, but it was always characteristic of Russia. This had a specially active character in Fedorov. His thought was very social; and this cannot be said of all those who took part in the religious philosophical gatherings; they were above all men of letters and they had had neither a theoretical nor a practical training for the solution of problems belonging to the social order, while at the same time they did pose questions about the conception of Christian community. Merezhkovsky said that Christianity did not reveal the mystery of the Three, that is to say the mystery of community. V. Tarnovtsev, who wrote a notable book on the Apocalypse, had a strong belief in the First Person of the Holy Trinity, God the Father, and in the Third Person, the Spirit, but very little belief in the Second Person, the Son. Among them all there was religious excitement, religious ferment and questing, but there was no real religious rebirth. That could arise out of literary circles less than anywhere, literary circles in which the elements of refined decadence were inherent. But the subject of religion, which among the Intelligentsia had for a long time been under an interdict, was brought forward and given the first place. It was very much *bien vu* to talk about religious subjects; it became almost fashionable. In accord with the nature of the Russians, the promoters of the Renaissance could not remain in the sphere of questions about literature, art and pure culture; the ultimate problems were posed. Problems of creativity, of culture, problems of art, of the order of society, of love and so on took on the character of religious problems. They were all the while problems of the same "Russian Boys," but after these had become more cultured. The religious philosophical gatherings lasted only for a short time, and that sort of meeting between the Intelligentsia and the clergy was never repeated; what is more the Intelligentsia themselves who took part in these gatherings broke up into various tendencies. At the beginning of the century there was a liberal movement among part of the clergy in Russia, chiefly the white clergy. The movement was hostile to episcopacy and monasticism, but there were no profound religious ideas in it, no ideas which bore upon Russian thought. The opposition of the official Church was very powerful; and efforts for ecclesiastical reform, of which there was a great need, met with no success. It is an astonishing thing that the Council of the year 1917, which became a possibility only thanks to the Revolution, displayed no interest whatever in the religious problems which had tormented Russian thought of the nineteenth century and the beginning of the twentieth. The Council was exclusively occupied with questions of ecclesiastical organization.

3

The third current of the Russian Renaissance is connected with the flowering of Russian poetry. Russian literature of the twentieth century did not create a great novel, like the novel of the nineteenth century, but it created most remarkable poetry and this poetry was very notable for Russian thought, and for the history of Russian tendencies in the realm of ideas. It was the period of symbolism. Alexander Blok, the greatest Russian poet at the beginning of the century, Andrei Byelii who had flashes of genius, Vyacheslav Ivanov, a universal man and a great theoretician of symbolism, and many poets and essayists of less stature, were all symbolists. The symbolists regarded themselves as a new line of development and they were in conflict with representatives of the old literature. The fundamental influence upon the symbolists was that of Vladimir Solovyov; he expressed the essence of symbolism in one of his own poems in this way:

> Everything visible to us
> Is only a flash, only a shadow
> From what cannot be seen by the eye.

Symbolism sees a spiritual reality behind this visible reality. The symbol is a link between two worlds, the mark of another world within this world. The symbolists believed that there is another world. Their faith was by no means dogmatic. Only one of them, Vyacheslav Ivanov, later on went over to Roman Catholicism. He was at one time very near to Orthodoxy. Vladimir Solovyov shared with the symbolists his belief in Sophia, but it is characteristic that, in contrast to Solovyov, the symbolists at the beginning of the century believed in Sophia and awaited its manifestation as the Beautiful Lady, but did not believe in Christ. And this must be regarded as the cosmic seduction under which that generation lived. The truth of it lay in the craving for the beauty of a transfigured cosmos. Andrei Byelii says in his reminiscences: "The symbol of 'the woman' became a dawn for us (the union of heaven and earth) which was intertwined with the teaching of the gnostics about concrete wisdom, with the name of a new muse, a fusing of mysticism with life."[1] The influence was not that of the daytime Solovyov with his rationalist theological and philosophical treatises, but the Solovyov of the night, expressing himself in verses and short essays, in the myth composed about him. Side by side with Solovyov there was the influence of Nietzsche; his was the strongest Western influence upon the Russian Renaissance. But what was accepted in Nietzsche was not that which for the most part they had written about him in the West, not his affinity with biological philosophy, not his fight for an aristocratic race and culture, not his will to power, but his religious theme. Nietzsche was accepted as a mystic and a prophet. Among the Western poets probably the most important was Baudelaire. But Russian symbolism was very different from the French. The poetry of the symbolists went beyond the boundaries of art and this was a very Russian trait. The period of what is called "Decadence" and aestheticism among us quickly came to an end, but there took place a transition to symbolism which indicated a search for spiritual order, and to mysticism. For Blok and Byelii, Solovyov was a window through which blew the winds of the future. Attention which is turned to the future, and with the expectation of extraordinary events in the future, is very characteristic of symbolist poets. Russian literature and poetry of the beginning of the century had a prophetic character. The symbolist poets with that sensitiveness which belonged to them felt that Russia is falling into an abyss, that the old Russia is coming to an end and that a new Russia which is still unknown must arise. Like Dostoyevsky they felt that an inward revolution is going on. Among the Russians of the cultured class in the nineteenth and twentieth centuries there was a swift replacement of generations of mentalities, and a constant quarrel between parents and children was specially characteristic of Russia. A. Byelii in his reminiscences describes the attention of his circle to symbolist poets as a waiting for the dawn and as a vision of the dawn. They were looking for the rising of the sun of a future day; it was the expectation not only of a completely new collective symbolist culture but also an expectation of the coming Revolution. A. Byelii calls "ours" only those who saw the "dawn," and

---

1. *Reminiscences of A. Blok* by A. Byelii, printed in four volumes. It is first-class material for the characteristic atmosphere of the Renaissance period. But there are in it many inaccuracies of fact.

had a presentiment of the dawning revelation. This also was one of
the forms of the expectation of the coming of the era of the Holy
Spirit. A. Byelii brilliantly describes the atmosphere in which Russian symbolism arose. It was a very remarkable time but an unpleas-
ant feature was the cliquishness, almost sectarianism, of the young
symbolists, a sharp division into "ours" and "not ours," and their
self-assurance and intoxication with themselves. Characteristic of
that time were overemphasis and a disposition to exaggeration, to
the puffing of sometimes insignificant events, to a lack of truthfulness with oneself and with others. Thus the quarrel between Byelii
and Blok reached extraordinary, almost cosmic, dimensions,
though behind it there were hidden feelings in which there was
nothing at all cosmic. Blok's wife at one time played the part of
Sophia. She was "The Very Beautiful Lady." In this there was a certain element of falsity and unpleasantness. It was playing with life,
a thing which belonged to that period generally speaking. To a
higher degree than Solovyov, Blok accepted the cult of "The Very
Beautiful Lady" and expressed it in his poem *Balaganchik*, and to
the same Very Beautiful Lady he dedicated a whole volume of his
poems. Later The Beautiful Lady went away and Blok was disillusioned about her. Byelii's indignation at what looked like the
treachery of Blok, and of Petersburg literature, to symbolist art, was
exaggerated and not entirely truthful, for behind it something personal was hidden. According to Byelii's reminiscences Blok made
the best of impressions. There was a greater simplicity in him,
greater truthfulness, less of the babbler than in the others. Byelii
was more complex and more varied in his gifts than Blok. He was
not only a poet but also a remarkable novelist; he was fond of philosophizing and later on became an anthroposophist. He wrote a
bulky book on symbolism which he built up with the help of Rickert's philosophy. He was the only notable futurist we had. In a very
original novel called *Petersburg* man and the cosmos were disinte-
grated into elements. The integrality of things disappears and the
boundaries that separate one thing from another can be transformed
into a lamp, the lamp into a street, and the street falls away into cosmic infinity. In another novel he depicts the life within the womb
before birth. In contrast to Byelii, Blok was not woven out of any
theories. He is nothing but a lyrical poet, the greatest poet of the

beginning of the century. He had a powerful feeling for Russia and an elemental genius devoted to Russia. Blok had a feeling that something dreadful was moving upon Russia:

> Wild passions are let loose
> 'Neath the yoke of the crescent moon.
>
> I see over Russia afar,
> A broad and gentle fire.

In the amazing poem *Russia* he enquires to whom will Russia yield herself and what will be the outcome of it:

> To any sorcerer's charm thou wilt
>   Thy devastating beauty yield!
> Let him entice, let him deceive thee
>   Thou wilt not perish. Passing fair
> In trouble, I shall still perceive thee,
>   Thy glory, veiled, will still be there.

But particularly remarkable are his verses *The Scythians*. This is a prophetic poem devoted to the theme of East and West:

> Millions of you, of us horde after horde;
>   Make the attempt; Loose war's harsh blows and cries
> Upon us, Yes, we own all Asia's Lord
>   Scythians are we who squint with greedy eyes.
>
> A sphinx is Russia; sorrow and joy embrace
>   Her both; and she is darkly drenched in gore
> She gazes, gazes, gazes in thy face
>   And in that look both love and hate implore.
> Yes, so to love as our own blood doth love
> None among you since long gone by has loved!
>
> All do we love: cold numbers hotly lit
>   And the far distance of the view divine
> All comes within our den: keen Gallic wit
>   And gloomy genius it sees across the Rhine.

Here are lines which are very painful for peoples of the West to read, and which may justify the uneasiness which Russia arouses:

> Is it our fault then that all your bones
> Rattle in our heavy tender paws?

In conclusion, some lines addressed to the West:

> For the last time, old world, bethink thee now
> Of the fraternal banquet, toil and peace.
> This last clear summons to it we allow,
> Barbarian trumpets sound it, then they cease.

Here the theme of Russia and Europe is stated with unusual trenchancy, the fundamental theme of Russian thought in the nineteenth century. It is not stated in terms of Christian categories, but Christian motifs remain. It might be said that the world sensitiveness of the symbolist poets was in touch with the cosmos, rather than with the Logos. For this reason with them the cosmos swallowed up personality; the value of personality was weakened. With them there were clear individualities, but personality was but feebly expressed. Byelii even said of himself that he had no personality. There was an anti-personalist element in the Renaissance. A pagan cosmism, though in a very much transformed shape, predominated over Christian personalism.

Vyacheslav Ivanov was a characteristic and brilliant figure of the Renaissance. He did not belong to the group of young poets who descried the dawn. At that time he was abroad; he was a pupil of Mommsen and he wrote a dissertation in Latin on the taxes of ancient Rome. He was a man of Western culture, of very great learning, which was not the case with Blok and Byelii. The principal influence on him was that of Schopenhauer, R. Wagner, and Nietzsche, and among the Russians, Solovyov, who knew him personally. He had the closest affinities with R. Wagner; he began to write poetry late in life. His poetry is difficult, erudite, sumptuous, full of expressions taken from old Church Slavonic, and makes a commentary necessary. He was not only a poet; he was also a learned philologist, the best Russian Hellenist, a brilliant essayist, a teacher of poets, and he was also a theologian, philosopher and theosophist; he was a universal man, a man of a synthetic spirit. In Russia he counted as a man of the most exquisite culture, such as did not exist even in the West. It was chiefly the cultured elite who recognized his worth. To broader circles he was inaccessible. He was not only a brilliant writer, but also a man of great versatility and charm. He could converse with everyone on the subjects in which they were specialists. His ideas apparently changed. He was a conservative, a mystic, an anarchist, an Orthodox, an occultist, a patriot, a communist, and he ended his life in Rome as a Catholic and a fascist. And among all these constant changes of his he always remained essentially the same self. There was much that was mere play in the life of this fascinating person. On his return from abroad he brought with him the religion of Dionysus about which he wrote a remarkable and very learned book. He wanted not only to reconcile Dionysus and Christ, but almost to identify them. Vyacheslav Ivanov, like Merezhkovsky, also introduced a great deal of paganism into his Christianity, and this was characteristic of the Renaissance of the beginning of the century. His poetry also hankered after being Dionysian, but it did not contain immediate elemental Dionysism. Dionysism with him was an attitude of mind. The problem of personality was alien to him. Vyacheslav Ivanov had an inclination towards occultism which, generally speaking, flourished in Russia round about the first decade of our century, as it did at the end of the eighteenth century and the beginning of the nineteenth. During these years people were looking for a real rosicrucianism. They looked for it sometimes in R. Steiner and at other times among secret societies. The more refined culture made the ascendency of occultism less convincing and less naive than at the beginning of the nineteenth century. Vyacheslav Ivanov was a many-sided and complex person and he could ring the changes in accordance with the various sides of his personality. He was saturated with the great cultures of the past, especially with Greek culture, and he lived in their reflections. He preached to some extent views which were almost Slavophil, but such hyper-culture, such decadent subtlety was not a Russian trait in him. He did not display that search for truth, that simplicity which captivates one in the literature of the nineteenth century; but in Russian culture there had to be revealed forms both of subtlety and of many-sided culture.

THE RUSSIAN IDEA ❖ 249

Vyacheslav Ivanov remains one of the most remarkable people of the beginning of the century, a man of the Renaissance *par excellence*.

L. Shestov, one of the most original and notable thinkers of the beginning of the twentieth century, was in every respect a contrast to Ivanov. In contrast to Ivanov, Shestov was a person of a single idea; he was a man of one subject which governed him entirely and which he put into everything he wrote. He was not a Hellene but a Jew; he represented Jerusalem, not Athens. He was a product of Dostoyevsky, Tolstoy and Nietzsche. His subject was connected with the destiny of personality, single, unrepeatable, unique. For the sake of this one and only personality he fought against the general, the universal, against the universal obligations of morals and of logic. He wants to take his stand beyond good and evil. The very rise of good and evil, the very distinction between them, is the Fall. Knowledge with its universal obligation, with the necessity which may be born of it, is the slavery of man. Being a philosopher himself he quarrels with philosophers, with Socrates, Plato, Aristotle, with Spinoza, Kant and Hegel. His heroes are just a few people who have passed through shattering experiences; they are Isaiah, the Apostle Paul, Pascal, Luther, Dostoyevsky, Nietzsche, Kierkegaard. Shestov's theme is religious in its nature; it is the theme of the unlimited possibilities of God. God can make what once existed non-existent; He can bring about that Socrates was not poisoned. God is not subject either to good or to reason; He is not subject to any kind of necessity. In Shestov's view the Fall was not ontological but gnosiological; it was due to the rise of the knowledge of good and evil, that is to say, the rise of the general and universally obligatory, the necessary. In Dostoyevsky he assigned particular importance to *Notes from the Underground*; he wants to philosophize like the man underground. The experience of shock brings a man out of the realm of the humdrum, to which the realm of tragedy is the opposite. Shestov sets the Tree of Life in opposition to the Tree of the Knowledge of Good and Evil, but he was always much more powerful in denial than in affirmation, the latter being with him comparatively meager. It would be a mistake to regard him as a psychologist. When he wrote about Nietzsche, Dostoyevsky, Tolstoy, Pascal and Kierkegaard, what interested him was not so much these men themselves as his own unique theme which he introduced into them. He was a fine writer; and by this he concealed the deficiencies of his thought; he never belonged to any school of thought; nor did he submit to the influence of the spirit of the age; he stood apart from the main channel of Russian thought; but Dostoyevsky connected him with basic Russia problems, above all the problem of the conflict of personality and world harmony. Towards the end of his life he met Kierkegaard, with whom he had close affinities. Shestov is a representative of original existential philosophy. His books have been translated into foreign languages and he has met with appreciation, but one cannot say that he has been accurately understood. In the second half of his life he gave more and more attention to the Bible. The kind of religion at which he arrived was biblical rather than evangelical, but he felt some kinship with Luther whom he had the originality to connect with Nietzsche (beyond good and evil). With Shestov the principal thing was faith, in antithesis to knowledge; he sought for faith but he did not express the faith itself. The figure of L. Shestov is most essential to the multiform Russian Renaissance of the beginning of the century.

4

A religious philosophical society was founded in Russia about the year 1908, in Moscow at the instance of S. Bulgakov, in Petersburg upon my own initiative, and in Kiev under that of the professors of the Ecclesiastical Academy. This religious philosophical society became a center of religious philosophical thought and spiritual enquiry. In Moscow the society was called "A Memorial to Vladimir Solovyov." This society reflected the birth of original religious philosophy in Russia. These societies were characterized by great freedom of thought and hatred of the traditions of the schools. Their realm of thought was not so much theological as religious and philosophical; this was characteristic of Russia. In the West there existed a sharp division between theology and philosophy; religious philosophy was a rare phenomenon and neither the theologians nor the philosophers were fond of it. In Russia at the beginning of the century philosophy, which was in a very flourishing condition, took on a religious character and confessions of faith were given a philosophical basis. Philosophy was in a position which was entirely independent of theology and of ecclesiastical authority. It was free but inwardly it depended upon religious experience. Religious philosophy embraced all questions of spiritual culture and even all the fundamental questions of social life. At the beginning the religious philosophical societies met with great success; public sessions at which papers were read and discussions took place were very well attended, and they were attended by people who had intellectual and spiritual interests, though these did not belong specially to the Christian religion. The central figure in the religious philosophical society of Moscow was S. N. Bulgakov, who had not yet taken holy orders. Contact was made with nineteenth-century currents of thought, chiefly with Khomyakov, Solovyov and Dostoyevsky. A quest for the true Orthodoxy began. They endeavored to find it in St. Seraphim Sarovsky, a favorite saint of that period, and in *starchestvo*. Attention was also given to Greek patristics. But among those who took part in the religious philosophical society there were also such men as V. Ivanov, and the anthroposophists also took part. There were various directions in which the way had been paved for Russian religious philosophy. A very characteristic figure of the Renaissance was Father Paul Florensky; he was a many-sided and gifted person; he was a mathematician, physicist, philologist, theologian, philosopher, occultist, poet. His was a very complex nature, not simple and direct. He came from the milieu of Sventitsky and Ern; he at one time tried to combine Orthodoxy with revolution, but gradually he became all the while more and more conservative and in the professorial chair at the Moscow Ecclesiastical Academy he was a representative of the right wing. As a matter of fact his conservatism and tendency to the right had a romantic rather than a realistic character. At that time this was a common occurrence. At the outset of his career Paul Florensky completed his course in the faculty of mathematics at Moscow University, and great hopes were centered upon him as a mathematician. After passing through a spiritual crisis he entered the Moscow Ecclesiastical Academy and later became a professor in the Academy, and wished to enter the monastic life. On the advice of a *starets* he did not become a monk, but simply took holy orders as a priest. At that time there were many men from the Intelligentsia who took orders: Paul Florensky, S. Bulgakov, V. Solovyov, S. Durilin and others. It was the outcome of a desire to enter deeply into

252 ❖ THE RUSSIAN IDEA

Orthodoxy, to enter into communion with its secret mystery. Florensky was a man of sensitive culture and there was an element of subtle tendency to decadence in him. Certainly he was not a person of simplicity and directness; there was nothing immediate and direct about him; there was all the while something in concealment; he spoke a great deal of set purpose, and displayed an interest in psychological analysis. I have described his Orthodoxy as stylized Orthodoxy.[2] He stylized everything. He was an aesthete and in that respect he was a man of his time, a man who was indifferent to the moral side of Christianity. It was the first time that such a figure had appeared in Russian Orthodox thought. This reactionary in aesthetic feeling was in many respects an innovator in theology. His brilliant book *The Pillar and Ground of the Truth* produced a great impression in a number of circles and had some influence upon many people, for instance upon S. N. Bulgakov, who was a man of quite different mental build and quite different spiritual makeup. By its music Florensky's book conveys the impression of falling autumn leaves; the melancholy of autumn flows through it; it is written in the form of letters to a friend. It might be numbered among books which belong to the type of existential philosophy. The psychological side of the book is of special value, particularly the chapter on $\varepsilon\pi o\chi\eta$. It is also a positive attack upon rationalism in theology and philosophy and a defense of antinomianism. Paul Florensky wants theology to be a matter of spiritual experience, but all the same his thought cannot be called a creative word in Christianity. He stylizes too much; he is too anxious to be traditional and orthodox; but, nevertheless, in his spiritual makeup he is a new man, a man of his times, and those were, moreover, the famous years of the beginning of the twentieth century. He understood the movement of the Spirit too much as reaction and not enough as movement forward. But he stated problems which were not traditional, and such above all was the problem of Sophia, the Wisdom of God; this was not one of the problems of traditional theology, however much Florensky tried to find support in the doctors of the Church. To pose the problem of Sophia indicates a different attitude to cosmic life and to the created world. The development

---

2. My essay in *Russian Thought* on Paul Florensky's book *The Pillar and Ground of the Truth* has been called "Stylized Orthodoxy."

of the theme of Sophia and the giving of theological shape to it was to be the work of S. Bulgakov, but Father Paul Florensky gave the first impetus to it. He spoke, in a fashion which was hostile and even contemptuous, about "the new religious consciousness," but all the same he produced too much the same impression as his contemporaries, Merezhkovsky, Ivanov, Byelii, Blok. He himself felt that he had a special affinity with Rozanov; he felt no concern for the subject of freedom and on that account was indifferent to the moral theme. It is characteristic that from a book which presents a complete theological system, albeit not in a systematic form, Christ is almost entirely absent. Florensky endeavored to conceal the fact that he lived under the cosmic lure and that with him man was crushed. But as a Russian religious thinker, he also in his own way is expecting a new era of the Holy Spirit. He expresses this with a great deal of caution, for his book was a dissertation for the Ecclesiastical Academy and he was a professor and priest at it. In any case Paul Florensky was an interesting figure in the years of the Russian Renaissance.

But the central figure in the movement of Russian thought towards Orthodoxy was S. Bulgakov. In his younger days he had been a Marxist and professor of political economy in a Polytechnic Institute. He came of clerical stock; his forebears had been priests and he began his education in a theological seminary. The foundations of Orthodoxy were deeply laid in him; he was never an orthodox Marxist; in philosophy he was not a materialist but a follower of Kant. An abrupt break which he experienced in his life is described in his book *From Marxism to Idealism*. He was the first of those who belonged to this school of thought to become a Christian and an Orthodox. At a certain moment Vladimir Solovyov exerted a particular influence upon him. He transferred his interests from economic questions to matters of philosophy and theology; he was always a dogmatist in his turn of mind. He was ordained priest in 1918. After his expulsion from Soviet Russia in 1922, with a group of scholars and writers, he became professor of dogmatic theology in Paris at the Orthodox Theological Institute. In Paris he is already working out a complete philosophical system of theology under the general title of *Concerning God-manhood*. The first volume is called *The Lamb of God*; the second *The Comforter* and the third has not yet been

published. Already before the war of 1914 he had committed his
religious philosophy to writing in a book called *The Light which is
not of Evening*. It is not now my purpose to give an exposition of
Father Bulgakov's ideas; he is a contemporary and is still going on
with his philosophical work at the time at which I write. I shall point
out only the most general outline. His line of thought has been called
sophiological and his sophiology gives rise to sharp attacks from
Orthodox circles of the right wing. He aims at giving abstract theological expression to Russian sophiological investigation; he aims at
being not a philosopher but a theologian, but in his theology there is
a large element of philosophy, and Plato and Schelling are of great
importance for his thought. He remains a representative of Russian
religious philosophy; he remains true to the basic Russian idea of
God-manhood. God-manhood is the deification of the creature. God-
manhood becomes real through the Holy Spirit. The subject matter
of sophiology is the theme of the divine in the created world. This is
above all a cosmological theme and one which has aroused the interest of Russian religious thought more than of Western religious
thought. There is no absolute division between the Creator and His
creation. The uncreated Sophia exists in God from all eternity; it is
the world of platonic ideas. Through Sophia our world was created,
and there exists a created Sophia which permeates creation. Father
Bulgakov calls this point of view "Panentheism" (a word of
Krause's) as distinct from Pantheism; it might also be called "Panpneumatism." There takes place, as it were, a descent of the Holy
Spirit into the cosmos. Panpneumatism in general is characteristic of
Russian religious thought. The chief difficulty for sophiology arises
from the problem of evil which is indeed inadequately stated and left
unsolved. It is an optimistic system; the fundamental idea is not that
of freedom but the idea of Sophia. Sophia is the eternal divine feminine principle, a view which in particular gives rise to objections.
Father Bulgakov's actual problem is of great importance and it does
not find an adequate solution in Christianity. The raising of the subject is an indication of creative thought in Russian Orthodoxy, but
the lack of clarity in defining what Sophia is gives rise to criticism.
Sophia appears to be the Holy Trinity and each of the Persons of the
Holy Trinity and the cosmos and humanity and the Mother of God.
The question arises: does there not result too great a multiplication

of intermediaries? Father Bulgakov reacts decisively against the identification of Sophia with the Logos. It is not clear what ought to be referred to revelation, what to theology and what to philosophy. Neither is it clear what philosophy should be considered necessarily linked with Orthodox theology. The volume of Bulgakov's theological system which is to be devoted to eschatological expectation is to be reconciled with sophiological optimism. There is an identification of the Church with the Kingdom of God and that contradicts eschatological expectation. I do not myself share the views of the sophiological school, but I place a high value on Bulgakov's line of thought in Orthodoxy and upon his statement of new problems. His philosophy does not belong to the existential type; he is an objectivist and a universalist and fundamentally a Platonist. He has too great a belief in the possibility of arriving at the knowledge of God through intellectual concepts. The kataphatic element predominates too much over the apophatic. Like the representatives of Russian religious philosophical thought he is striving towards what is new, towards the kingdom of the Spirit, but it remains obscure to what extent he recognizes the possibility of a new and third revelation. Father Bulgakov represents one of the tendencies of Russian religious thought and especially of those which are focused upon the theme of the divineness of the cosmos. But the greatest truth about him is his belief in the divine principle in man. In this sense his thought stands in opposition to Thomism and especially Barthianism and also to the monastic ascetic theology of traditional Orthodoxy.

I myself belong to the generation of the Russian Renaissance. I have taken part in that movement. I have been in close contact with the active and creative minds of the Renaissance, but in many respects I have parted company with the men of that remarkable period. I am one of the founders of the religious philosophy which was established in Russia. It is not my purpose now to expound my philosophical ideas; those who are interested in them may become acquainted with them in my books. The books which I have written while abroad among the *émigrés* are very important to me, butthey have appeared outside the limit of the period of the Renaissance about which I am writing. But I think it worthwhile in describing the characteristics of our many-sided Renaissance epoch to point out the traits which distinguish me from others with whom I have sometimes acted in concert. The original contribution of my general outlook was expressed in my book *The Meaning of Creativity, an Essay of the Justification of Man* which was written in 1912–13. It was *Sturm und Drang*. The book was devoted to the fundamental theme of my life and my thought, the subject of man and his creative vocation. The idea of man as creator was later on developed in my book *The Destiny of Man, an Essay in Paradoxical Ethics* which was published in the West. It was better developed but with less passion. It is not without grounds that I have been called the philosopher of freedom. The subject of man and creativity is linked with the subject of freedom; that was for me the basic problem, and it has frequently been but poorly understood. Jacob Boehme was of great importance to me; at a certain time in my life I read him with enthusiasm. Among pure philosophers I read more of Kant than of any other, in spite of the fact that in many respects I have parted company with Kantianism. But it was Dostoyevsky who had the primarily decisive significance for me. Later on Nietzsche and especially Ibsen became important to me. In the attitude I took in my very young days towards the wrongness of the world which surrounds us, the wrongness of history and civilization, Tolstoy was of great significance to me; and later on Marx. My subject of creativity which had affinities with the Renaissance period, but not with the majority of the philosophers of that time, is not the theme of the creativity of culture, not the creativity of man in the "sciences and arts." It is a subject which goes deeper than that; it is metaphysical; it is concerned with the continuation by man of the creation of the world, with the answer given to God by man, who is able to enrich the very divine life itself. Superficially my views may have changed, particularly as they depended upon my sometimes too sharp and passionate reactions to what at a given moment dominated my mind, but all my life I have been a defender of freedom of the spirit and of the highest dignity of man; my thought has been orientated anthropocentrically, not cosmocentrically. Everything that I have written has been related to the philosophy of history and to ethics; I am above all else a student of history and a moralist and perhaps a theosophist in the sense of the Christian theosophy of Franz Baader, Cieszkowski or Valdimir Solovyov. I have been called a modernist and this is true in the sense that I have believed and I believe in the possibility of a new era in Christianity,

an era of the Spirit, and that this will also be a creative era. To me
Christianity is a religion of the Spirit. It is truer to call my religious
philosophy eschatological, and I have for a long period of time tried
to perfect my understanding of eschatology. My interpretation of
Christianity is eschatological and I place it in antithesis to historical
Christianity. But my interpretation of eschatology is active and creative, not passive. The end of this world, and the end of history,
depend also upon the creative act of man. At the same time I have
shown the tragedy of human creativeness, which consists in the fact
that there is a lack of correspondence between creative purpose and
created product. Man is not creating a new life nor a new form of
existence, but cultural products. In my view the fundamental philosophical problem is the problem of an objectivization which is based
upon alienation, the loss of freedom and personality, and subjection
to the general and the necessary. My philosophy is decisively personalist and according to the fashionable terminology now established it might be called existential, although in quite a different
sense from the philosophy of Heidegger, for example. I do not
believe in the possibility of a metaphysics and theology based upon
concepts and I have certainly no desire to elaborate an ontology.
Being is only the objectivization of existence. God the Father, God
the Son and God the Holy Spirit are images and symbols of the inex-
pressible Godhead, and this fact has an immense existential significance. Metaphysics is only the symbolism of spiritual experience; it
is expressionist. The revelation of the Spirit is the revelation of spirituality in man. I affirm the dualism of the phenomenal world, which
is the world of objectivization and necessity, and the noumenal
world which is the real world of life and freedom. This dualism is
resolved only eschatologically. My religious philosophy is not
monistic and I cannot be called a Platonist like Bulgakov, Florensky,
Frank and others. Above all I dispute what may be called false objec-
tivism, which leads to the subjection of the individual to the general.
Man, personality, freedom, creativity, the eschatological and messianic solution of the dualism of the two worlds are my basic themes.
The social problem plays a much greater part with me than with
other representatives of Russian religious philosophy. I have close
affinity with that school of thought which in the West is called religious socialism, but the socialism is decisively personalist. In many

respects, some of them very serious, I have remained and I remain a
lonely figure; I represent the extreme left in the Russian religious
philosophy of the time of the Renaissance, but I have not lost and I
do not wish to lose my links with the Orthodox Church.

To the religious philosophical school of thought of the beginning
of the century there belonged also Prince E. Trubetskoy and V. Ern.
Prince E. Trubetskoy had close affinities with Vladimir Solovyov
and was an active member of the Moscow religious philosophical
society. His line of thought was more academic. His *World Outlook
of Vladimir Solovyov*, which contains an interesting criticism, is of
special interest. The world outlook of Prince E. Trubetskoy underwent the influence of German idealism, but he aims at being an
Orthodox philosopher; he adopts a very critical attitude to the sophiological line of Florensky and Bulgakov, and he developed a tendency to Pantheism. V. Ern, who has left us no complete and final
expression of himself, on account of his early death, stood particularly close to the sophiology of Florensky and Bulgakov, but his criticism was often unfair and was directed in the main against German
philosophy which had become particularly popular among groups of
young Russian philosophers. The Russian Renaissance was also a
renaissance of philosophy. Never, I think, had there been hitherto
such an interest in philosophy among us. Philosophical circles were
organized in which an intense philosophical life went on. The most
notable representatives of pure philosophy were N. Lossky and S.
Frank, who created an original philosophical system which might be
called ideal realism. Their actual method of conducting philosophical thought is, however, reminiscent of the Germans, but their line of
thought was metaphysical at a time when in Germany neo-Kantian-
ism, which was hostile to metaphysics, still held sway. Lossky created his own original form of intuitivism which might be called a
critical rehabilitation of naive realism. He was not a disciple of the
philosophy of Kant, Fichte, Schelling and Hegel; his sources were
other than these and closer akin to Leibnitz, Lotze and Kozlov. S.
Frank is nearer to classical German idealism. Like Vladimir
Solovyov he aimed at constructing a philosophy of the all-embracing
unity. He calls himself a continuator of Plotinus and Nikolai
Kuzansky and especially of the latter. In general his philosophy
belongs to the platonic stream of Russian philosophy. His book *The*

Object of Knowledge is a very valuable contribution to Russian philosophy which later on N. Hartmann was to defend in Germany; it represents a point of view very near to S. Frank. Both Lossky and Frank in the last resort pass over to a Christian philosophy and flow into the common channel of our religious philosophical thought of the beginning of the century. The basic theme of Russian thought at the beginning of the twentieth century is the theme of the divine in the cosmos, of cosmic divine transfiguration, of the energies of the Creator in creation. It is the theme of the divine in man, of the creative vocation of man and the meaning of culture. It is an eschatological theme of the philosophy of history. The Russians meditated upon all problems in their essential nature, as if they were standing face to face with the mystery of being, whereas the Westerns, burdened with the weight of their past, meditated upon all problems with too much regard to their cultural reflections, that is to say, there was in Russia more freshness and immediacy; and it is possible to see something in common between the search for God among the masses of the people and the search for God at the higher level of the Intelligentsia.

Yet all the same it must be acknowledged that there was a breach between the interests of the higher cultural classes of the Renaissance, and the interests of the revolutionary social movement among the people and in the left Intelligentsia, which had not yet passed through the intellectual and spiritual crisis. They lived at different levels of culture, almost in different centuries. This had fateful results upon the character of the Russian Revolution. The paper *Problems of Life*, edited by me and by S. Bulgakov, tried to combine the various tendencies. Those were the days of the first small revolution, and the paper was unable to continue its existence for more than a year. Politically the paper belonged to the left, the radical school of thought, but it was the first in the history of Russian periodicals to combine that sort of social and political ideas with religious enquiry, with a metaphysical outlook and a new tendency in literature. It was an attempt to unite those who had been Marxists and, becoming idealists, were moving towards Christianity, with Merezhkovsky and the symbolists, in part with the representatives of the academic philosophy of the idealist and spiritual school, and with journalists of a radical tendency. The synthesis was not organic enough and could not be durable. That was a time of great interest and tension, when new worlds were opening out before the most cultured section of the Intelligentsia, when souls were set free for creative spiritual culture. The most essential feature of the situation was that some spirits came to light who emerged from the enclosed immanent circle of earthly life and turned towards the transcendental world. But this went on only among a section of the Intelligentsia; the greater part continued to live by the old materialist and positivist ideas which were hostile to religion, to mysticism, metaphysics, aesthetics and the new movement in art. Such a position was regarded as obligatory for all those who took part in the emancipation movement and fought for social truth and right. I call to mind a clear picture of the breach and schism in Russian life. The cultured elite, poets, novelists, philosophers, savants, artists, actors, used to meet on Wednesdays for several years at Vyacheslav Ivanov's "Tower"; that was what they called his flat at the corner of the very top storey of a high house opposite the *Tavrichesky Dvorets*. At this circle of Ivanov's they would read papers and engage in very subtle disputes. They talked not only about literary matters but also about philosophical, religious, mystical subjects and the occult. The flower of the Russian Renaissance was present. At the very same time down below in the *Tavrichesky Dvorets* and round about, revolution was raging. The actors in the Revolution were entirely uninterested in the subjects discussed in Ivanov's circle; but the people of the cultural Renaissance who were squabbling on Wednesdays in the "Tower," so far from being conservatives belonging to the right wing, were many of them even of a left tendency and prepared to sympathize with the Revolution. But the majority of them were asocial and very remote from the interests of the blustering Revolution. When in 1917 the promoters of the Revolution were victorious, they regarded the promoters of the cultural Renaissance as their enemies and overthrew them, destroying their creative work. The blame for this rests upon both sides. Among the promoters of the Renaissance who were opening up new worlds, there existed a feeble moral will and too much complacency regarding the social side of life, whereas the promoters of the Revolution lived by a backward and elemental idea. There is a contrast in this respect with the French Revolution. The makers of the French Revolution lived by the up-to-date ideas of the time, the ideas of J. J. Rousseau, of the eighteenth-century philosophy of the Enlightenment. Those who made the Russian Revolution lived by the ideas of Chernishevsky, Plekhanov, by a materialist and utilitarian philosophy, by an outworn and tendentious literature; they were not interested in Dostoyevsky, Tolstoy, Solovyov; they knew nothing of the new movements of Western culture. For that reason the Revolution with us was a crisis in and a cramping of spiritual culture. The militant godlessness of the communist Revolution is to be explained not only by the state of mind of the communists which was very narrow and dependent upon various kinds of *ressentiment*, but also by the historical sins of Orthodoxy which had failed to carry out its mission for the transfiguration of life, which had been a support of an order which was based upon wrong and oppression. Christians must recognize their guilt and not be content to accuse the adversaries of Christianity and consign them to perdition. What was hostile to Christianity and to every form of religion was not the social system of communism which answered more truly to Christianity than capitalism, but the false religion of communism which aimed at taking the place of Christianity, and that false religion of communism took shape because Christianity had not done its duty and was distorted. The official Church occupied a conservative position in relation to the State and social life and was slavishly subject to the old regime. For some time after the Revolution of 1917 a considerable section of the clergy and the laity who considered themselves particularly Orthodox adopted a counter-revolutionary frame of mind, and only later on there appeared priests of a new type. No ecclesiastical reform and no rehabilitation of Church life by the creative ideas of the nineteenth century and the beginning of the twentieth century took place. The official Church lived shut up in a world of its own. The *vis inertiae* in it was enormous. This also was one of the manifestations of the breach and schism which runs all through Russian life.

5

In the year 1917 in the atmosphere of unsuccessful war everything was ripe for revolution. The old regime had rotted away and had no reputable defenders. The holy Russian Empire collapsed, that holy Russian Empire which the Russian Intelligentsia had for centuries repudiated and combatted. Among the people, those religious beliefs which had been a support of the autocratic monarchy became weakened and were liable to dissolution. The real content disappeared from the official phrase: "Orthodoxy, autocracy and the people"; such an expression had become insincere and false. In Russia a liberal, bourgeois revolution, requiring a right wing organization, was a utopia which did not correspond either with Russian traditions or with the revolutionary ideas which prevailed in Russia. In Russia the revolution could only be socialist. The liberal movement was connected with the *Duma* and the cadet party, but it found no support among the masses of the people and was lacking in inspiring ideas. In accordance with the Russian spiritual turn of mind the revolution could only be totalitarian. All Russian ideology has always been totalitarian, theocratic or socialist. The Russians are maximalists and it is precisely that which looks like a utopia which in Russia is most realistic. As the well-known word "bolshevism" took its origin from the "majority" (*bolshinstvo*) at the meeting of the Social Democratic Party in 1903, so the word "menshevism" arose from the "minority" at that meeting. The word "bolshevism" was an admirable slogan for the Russian Revolution, whereas the word "menshevism" was good for nothing. To the Russian Intelligentsia of the left the Revolution had always been both a religion and a philosophy. The revolutionary idea was an integrated idea. The more moderate schools of thought did not grasp this. It is very easy to show that Marxism is a completely unsuitable ideology for revolution in an agricultural country with an overwhelming predominance of the peasantry, with an out-of-date commercial life and with a proletariat very insignificant in numbers. But symbolism in the revolution was conventional; there is no need to interpret it too literally. Marxism was adapted to Russian conventions and was Russified. The messianic idea of Marxism, which was connected with the mission of the proletariat, was combined and identified with the Russian messianic idea. In the Russian communist revolution it was not the actual proletariat of experience which was in control but the idea of the proletariat, the myth of the proletariat. But the communist revolution which was also the actual Russian Revolution was a universal messianism; it aimed at bringing happiness and liberation from oppression to the whole world. It is true that it established the greatest oppression and annihilated every trace of freedom, but it did this under the sincere impression that this was a temporary means which was necessary in order to give effect to its highest purposes. The Russian communists went on regarding themselves as Marxists and turned towards certain *narodnik* ideas which had prevailed in the nineteenth century; they acknowledged that it was possible for Russia to avoid a capitalist stage of development and to arrive at socialism directly, at a bound. Industrialization had to go forward under the banner of communism, and so it did. The communists showed that they were more akin to Tkachev than to Plekhanov or even to Marx and Engels, they rejected democracy as many of the *narodniks* had rejected it. At the same time they put into practice despotic forms of government which were characteristic of the old Russia; they introduced changes into Marxism which had to be brought in to fit in with the era of proletarian revolutions which were still unknown to Marx. Lenin was an admirable theoretician and practician of revolution; he was a characteristic Russian with an alloy of Tartar traits. Followers of Lenin exalted the revolutionary will and regarded the world as plastic and fit for any changes you like, which came from the side of the revolutionary minority. They began to assert a form of dialectic materialism, from which that determinism which so plainly leapt to the eyes earlier in Marxism had disappeared. Matter also almost disappeared; it was assigned spiritual qualities, a possibility of automatic movement from within, of inward freedom and intelligence. There also took place a sharp nationalization of Soviet Russia and a return to many traditions of the Russian past. Leninism and Stalinism are not classical Marxism.

Russian communism is a distortion of the Russian messianic idea; it proclaims light from the East which is destined to enlighten the bourgeois darkness of the West. There is in communism its own truth and its own falsehood. Its truth is a social truth, a revelation of the possibility of the brotherhood of man and of peoples, the suppression of classes, whereas its falsehood lies in its spiritual foundations which result in a process of dehumanization, in the denial of the worth of the individual man, in the narrowing of human thought, a thing which had already existed in Russian nihilism. Communism is a Russian phenomenon in spite of its Marxist ideology. Communism is the Russian destiny, it is a moment in the inner destiny of the Russian people and it must be lived through by the inward strength of the Russian people. Communism must be surmounted but not destroyed, and into the highest stage which will come after communism there must enter the truth of communism also but freed from its element of falsehood. The Russian Revolution awakened and unfettered the enormous powers of the Russian people. In this lies its principal meaning. The Soviet constitution of the year 1936 has established the best legislation on property in the world; personal property is recognized, but in a form which does not allow of exploitation. A new spiritual type has come to maturity, but the freedom of man still does not exist. With all the disruptedness of Russian culture and the antithesis between the revolutionary movement and the Renaissance, there was something in common between them. The dionysiac principle broke through in both spheres although in different forms. What is called the Russian Renaissance is that creative exalting impulse which took place among us at the beginning of the century, but it was not like the great European Renaissance in character; there was no Middle Ages behind it; behind it was the era of enlightenment experienced by the Intelligentsia. The Russian Renaissance compares more truly with the German romanticism of the beginning of the nineteenth century which was also preceded by an era of enlightenment. But in the Russian movement at that time there were specifically Russian traits which were connected with the Russian nineteenth century, that is to say above all the religious unrest and the religious questing, the constant movement in philosophy across the frontiers of philosophical knowledge, in poetry beyond the boundaries of art, in politics beyond the boundary of politics, in the opening-up of an eschatological outlook. Everything flowed in an atmosphere of mysticism. The Russian Renaissance was not classical, it was romantic, if one uses this generally accepted terminology. But this romanticism was of another kind than that of the West. There was in it a striving towards religious realism, although this realism itself was not attained. There did not exist in Russia that complacent self-containedness in culture which was so characteristic of Western Europe. In spite of Western influences and especially that of Nietzsche, although he was understood in a special way among Western symbolists, there was a striving towards Russian self-consciousness. At this period Blok's verses *The Scythians,* which I have already quoted, were written. Only in the Renaissance period did it come about that we really drew near to Dostoyevsky and came to love the poetry of Tyutchev and to value Solovyov. But at the same time the nihilist negativeness of the nineteenth century was overcome; the Russian revolutionary movement, the Russian bent towards a new social life, was a powerful cultural Renaissance movement, a movement which relied upon the masses which were rising from below and was connected with the strong traditions of the nineteenth century. The cultural Renaissance was broken off and its creators swept away from the forefront of history, and in part compelled to go abroad. For some time the most superficial materialist ideas triumphed and in the realm of culture there was a return of the old rationalist enlightenment; the social revolutionary was a cultural reactionary. But all this, witnessing as it does to the tragic fate of the Russian people, by no means indicates that the whole stock of creative energy and creative ideas has collapsed and failed of any purpose, nor that it will not have any importance for the future. It is not thus that history is fulfilled; it flows on in varied psychic reactions in which thought at one time contracts and at another time expands, which at one time sinks into the depth and disappears from the surface, which again at another time rises up and finds expression for itself in the external world. So it will be with us also. The havoc which has taken place in spiritual culture among us is only a dialectic moment in the destiny of Russian spiritual culture, and witnesses to the problematic nature of culture for the Russians. All the creative ideas of the past will again have their creatively fruitful importance. In the emigration the reaction against the Revolution has created the reactionary religious spirit, but this is a phenomenon which becomes insignificant when viewed in the larger perspective.

Russian thought and the Russian quest at the beginning of the nineteenth century and the beginning of the twentieth bear witness to the existence of a Russian Idea, which corresponds to the character and vocation of the Russian people. The Russian people belong to the religious type and are religious in their spiritual makeup. Religious unrest is characteristic even of the unbelievers among them. Russian atheism, nihilism, materialism have acquired a religious coloring;

Russians who belong to the working masses of the people, even when they have abandoned Orthodoxy, have continued to search for God and for divine truth and to enquire into the meaning of life. The refined skepticism of the French is alien to the Russians; they are believers even when they profess materialist communism. Even among those Russians who not only do not hold the Orthodox faith but even carry on a persecution against the Orthodox Church, there remains a stratum in the depth of their souls which is shaped by Orthodoxy. The Russian Idea is eschatological, it is orientated to the end; it is this which accounts for Russian maximalism. But in Russian thought the eschatological idea takes the form of striving after universal salvation. The Russians rank love higher than righteousness. The Russian spirit of religion bears a communal character. Western Christians have no knowledge of that sort of community which belongs to the Russians. All these are traits which find their expression not only in religious tendencies but also in social tendencies. It is a well-known fact that the chief festival of Russian Orthodoxy is the Festival of Easter. Christianity is interpreted as above all the religion of the Resurrection. If we take Orthodoxy not in its official, governmental, distorted form, there is to be found in it more freedom, more feeling of the brotherhood of man, more kindliness, more true humility and less love of power, than in the Christianity of the West. Behind their external hierarchical system the Russians in their ultimate depth have always been antihierarchical, almost anarchist. There is not among the Russians that love for historical grandeur which has so captivated the peoples of the West. The people who are in possession of the greatest State in the world have no love for the State or for power, and bend their energies to a different end. The Germans have for long propounded the theory that the Russian people is feminine and psychic in contrast to the masculine and spiritual German people. The masculine spirit of the German people ought to subdue the feminine soul of the Russian people. This theory has been linked to a practice which corresponds with it. The whole theory is constructed for the justification of German imperialism and the German will to power. In actual fact the Russian people has always been capable of displaying great masculinity and it is proving this to the Germans. There has been a heroic principle in it. The Russian quest bears a spiritual rather than a psychic character. Every

people ought to be both masculine and feminine; the two pr
should be combined in it. It is true that there is a predomin
the masculine principle in the German people, but this is rather a dis-
figurement than a quality to be proud of and it leads to no good. The
significance of these judgments is of course limited. During the
period of German romanticism the feminine principle made its
appearance also. But it is true that the German and Russian ideas
stand in opposition to each other. The German idea is the idea of
rule, dominance, of might, whereas the Russian idea is the idea of
community and the brotherhood of men and peoples. In Germany
there has always been an acute dualism between its State, its military
and aggressive spirit, and its spiritual culture, the immense freedom
of its thought. The Russians have owed very much to German spiritual culture, especially to its great philosophy. But the German State
is the historical enemy of Russia. In German thought itself there is
an element which is hostile to us; this is especially the case in Hegel,
Nietzsche and, however strange it may be, in Marx. We are bound to
desire brotherly relations with the German people, who have
achieved much that is great, but on condition that it repudiates the
will to power. To the will to power and dominance there must be
opposed the masculine power of defense. The ethical ideas of the
Russians are very different from the ethical ideas of Western peoples, and they are more Christian ideas. Russia's moral values are
defined by an attitude towards man, and not towards abstract principles of property or of the State, nor towards good in the abstract. The
Russians adopt a different attitude towards sin and crime; there is
pity for the fallen and debased; nor is there any love for grandeur.
The Russians have less of the sense of family than Western peoples,
but immeasurably more of the community spirit; they are seeking
not so much an organized society as the sense and experience of
community, and they are less academic. The Russian paradox is
summed up in this, that the Russian people are much less socialized
than the peoples of the West, but also much more community conscious, more ready for the life in common. Any mutations and abrupt
changes may take place under the influences of revolutions and it is
possible that this may be a result of the Russian Revolution. But the
divine purpose for the people remains the same and the task of struggling for the freedom of man remains true to that design. There is

something which does not belong to the realm of determinism in the life of the Russians, something which is too little grasped by the more rationally determined life of the men of the West. But this indeterminate element reveals many possibilities. Among the Russians there are not to be found such divisions, classifications and groupings into various spheres which there are among the peoples of the West. There is more integrality. But this in its turn creates difficulties and possibilities of confusion. It must be remembered that the nature of the Russians is highly polarized. On the one side it is humble and self-denying; on the other side there is revolt aroused by pity and demanding justice; on the one hand sympathy, compassion, on the other hand the possibility of cruelty. Among the Russians there is a different feeling for the soil and the very soil itself is different from soil in the West. Mysticism of race and blood is alien to the Russians, but the mysticism of the soil is very much akin to them. The Russian people, in accordance with its eternal Idea, has no love for the ordering of this earthly city and struggles towards a city that is to come, towards the new Jerusalem. But the new Jerusalem is not to be torn away from the vast Russian land. The new Jerusalem is linked with it, and it, the soil, leads to the new Jerusalem. The spirit of community and the brotherhood of mankind are a necessity for the new Jerusalem, and for the attainment of these it is still endeavoring to have the experience of an era of the Holy Spirit, in which there will be a new revelation about society. For this the way is being prepared in Russia.

INDEX

provides religious basis for state, 160
Khomyakov on, 58, 178
and Rozanov, 241
Orthodoxy, 21, 23, 24, 25-27, 30, 31, 36, 45,
109, 114, 153, 157, 202, 213, 230, 265,
266
and Alexander I, 38, 39
opposed to natural sciences, 47-48
and philosophy, 48
Chaadaev and, 52, 54
Slavophils on, 57, 60, 65, 67, 68, 83
Kireevsky on, 59, 64-65
freedom and, 63
Khomyakov on 66, 178, 179, 180, 181
as essential of Russian vocation, 68
paganism in 68
and Danilevsky, 83
and humanism, 114-115
and *narodniks*, 119
and Dostoyevsky, 139, 169, 171, 218-219
Zhelabov and, 143
and nihilism, 146
obscurantism in, 147
and Dobrolyubov, 148-149
and Tolstoy, 155, 156, 197
K. Aksakov on, 162
and theology, 173, 179, 181
sobornost and, 178-181
and Solovyov, 182, 189, 193
and Bukharev, 199
and Archibishop Innocent, 201
and Tareev, 205-206
and eschatology, 146, 152, 230
and asceticism, 152, 207, 230
and Marxism, 237
and Merezhkovsky, 238-239
and religious philosophical meetings at
Petersburg, 240
and Ivanov, 243, 248
and religious philosophical society of
1908, 251-252
and Bulgakov, 253-255
and E. Trubetskoy, 258
its relation to Russian Renaissance, 261

Paganism, 21, 24, 68, 157, 236
Khomyakov on, 61
and God-manhood, 188
Nesmelov on, 204
Rozanov and, 229, 239
Merezhkovsky and, 239, 248
and Russian Renaissance, 247

and Ivanov, 248
see also Dionysism
Pankova, E. D., 51
Paracletism, 181, 227-228
Pascal: and Shestov, 249
Pavlov, M. G., 49
Pechorin, 44, 55, 117
Penal legislation, 69, 105
People's Will, 118
and murder of Alexander II, 143, 236
Personalism, 112, 131
and Herzen, 79-82, 121, 166
Hegel against, 92
clashes with world harmony, 93-98
and Pisarev, 128, 150, 152, 153
and Mikhailovsky, 131-133
and Lavrov, 133-134
and Dostoyevsky, 139
and utilitarianism, 153
and Bakunin, 166
and Tolstoy, 198
and Nesmelov, 205
and Russian Renaissance, 247
and Ivanov, 248
and Berdyaev, 257
Pessimism, 24, 89, 219
regarding past and present, 51
of Herzen, 79, 81, 122
of Leontyev, 86, 111, 219, 220
of Solovyov, 109-110, 221
Pestel, 41, 42, 117
Peter the Great, 21, 22, 27, 31, 46, 53, 54,
65, 85, 120, 235
his character, 33
reforms of, 23, 32-34, 56-57, 58, 74
as antichrist, 31, 34, 211
Petrashevsky, M. V.
a follower of Fourier, 117
and Dostoyevsky, 139
Philaret the Metropolitan, 39, 201
Philosophy of history, 26, 30, 49, 89
importance of problem of, 51-55
and significance of Peter's reforms, 56-
57
of Slavophils, 60-61, 62
of Khomyakov, 61-63
of Herzen, 78-82
of Leontyev, 84
of Solovyov, 187
and Tareev, 206
and Cieszkowski, 226-227
and Marxism, 237

ESALEN INSTITUTE / LINDISFARNE PRESS
LIBRARY OF RUSSIAN PHILOSOPHY

Though it only began to flourish in the nineteenth century, Russian philosophy has deep roots going back to the acceptance of Christianity by the Russian people in 988 and the subsequent translation into church Slavonic of the Greek Fathers. By the fourteenth century religious writings, such as those of Dionysius the Areopagite and Maximus the Confessor, were available in monasteries. Until the seventeenth century, then, except for some heterodox Jewish and Roman Catholic tendencies, Russian thinking tended to continue the ascetical, theological, and philosophical tradition of Byzantium, but with a Russian emphasis on the world's unity, wholeness, and transfiguration. It was as if a seed were germinating in darkness, for the centuries of Tartar domination and the isolationism of the Moscow state kept Russian thought apart from the onward movement of Western European thinking.

With Peter the Great (1672–1725), in Pushkin's phrase, a window was cut into Europe. This opened the way to Voltairian freethinking, while the striving to find ever greater depths in religious life continued. Freemasonry established itself in Russia, inaugurating a spiritual stream outside the church. Masons sought a deepening of the inner life, together with ideals of moral development and active love of one's neighbor. They drew on wisdom where they found it and were ecumenical in their sources. Thomas à Kempis's *Imitation of Christ* was translated, as were works by Saint-Martin ("The Unknown Philosopher"), Jacob Boehme, and the pietist Johann Arndt. Russian thinkers, too, became known by name: among others, Grigory Skovoroda (1722–1794), whose biblical interpretation drew upon Neoplatonism, Philo, and the German mystics; N.I. Novikov (1744–1818), who edited Masonic periodicals and organized libraries; the German I.G. Schwarz (1751–1784), a Rosicrucian follower of Jacob Boehme; and A.N. Radishchev (1749–1802), author of *On Man and His Immortality*.

There followed a period of enthusiasm for German idealism and, with the reaction to this by the Slavophiles Ivan Kireevksy and Alexei Khomyakov, independent philosophical thought in Russia was born. An important and still continuing tradition of creative thinking was initiated, giving rise to a whole galaxy of nineteenth and twentieth-century philosophers, including Pavel Yurkevitch, Nikolai Fedorov, Vladimir Solovyov, Leo Shestov, the Princes S. and E. Trubetskoy, Pavel Florensky, Sergius Bulgakov, Nikolai Berdyaev, Dmitri Merezhkovsky, Vassili Rozanov, Semon Frank, the personalists, the intuitionists, and many others.

Beginning in the 1840s, a vital tradition of philosophy entered the world stage, a tradition filled with as-yet unthought possibilities and implications not only for Russia herself but for the new multicultural, global reality humanity as a whole is now entering.

Characteristic features of this tradition are: *epistemological realism*; *integral knowledge* (knowledge as an organic, all-embracing unity that includes sensuous, intellectual, and mystical intuition); the celebration of *integral personality* (*tselnaya lichnost*), which is at once mystical, rational, and sensuous; and an emphasis upon the *resurrection* or *transformability* of the flesh. In a word, Russian philosophers sought a theory of the world as a whole, including its transformation.

Russian philosophy is simultaneously religious and psychological, ontological and cosmological. Filled with remarkably imaginative thinking about our global future, it joins speculative metaphysics, depth psychology, ethics, aesthetics, mysticism, and science with a profound appreciation of the world's movement toward a greater state. It is *bolshaya*, big, as philosophy should be. It is broad and individualistic, bearing within it many different perspectives—religious, metaphysical, erotic, social, and apocalyptic. Above all, it is universal. The principle of *sobornost* or all-togetherness (human catholicity) is of paramount importance in it. And it is future oriented, expressing a philosophy of history passing into *metahistory*, the life-of-the-world-to-come in the Kingdom of God.

At present, in both Russia and the West, there is a revival of interest in Russian philosophy, partly in response to the reductionisms implicit in materialism, atheism, analytic philosophy, deconstructionism, and so forth. On May 14, 1988, *Pravda* announced that it would publish the works of Solovyov, Trubetskoy, Semon Frank, Shestov, Florensky, Lossky, Bulgakov, Berdyaev, Alexsandr Bogdanov, Rozanov, and Fedorov. According to the announcement, thirty-five to forty volumes were to be published. This is now taking place.

The Esalen Institute–Lindisfarne Press Library of Russian Philosophy parallels this Russian effort. Since 1980 the Esalen Russian-American Exchange Center has worked to develop innovative approaches to Russian-American cooperation, sponsoring nongovernmental dialog and citizen exchange as a complement to governmental diplomacy. As part of its program, seminars are conducted on economic, political, moral, and religious philosophy. The Exchange Center aims to stimulate philosophic renewal in both the East and West. The Esalen-Lindisfarne Library of Russian Philosophy continues this process, expanding it to a broader American audience.

It is our feeling that these Russian thinkers—and those who even now are following in their footsteps—are world thinkers. Publishing them will not only contribute to our understanding of the Russian people, but will also make a lasting contribution to the multicultural philosophical synthesis required by humanity around the globe as we enter the twenty-first century.